COLLINS ENCYCLOPEDIA
OF
HOME SEWING

First published 1976
Reprinted 1977
Published by William Collins Sons and Company Limited
Glasgow and London
Copyright © J & P Coats Limited 1976
Designed by Ian Harley
Cover photography by Eric Thorburn
Full page colour drawings by Barry Rowe
Zip fastener diagrams by permission of Lightning Fasteners
Rug designs by courtesy of Stitchcraft
Tie-and-dye designs and photographs
by permission of Dylon International Limited
Curtains chapter by permission of 'Rufflette' Limited

Set in Monophoto Photina 11/12pt
Printed in Great Britain
ISBN 0 00 434603 3

COLLINS ENCYCLOPEDIA
OF
HOME SEWING

Edited by Jean Kinmond

Contents

Collins   Glasgow and London

Chapter 1

Diagram 1
Notched Guide

SEWING EQUIPMENT, FABRICS & TECHNIQUES

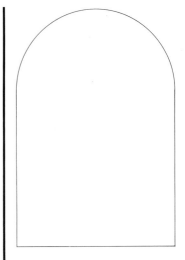

Diagram 3
Pattern for Pressing Mitt

A home is the background for the people who live in it. What does your home 'say' about you? That you have a good sense of colour; a fund of clever furnishing ideas; a talent for arranging your possessions to create an interesting and friendly atmosphere? This book will show you how to make your own furnishings and introduce you to the enjoyment that can be found in selecting colours and fabrics to enhance each room and give lasting pleasure and satisfaction.

Colour, pattern and originality of ideas are the main elements in any decorative scheme. Perhaps the most exciting of these is colour. A well designed piece of chintz can dictate your decorating scheme. Chosen first for curtains, its predominant colour can be used for your divan cover and its secondary colours as accents for cushions and rugs, with its background tones serving as a guide for walls and paintwork.

Another way of using colour is to select a monochromatic scheme. In this, a colour is used throughout your room in matching or varying tones but with strong accents of white to give an over-all sparkle.

If something brighter is preferred, then green and yellow go together beautifully, especially when you use yellowy greens and greeny yellows and set them off against white paintwork. Alternatively, greens can be blended with blues, or blues with lilacs. As a further example, you can work with complementary colours. Red with muted green is effective and very gay in a small dark room; blue-violet with lime is cool and pretty in a room which gets the sun all day.

Generally, it must be remembered that too many different colours used haphazardly create an air of unrest and disharmony and this style of background is not relaxing.

Pattern, if used too liberally, is also unpleasant and ineffective. It must be introduced with restraint and with full awareness of the value of contrast. Large flowers in fabrics look better against plain coloured walls. Strong horizontal or vertical stripes will clash with other dominant patterns in your furnishings and need to be handled carefully.

You must also ensure that your fabric and wallpaper patterns are scaled to the size of your furniture and room. Rosebud chintz may be charming when framing a small window in a tiny cottage room, but would be out of place on tall windows in a high-ceilinged room.

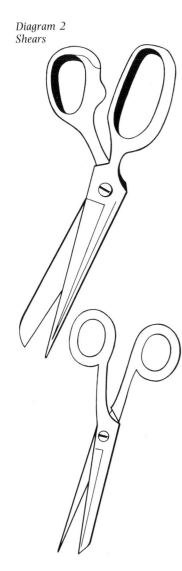

Diagram 2
Shears

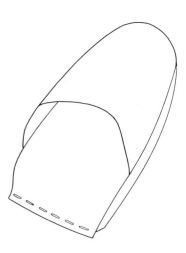

Diagram 4
Completed Pressing Mitt

Diagram 5
Quick Unpick

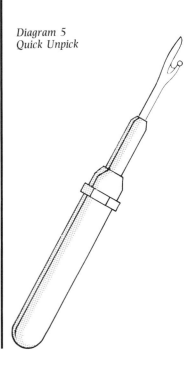

This book provides many practical suggestions for furnishing and decorating every room in your home. Now you can make your own bed and table linen, bed covers, curtains, cushions, loose covers and also the little extras such as bedheads and lampshades. In this chapter, there is a chart to guide you to correct stitching, and a section devoted to all the necessary hand sewing techniques, which will enable you to produce work that will be expertly made and long lasting. Decorative furnishing has not been forgotten, and full instructions for the basic hand embroidery stitches are given. The old crafts of patchwork and quilting have recently been revived, and they are also included in this section.

Crochet lace forms another decorative finish. Don't worry if this craft is new to you; it is very easy to learn, particularly when you follow the simplified learn-to-crochet course included.

Equipment

Before you begin to sew you must have the correct equipment. It is false economy to try and make do with blunt scissors or a stretched tape measure which could result in inaccurate measuring. Below we give the main tools you will require.

For Measuring

Tape Measure – We recommend a steel tape or a Milward fabric tape 150 cm (approx. 60 in) long.
Ruler – A 30 cm (12 in) ruler; useful for measuring hems.
Notched Guide – This is a most useful aid for marking as it is simple to use and simple to make. Make the guide from stiffish paper or cardboard (diagram 1). The best way to use the guide is to hold it in your left hand, having laid the article to be marked on a flat surface, right side up. Baste along the edge using the card as a guide for stitching, the first notch running along the edge to be marked. The second notch may be used to mark lines or tucks equal distances apart.

For Cutting

Keep cutting tools sharp.
Shears – These have long cutting blades and different size handles. Shears with bent handles make cutting simpler and more accurate as they lift the fabric less (diagram 2).
Small Scissors – They are useful for snipping seams etc.
An old pair of Scissors – These are kept specially for cutting paper. Never use your shears for cutting paper as this would make them blunt.

For Sewing

Needles – The sizes of Milward needles are indicated by numbers. There are two types of sewing needles; Sharps and Betweens. For most hand sewing use Sharps which are of medium length and have small round eyes. Betweens have the same size of eye, but are shorter in length and are used for fine handwork.
Needle Book – Make a needle book of wool flannel in which to keep your needles. This will prevent them rusting.
Pins – Always buy fine-quality steel dressmaker's pins with sharp points. They will not mark the fabric.
Pin Cushion – You will need a pin cushion to keep pins within easy reach.
Sewing Machine – A good and reliable sewing machine is invaluable. It is therefore extremely important to understand its working processes thoroughly, to be able to handle it with care and thus keep it in good working order. Sewing machines are operated by either hand wheel, foot treadle or electricity. All are efficient, but the latter is by far the best owing to the speed and simplicity of the operation.

The machine should be dusted each time it is used, to prevent soiling the fabric which is to be stitched. Clean the visible working parts as often as is necessary to free them from dust and dirt. The frequency of this cleaning operation will depend upon the amount of sewing done and the type of fabric used. Fabric with a woolly or hairy surface will soon clog the mechanism. A lintbrush or a 2.5 cm (1 in) paintbrush dipped in a good machine oil, may be used to free the revolving parts from dust. Remove the throat or needle plate occasionally and clear fluff from the claw. Oil the machine frequently but sparingly. Too much oil will clog the machine and the excess oil will seep through and mark the fabric. For detailed instructions on oiling and cleaning, consult the manual supplied with the machine, where clear explanatory directions and diagrams are given. After oiling the machine, run the machine unthreaded over a scrap of fabric in order to absorb any slight trace of oil.
Thimble – A thimble is a must for sewing. It protects the middle finger when pushing the needle and so increases the speed of sewing. Buy a good-quality one that fits well – metal (preferably steel) or plastic. Milward make thimbles, size large 0 to small 7.
Threads – These are very important. The introduction of Coats Drima has simplified the sewing on all types of fabric. Refer to the chart on page 9 as your complete guide for stitching.

For Pressing

Iron – Use a dependable iron, if possible with a temperature control for various fabrics. Rayons and synthetic fabrics require a low temperature and silks and woollens scorch easily. A steam iron, which steams as it presses, is useful.
Ironing Board – A good ironing board should be well padded and should have an easily removable cover. Keep the cover clean by washing it regularly.
Pressing Mitt – A pressing mitt is useful for pressing inaccessible and curved seams and may be made from 30 cm ($\frac{1}{4}$ yd) white cotton and 30 cm ($\frac{1}{4}$ yd) wadding. Make a pattern as shown in diagram 3 (1 sq = 2.5 cm (1 in)) and cut six pieces from pattern, three in cotton, three in wadding. Baste the three wadding sections

together, edges even. Place two cotton sections, wrong sides together, edges even, sandwiching the wadding between them. Make a hem on short straight edge of the remaining cotton section, place to one side of the mitt, right sides together. Baste. Stitch round the outside edge, leaving the short straight edges open. Trim seam and turn the single cotton section to the right side. Turn in raw edges to enclose wadding, and sew. See diagram 4.

Sleeve Board – This is used to press small seams. It is sometimes incorporated in the ironing board.

Quick Unpick – A good gadget for unpicking stitching. Be careful not to snip the fabric when using it (diagram 5).

Fabrics Natural and Synthetic

Furnishing fabrics today present an irresistible choice of colour and texture. They are made from natural yarns including cotton, linen, silk, wool, and synthetic yarns such as nylon, polyester, acrylic – also plastic and glass fibre and a wide range of mixtures. A wide choice that combines to make a visit to the fabric department a really exciting event. The choice, in fact, is so wide that it may prove bewildering. How is one to select the most suitable material and, almost of equal importance, the appropriate sewing thread? This section gives guidance in the selection and care of today's fabrics.

Natural Fabrics

Cotton

Cotton has been cultivated for thousands of years. It is a fibre obtained from the seed pod of the cotton plant, and it is a popular fabric. The most famous cotton, renowned for its silky appearance, is Sea Island cotton from the West Indies, but there are many other cottons which come from India, the Sudan, Africa, South America and the United States. Cotton will always be popular, as scientific methods have been used to give it numerous finishes, of which the best known are 'crease- or stain-resistant', 'water-repellent', 'flare-resistant', 'drip-dry', 'non-shrink', and the glazed and embossed effects. Indeed, cotton fabrics with their unlimited designs, colours and textures are a favourite choice of the discerning buyer. They are easy to handle and devoid of sewing difficulties.

Linen

This yarn is spun from the long fibres found in the stem of the flax plant. It is grown in many parts of the world, including France, Belgium and Holland, and the finished fabric is easily recognizable by its coolness and smoothness to the touch, by its natural glaze and by the sudden irregular thickening of single threads, even in the finest weaves. Linen does not tear easily, it is very absorbent and has the unusual quality of being about 20% stronger wet than dry. By variation in the manner of weaving, many different types of linen are produced. Each weave has its own special quality, suited for a particular purpose. The sewing of linen fabric presents no problems, except that as open weave linens are apt to fray, the raw edges should be finished at once.

Silk

This is one of the oldest textile fibres known to man, and was discovered by the Chinese almost 5,000 years ago. It is a natural fibre produced by the silkworm; a continuous thread, gossamer-fine, yet so strong that it can be woven into long-lasting fabrics of exceptional beauty. For some 3,000 years the Chinese kept it a secret; but eventually it was smuggled into Japan and from there to India and north-west to Europe. It would be impossible to name all the fabrics that are made from silk but they include satin, brocade, dupion, taffeta and velvet.

Wool

Woollen yarn is spun from the fleece of sheep. There are numerous breeds of sheep which produce different types and grades of woollen yarn, to be spun, woven, knitted or felted according to the effect required. Weights range from fine to heavy, flannel to tweed, and textures are worth noting in bouclés and pile fabrics. Nowadays, woollens can be chemically processed to become water-repellent, mothproof and shrink-resistant.

Synthetic Fabrics

Man-made fibres result from the chemical processing of raw materials such as wood pulp and coal. Today the variety of such fabrics is endless and we have a choice of hundreds. There are, as well as pure synthetics, mixtures and blends used with each other and with natural fibres to produce a still larger and almost limitless range of types and textures. To explain this further, a mixture is a fabric constructed of two or more different yarns during weaving or knitting: for example, a woven fabric with a nylon warp and a rayon or cotton weft. A blend is a fabric woven or knitted from a blended yarn – a yarn spun from viscose staple fibre and a natural fibre. Mixtures and blends often improve the properties of fabrics with regard to strength, wear and laundering.

Synthetic fabrics are a boon to everyone; they wash easily and are often crease-resistant. All man-made fibres have their own characteristics, and as they should not be compared with natural fibres, it's as well to find out about them before buying. Generally, most man-made fibres will neither shrink nor stretch, and need little or no ironing.

Threads and Stitching

Beautiful impeccable stitching is the perfect union of thread and fabric, based on the correct thread, the proper needle size, the right tension, the appropriate number of stitches to the cm (in), and the correct pressure of the presser foot. These basic points must be understood before you begin to sew.

For over a hundred years the manufacturers have been producing and improving thread. Every advance in sewing machines and the methods of using them has called for the production of a suitable thread. With the introduction of Coats Drima, thread selection is simplified. In this book you are given the correct guide to perfect stitching. Thread selection includes the choice of colour, which is extremely important; fabric and thread should be well matched, otherwise much painstaking work will be ruined. When thread is matched to a fabric, the thread on the reel will appear slightly darker than the single strand as it is sewn into the fabric, so buy thread a tone darker than the fabric. This advice applies to all colour matching.

Coats Drima

Being a multi-purpose sewing thread, Coats Drima can be used to sew both natural and synthetic fabrics by hand or by machine. It will give successful results on practically any weight or texture of fabric including the wide range of synthetic dress and furnishing fabrics and the many types of natural fabrics such as wool, linen, cotton and silk.

Drima is made in a selection of over 190 scientifically graded shades to make colour matching easy. Its small compact spool takes up little space in the workbox, yet holds a full 92 m (100 yd) of thread. A 183 m (200 yd) spool is available in black and white only. A 457 m (500 yd) economy buy spool is also available in black, white and a limited shade range. Whatever the fabric, Drima will give neat, inconspicuous seams. Although fine, this thread has great strength, which means that while stitches have a dainty, delicate appearance, seams are more than strong enough to withstand all the stress and strain which may be imposed on them.

Sewing with Coats Drima will present no difficulties if the simple instructions given below are followed:

Hand Sewing

Use a fairly short length of thread. Constantly pulling a long thread through the fabric may cause it to twist and snarl.

Machine Sewing

Use 3–6 stitches per cm (8–14 per in) depending upon the fabric type – see Fabric and Thread chart on page 9. To prevent any tendency to puckering, reduce tensions on the machine, watch that the pressure of the presser foot is not too great, and feed the fabric into the machine smoothly and evenly. Remember that Drima must be used on both the top thread and the bobbin.

Needle Size

Needles, like thread, are taken for granted, yet there are many sizes and types, each with its individual purpose.

First of all, there are sewing machine needles which come in a range of sizes from fine to heavy. Like thread, needles should be chosen with a view to how they are going to be used. The size of a needle's eye is in proportion to its thickness (diagram 6), therefore a fine needle demands a fine thread for a fine fabric, otherwise friction will cause the thread to fray in the needle eye. If a fine needle is used on thick material, the needle will probably break. Similarly, don't use a thick needle on a fine fabric; it will make holes in the weave, and the seam will be inclined to split. This applies to both machine and hand sewing. There are many kinds of hand sewing needles. The most widely known are Crewel for embroidery, Sharps for everyday sewing, and Betweens for tailoring.

Stitch Length

The length of a machine stitch is too often overlooked; but it also is an important factor in machine stitching. If the stitch length is too small the needle makes too many punctures too close together and the weave or body of the fabric is damaged. Again, when the stitch is too large, the seam is not held together securely and it will split.

Tension

To obtain a good stitch that will neither pucker nor pull out of the fabric, an evenly balanced tension is essential. On a sewing machine there are two tensions: the upper, which controls the thread from the needle, and the lower, which controls the thread from the spool or bobbin. The spool must always be wound evenly for the best stitching results. You get a balanced stitch when the formation of it is the same on both sides and the stitches are firmly embedded in the fabric (diagram 7A). It's a good plan to take a scrap of the fabric you propose to use, and run a row of stitching along it in order to check the tension. Always practise on the number of layers of fabric you are going to use, and stitch at an even, steady pace, avoiding sudden spurts of speed.

If the thread lies in a line on the top of the fabric, the upper tension is too tight and the stitches are not locked together evenly, or else the lower tension is too slack (diagram 7B); in the same way, if the thread lies in a line on the under side of the fabric, the lower tension is too tight or the top tension too loose (diagram 7C).

In both these cases, check the tension of each thread by gently pulling the reel thread (removed from the needle eye) and the shuttle thread. Your sewing machine instruction book will explain how to adjust and correct any fault.

Diagram 6 Machine Needles

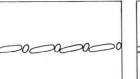
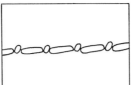

Diagram 7A Balanced Stitch

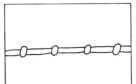
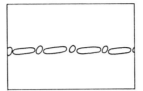

Diagram 7B Slack Lower Tension

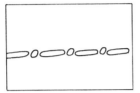
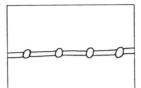

Diagram 7C Tight Lower Tension

Drima Bold Stitch

Drima Bold Stitch is a new extra-strong thread on a distinctive orange-coloured spool, which has been produced for decorative top stitching, sewing on buttons and hand-made buttonholes. It is available in 38 shades plus black and white.

Hand Sewing

To outline and give a decorative effect use Drima Bold Stitch for saddle stitching edges. Saddle stitching is formed with long evenly spaced Running Stitches.

Sewing on Buttons

For extra strength use Drima Bold Stitch to sew on buttons.

Machine Sewing

This thread makes good bold decorative machine stitching. Use the largest stitch on your sewing machine and a No. 100/16 machine needle. When decorative stitching the machine should be threaded with Drima Bold Stitch, while the bobbin must be filled with ordinary Drima in a matching colour.

Stitch Problems

The use of the Fabric and Thread chart on the right and the careful study of your sewing machine should make sewing virtually fault-free. However, faults can and do occur occasionally. Here are some of the most common problems and their remedies.

Needle Thread Breaks

There are several causes:
a) The needle tension is too tight.
b) The machine is wrongly threaded.
c) The needle is too fine for the thread used.

FABRIC AND THREAD CHART

	Fabrics	Thread	Machine Needle No. B: British C: Continental B	C	Milward Hand Needle No.	No. of Stitches to the cm (in)
Fine Fabrics	Organdie	Coats Drima	9 or 11	70	8 or 9	3–4 (8–10)
	Voile		9 or 11	70	8 or 9	3–4 (8–10)
	Lace		9 or 11	70	8 or 9	3–4 (8–10)
	Silk		9 or 11	70	8 or 9	3–4 (8–10)
	Lawn		9 or 11	70	8 or 9	3–4 (8–10)
	Crepe		9 or 11	70	8 or 9	3–4 (8–10)
	Tulle		9 or 11	70	8 or 9	3–4 (8–10)
	Net		9 or 11	70	8 or 9	3–4 (8–10)
Fine/ Medium Fabrics	Cotton	Coats Drima	9 or 11	70 or 80	7 or 8	4–5 (10–12)
	Linen		9 or 11	70 or 80	7 or 8	4–5 (10–12)
	Satin		9 or 11	70 or 80	7 or 8	4–5 (10–12)
	Crimplene		9 or 11	70 or 80	7 or 8	4–5 (10–12)
	Glass Fibre		9 or 11	70 or 80	7 or 8	4–5 (10–12)
	Plastic		9 or 11	70 or 80	7 or 8	3–4 (8–10)
Medium/ Heavy Fabrics	Bonded Fabric	Coats Drima	14	90	7 or 8	3–4 (8–10)
	Vinyl		14	90	7 or 8	3–4 (8–10)
	Jersey		14	90	7 or 8	5–6 (12–14)
	Brocade		14	90	7 or 8	5 (12)
	Wool		14	90	7 or 8	5 (12)
	Corduroy		14	90	7 or 8	5 (12)
	Velvet		14	90	7 or 8	5 (12)
	Terry Cloth		14	90	7 or 8	5 (12)
	Flannel		14	90	7 or 8	5 (12)
	Tweed		14 or 16	90 or 100	5 or 6	4–5 (10–12)

d) The needle is bent.
e) The point of the needle is broken.

Skipped Stitches

These result from four possible causes:
a) The needle has been incorrectly inserted.
b) The needle has become blunt.
c) The needle is the wrong size for the fabric.
d) Fabric finish — use a ballpoint needle.

Top and Under Thread not catching

When the needle has been wrongly inserted the top thread will not pick up the under thread. The needle must always be inserted properly.

Looped Stitches on under side of Fabric

Incorrect threading can cause this. Or perhaps the

upper tension is too light. Alternatively the presser foot is not being let down correctly.

Bobbin (under) Thread Breaks

Here there are three possible causes:
a) The lower tension is too tight.
b) The bobbin has been unevenly wound.
c) The bobbin has been overwound and is too full.

Puckered Fabric

Both upper and lower tensions are probably too tight. If it is certain that the stitching is properly balanced, ease both tensions slightly. Watch that the pressure of the presser foot is not too great.

Stitching Uneven

This may be due to:
a) Using a needle that is too fine with a thread that is too thick.
b) The presser foot not resting fully on the fabric.
c) Fabric being pulled through the machine.
d) Insufficient pressure on the presser foot.
e) The machine is threaded wrongly.
f) The thread has not been wound on the bobbin evenly.

Machine not Feeding Properly

The causes of this are:
a) The feed dog may be lowered.
b) Not enough pressure on the presser foot.

Machine Sews Badly

a) Needle bent, blunt or incorrectly inserted.
b) Bobbin wound unevenly.
c) The thread is too heavy for the needle or the needle is the wrong size.
d) Tension badly adjusted.

Machine Working Heavily

This may be caused by:
a) Machine being oiled too much.
b) Machine requires oiling or needs cleaning.

Hand Sewing Stitches, Seams and Techniques

In all sewing it is necessary to know some hand sewing stitches. Below, are given a few of the basic stitches including seams. A few helpful techniques are also included in this section.

Basting

Basting is a temporary stitch used to hold two or more thicknesses of fabric together, while they are machine stitched. Stitches and the spaces between them should be about 1.5 cm ($\frac{1}{2}$ in). Begin and finish off with two small back stitches (diagram 8). Basting can also be done on the machine – see machine instruction book.

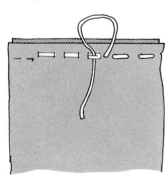

Diagram 8
Basting

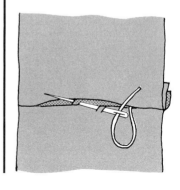

Diagram 9
Slip Basting

10

Diagram 10
Hemming

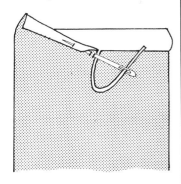

Diagram 11
Slipstitching

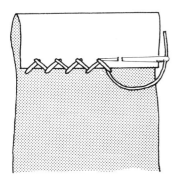

Diagram 12
Herringbone Stitch

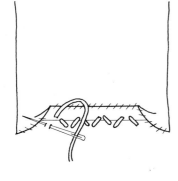

Diagram 13
Catch Stitch

Slip Basting

This type of basting is used to join striped or checked fabric. Fold back seam allowance on one section and place to the fitting line on other section, right sides up. Take a small stitch on under section then on upper section slipping needle through fold (diagram 9).

Hemming

Make small slanting stitches picking up only a thread or two of the fabric, then catching in the fold of the hem. The stitching is visible on the inside only (diagram 10).

Slipstitching

Pick up a thread or two of fabric, then slide the needle along the fold of the hem for 6 mm ($\frac{1}{4}$ in) so that the stitching is invisible on both sides. Do not pull the thread tightly (diagram 11).

Herringbone Stitch

Herringbone stitch is a suitable way of securing hems on heavy fabrics, which do not fray easily. Bring the needle out on the lower line at the left side and insert it on the upper line a little to the right taking a small stitch to the left. Next insert the needle on the lower line a little to the right and take a small stitch to the left. These two movements are worked throughout (diagram 12).

Catch Stitch

This is a neat stitch for finishing a hem edge. Take a small stitch on each side of the fabric (diagram 13). Keep stitches loose so that they do not pull the fabric.

French Tack

Take a small stitch into the fabric of each edge to be caught, making the length about 2.5 cm (1 in). Repeat three or four times, then cover the threads with Buttonhole Stitch (diagram 14).

Flat Seam

Place the two sections, right sides together, edges even. Baste and stitch on the seam line (diagram 15A). Press the seam open (diagram 15B).

Machine Fell Seam

With wrong sides together and raw edges even, baste and stitch the two sections on the fitting line. Trim one raw edge to 3 mm ($\frac{1}{8}$ in) (diagram 16A). Press the raw edges flat so that the wider edge lies on top. Turn in this raw edge, press flat and edge stitch close to the folded edge (diagram 16B).

French Seam

Place the two sections wrong sides together, raw edges even. Baste and stitch approximately 6 mm

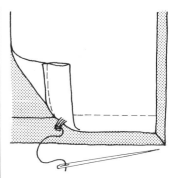

Diagram 14
French Tack

Diagram 15
Flat Seam

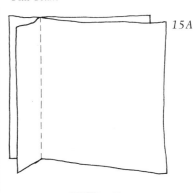

15A

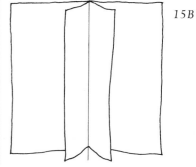

15B

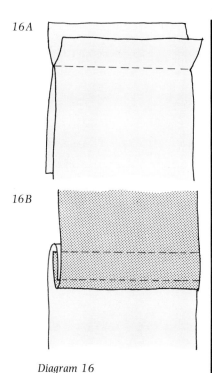

16A

16B

Diagram 16
Machine Fell Seam

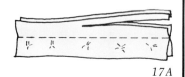

17A

17B

Diagram 17
French Seam

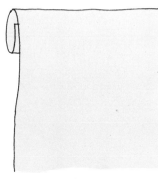

Diagram 18
Double Hem

($\frac{1}{4}$ in) from the seam line. Trim seam and press open (diagram 17A). With the seam on the edge, place the sections right sides together, enclosing the raw edges, and machine stitch on the seam line (diagram 17B).

Double Hem

This type of hem is for use on fine transparent fabric where the raw edge should not be seen. Make the hem turning the same width as the hem (diagram 18).

Mitred Corner

A mitre is a fold used on a hem to achieve smooth shaping at a corner. A true mitre is made when the hems are the same size.

Fold and press the hem, open out the fold and fold the corner inwards on the inner fold line. Cut off the corner leaving a small seam allowance (diagram 19A). Refold the hem, baste and slipstitch the diagonal line of the mitre. Stitch or slipstitch the hems (diagram 19B). When the hems are of different depths as on curtains, make the mitre by turning up the hem and folding on the dotted line (diagram 19C). Trim if necessary and finish as in diagram 19D.

Sewing Notions

Press Studs

Press studs can be used to close an overlapping opening where not too much strain is likely to occur. They provide a neat flat closure and, if sewn reasonably close together (3–4 cm (1–1$\frac{1}{2}$ in)), will not allow gaping.

Press studs are available in various sizes in black and silver metal, and in one size in colourless nylon, which blends with all shades of fabric and is specially suitable for man-made sheer fabrics and fine knitwear. (The nylon type should not be allowed to come in contact with a hot iron, only a heat suitable for nylon fabric).

Press studs have a guide hole in the centre of both halves through which the needle can be passed to ensure correct alignment on both sides of the opening. The smaller half, the stud with a little knob in the centre, should be sewn to the underside of the opening so that the other half can be pressed down on to it.

Mark position of both halves of press stud by pins or tailor's chalk. The ball part is sewn through all thicknesses on the underside of the opening by oversewing or buttonholing. The socket part is sewn through the turning, picking up only a thread of the main fabric to prevent stitching showing on the right side.

For loose covers, curtain linings, etc, press studs already attached to tapes at 4–5 cm (1$\frac{1}{2}$–2 in) intervals are available, so that it is only necessary to align the 2 sides correctly and machine stitch along both edges of the tapes. These tapes can be bought in 3 widths and 4 neutral shades.

Diagram 19
Mitred Corner

19A

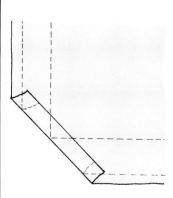

19B

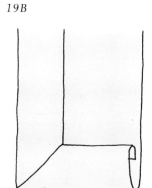

19C

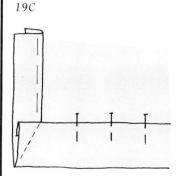

19D

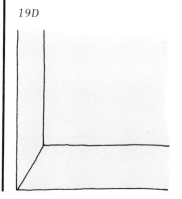

Hooks and Eyes

Included among the original types of clothing fastenings, pins, brooches, buttons and lacings, were crude metal prong fastenings, but hook and eye fasteners really came into use in the 16th century to secure tight-waisted full-skirted garments.

They remain today probably the cheapest secure fastening where strain occurs and are often used in conjunction with other types of fasteners, such as press studs and zips.

The main drawback to using hooks and eyes for a long opening on anything which is tight fitting is that gaps appear between each hook unless they are sewn very close together.

Hooks and eyes and hooks and bars are available in black and silver metal in a variety of sizes to suit all fabrics.

Hooks and eyes should always be sewn in position with Buttonhole Stitches. Secure the band of the hook with a few straight stitches; then Buttonhole Stitch through the rings of the hook. The position for the eye, bar or buttonhole loop may be determined by placing the hook over a pin. Sew the eye or bar with Buttonhole Stitches or work a small fine Buttonhole Bar.

Velcro

The idea was born about 1957 when a Swiss inventor George de Hestral was fascinated by the plant burrs which clung tenaciously to both his clothes and the coat of his dog, when walking or hunting. He studied the mechanism of this attraction under the microscope and set out to reproduce the action in a textile fastener. The result is Velcro. It consists of two nylon strips, one with thousands of tiny hooks, and the other with thousands of tiny loops. When pressed together, the hooks grip the loops to give a tight secure closure. Yet the two strips can be easily separated by simply pulling them apart.

Velcro can be opened and closed without losing its power of adhesion and normally will outlast the life of the article on which it is used. It can be washed, dry cleaned, ironed (preferably in closed position), cut to any length, pinked or notched, and sewn by hand or machine to almost any fabric including leather, plastic etc. Velcro strips do not fray. Therefore, they can be cut into separate pieces and sewn at regular intervals, thus reducing cost.

It is available in 17 shades in 4 widths − 1.5 cm ($\frac{1}{2}$ in), 2.5 cm (1 in), 3 cm (1$\frac{1}{4}$ in) and 5 cm (2 in).

The soft strip is loops, the firm one, hooks. As a general rule, *it is preferable to attach the hook strip to the fixed part, and the loop strip to the removable part.* The choice of width depends on the weight of the fabric and the behaviour of the fixed part. The best method of attaching is by means of a row of stitching along each edge using any strong thread, such as Drima. You will find that it passes easily under the machine foot like any other textile material.

Zip Fasteners

For most purposes, zip fasteners form the best method of closing an opening. Cushion covers and duvet covers can be fitted with zips to make it easier to remove the cover for washing. Zips are also used on one or both side backs of loose covers and are fitted with the bottom stop at the top of the opening (See loose covers page 108, diagram 2).

Three methods of fitting a zip fastener are as follows.

Diagram 20

Visible Method (diagram 20)

This is the original and simplest way of fitting a zip. The teeth and 3 mm ($\frac{1}{8}$ in) of tape on either side are visible and the two rows of stitching are worked close to the edges of the fabric.

Diagram 21

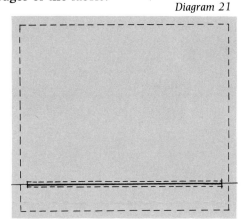

Semi-Concealed Method (diagram 21)

Two rows of stitching, each 6 mm ($\frac{1}{4}$ in) from the centre of the opening, and a double row below the bottom stop, show on the outside. The two edges of the opening overlap slightly and conceal all but the cap of the slider.

Diagram 22

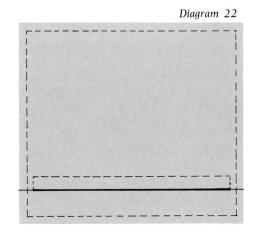

13

Concealed Method (diagram 22)

One row of stitching and a double row just below the bottom stop shows on the right side. The first row of stitching 3 mm ($\frac{1}{8}$ in) from the zip teeth and the zip are completely covered by the overlap.

Cushion covers have been chosen to illustrate the principles of handling zip fasteners, because the openings are cut on a straight thread, and there are no fitting problems such as arise in skirts and dresses.

Points to Remember

1. For bulky or easily frayed fabric, allow turnings of at least 2.5 cm (1 in). For other fabrics 2 cm ($\frac{3}{4}$ in) is sufficient.
2. When the semi-concealed or concealed methods are to be used for a box cushion, the part of the border in which the zip is to be sewn must be cut 4–5 cm ($1\frac{1}{2}$–2 in) wider than the rest of the border to allow for sufficient turnings to cover the zip.
3. In all cases the zip is fitted first before making up the cover.
4. Attach a piping or cording foot to the sewing machine before fitting the zip.
5. Make sure that no raw edges of fabric come in contact with the zip teeth.

Fitting Instructions for Box Cushion Cover with Nylon Zip (Visible Method)

1. Cut 2 squares or rectangles of fabric, the size of cushion plus turnings.
2. Length of zip – length of back of cushion plus 10–15 cm (4–6 in).
3. Width of border – depth of cushion plus turnings.
4. Length of border – overall measurement of the four sides of cushion plus 10 cm (4 in). Cut the border in 2 pieces. 1st strip – length of zip plus 5 cm (2 in). 2nd strip – remaining length of border plus 5 cm (2 in).
Note – If it is not possible to cut the longer strip in one continuous length, two joins should be made to match the two front corners of cushion.

Method

1. Cut along centre of 1st strip of border lengthwise.
2. Turn 6 mm ($\frac{1}{4}$ in) lays on to wrong sides along the newly cut edges.
3. Place zip centrally between those two narrow strips, right side of zip to wrong sides of fabric, with the top of the slider and the bottom stop 2 cm ($\frac{3}{4}$ in) from the ends of the fabric. Adjust width of border to its original width. (The zip teeth and about 3 mm ($\frac{1}{8}$ in) of tape on either side will now be visible between the two strips of fabric).
4. Tack into position and stitch on the right sides close to the folded edges of the fabric (diagram 23).
5. Join the two lengths of border together at the slider end of the opening, two right sides together. Pin and

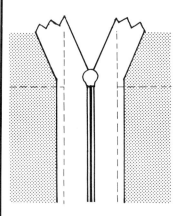

Diagram 24

Diagram 25

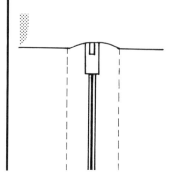

Diagram 23

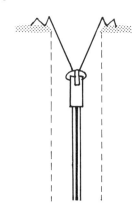

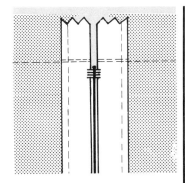

Diagram 26

tack into position. Stitch on a line with the bottom of the slider, leaving a gap between the two rows of stitching on the zip tape (diagram 24).

This forms, on the right side, a small tunnel into which most of the slider will disappear when the zip is fully closed. The pull cannot then be damaged (diagram 25).

6. Place centre of zip-fitted border to centre back of one half of the cover, right sides together. Pin whole of border into position and mark where last border join will have to be made.

7. Join two ends of border by placing right sides together and tacking. Stitch across the width close to and just below the bottom stop with two rows of stitching (diagrams 26 and 27).

8. Tack and stitch the whole of the border on to one half of the cover (diagram 28).

9. Open the zip about 5 cm (2 in).

10. Tack and stitch border on to the other half of the cover.

11. Trim the turnings at all corners.

12. Open the zip fully and turn inside out (diagram 29).

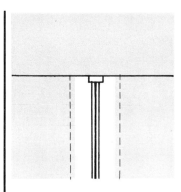

Diagram 27

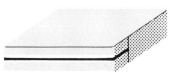

Diagram 29

Diagram 28

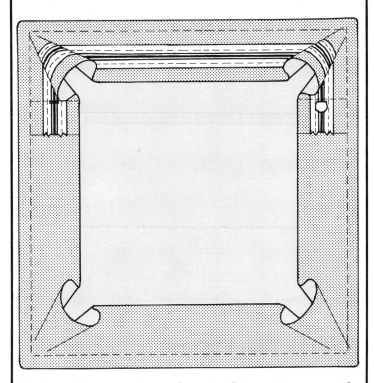

Fitting Instructions for Cushion Cover with Nylon or Metallic Zip (Semi-Concealed Method)

This method is not suitable for a one-way patterned fabric.

The zip is fitted 4 cm (1½ in) from the lower edge of the back of the cushion.

Make the opening as long as possible, bearing in mind that zips over 25 cm (10 in) lengths are available in 5 cm (2 in) increments only. In the finished cover the slider and bottom stop should be between 2.5 cm (1 in) and 4 cm (1½ in) from the outside edges so that the tape ends will lie flat.

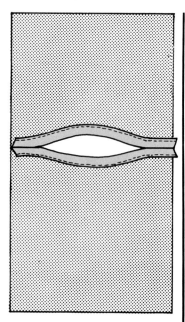

Diagram 30

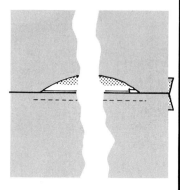

Diagram 31

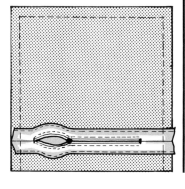

Diagram 34

Preparation

Cut one piece of fabric, width of cushion plus turnings and twice the depth of cushion plus turnings. Cut into two so that one piece is 8 cm (3 in) longer than the other.

Length of zip = width of cut-out fabric less 10–15 cm (4–6 in).

Method

1. Place two right sides of fabric together widthways with top edges level.
2. Tack and stitch two short seams of equal length at either end to leave an opening of 6 mm (¼ in) longer than the zip. These seams will be between 3–5 cm (1¼–2 in).
3. Open the seams and finish the raw edges of both turnings (diagram 30).
4. Place the right side of the zip to the wrong side of the opening so that the top of the slider fits into one corner and the bottom stop into the other. Pin at either end. (Because of the extra 6 mm (¼ in) allowed, the fabric can now be eased on to the zip tape).
5. Place one folded edge so that it almost covers the zip teeth. Tack and stitch 6 mm (¼ in) from this edge (diagram 31).
6. Place the other folded edge so that it almost covers the zip teeth. There should now be a slight ridge of fabric over the centre of the zip. Tack and stitch 6 mm (¼ in) from the folded edge.
7. Still working on the right side, finish by stitching across the top of the slider and close to, and just below, the bottom stop with a double row (diagram 32).
8. Fold two right sides of cover together (diagram 33).
9. Stitch down the two sides, just catching the tape ends in the seam. Open the zip about 5 cm (2 in). Stitch across the top (diagram 34).
10. Trim all turnings, and remove surplus bulk at corners. Open zip fully and turn right side out. Close zip.
11. Stitch round all four sides of cover. The width of these seams should be sufficient to cover the raw edges of fabric in the inside (diagram 35).

Fitting Instructions for Cushion Cover with Nylon or Metallic Zip (Concealed Method)

This method of making a cushion cover is not suitable for a one-way patterned fabric.

Allow turnings of at least 2.5 cm (1 in) at opening edges. The zip is completely concealed and is fitted 4 cm (1½ in) from the lower edge of the back of the cushion. Make the opening as long as possible. Zips over 25 cm (10 in) lengths are available in 5 cm (2 in) increments only and this has to be taken into account when deciding on the length of the opening. As a guide the zip should be 5–8 cm (2–3 in) less than the width of the finished cover.

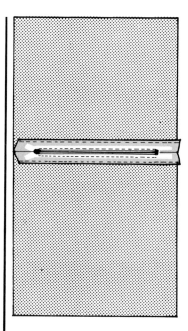

Diagram 32

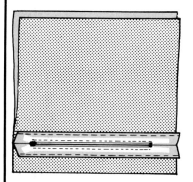

Diagram 33

Diagram 35

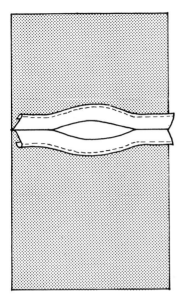

Diagram 36

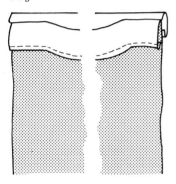

Diagram 37

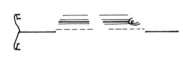

Diagram 38

Diagram 39

Preparation

Cut one piece of fabric, width of cushion plus turnings and twice the depth of cushion plus turnings.
Cut into two so that one piece is 8 cm (3 in) longer than the other.
Length of zip = width of cut-out fabric less 10–15 cm (4–6 in).

Method

1. Place two right sides of fabric together widthways, with top edges level.
2. Tack and stitch two short seams of equal length at either end to leave an opening 6 mm ($\frac{1}{4}$ in) longer than the zip. These seams will be between 4–5 cm ($1\frac{1}{2}$–2 in).
3. Open the seams and finish raw edges of both turnings (diagram 36).
4. Still working from the wrong side, and with the longer piece of material uppermost, lay the two edges of the opening together. Then extend the line of the shorter piece by 6 mm ($\frac{1}{4}$ in) beyond the original seam line (diagram 37).
5. Place the zip, right side uppermost, behind this extended seam allowance so that the top of the slider is in line with one end of the opening, and the bottom stop in line with the other. (Because of the extra 6 mm ($\frac{1}{4}$ in) allowed, the fabric can now be eased on to the zip tape.) Making sure that there will be 3 mm ($\frac{1}{8}$ in) between the edge of the fabric and the teeth, tack and stitch the whole length of the fastener tape (diagram 38).
6. Turn to the right side of the fabric and open out so that the free edge of the opening lies along the original seam line and the zip is completely hidden. Tack this free edge along the seam line with a catch stitch (diagram 39).
7. Measure 2 cm ($\frac{3}{4}$ in) in from this edge and mark a line parallel to the seam line.
8. Tack and stitch across the top of slider along the marked line and below the bottom stop (diagram 39).
9. Fold two right sides of cover together (diagram 40).
10. Stitch down the two sides just catching the tape ends in the seams. Open the zip about 5 cm (2 in). Stitch across the top (diagram 41).
11. Trim all turnings and remove surplus bulk at corners. Open zip fully and turn cover right side out. Close zip.
12. Stitch round all four sides of cover. The width of these seams should be sufficient to cover the raw edges in the inside (diagram 42).

Embroidery

Free Style Embroidery

The most popular type of embroidery is Free Style embroidery which is worked over a traced or hot-iron transfer design or from a stamped linen.

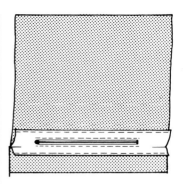

Diagram 40

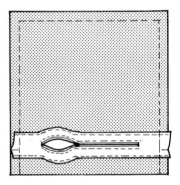

Diagram 41

Diagram 42

Counted Thread Embroidery

In contrast to Free Style embroidery, Counted Thread embroidery requires no tracing or transfer and is worked by counting the threads of the fabric and working each stitch over an exact number of threads. Evenweave fabric or canvas must be used.

Use of Stitches

Many of the embroidery stitches are used only in Free Style embroidery and others are used only in Counted Thread embroidery. In certain cases, stitches may be used for both types, eg Satin Stitch and Back Stitch.

Hardanger Embroidery

Hardanger embroidery should always be worked on an evenweave fabric. Satin Stitch is the basic stitch and is worked in groups (blocks) comprising an uneven number of stitches. When all the Satin Stitch blocks have been completed, the fabric threads are then cut and withdrawn as required. The loose threads are overcast or woven to form bars, and various filling stitches worked within the spaces left by the drawn threads. Satin Stitch blocks are worked with Anchor Pearl Cotton No. 5; bars and fillings with Anchor Pearl Cotton No. 8.

Canvas Embroidery

There are various types of canvas: single thread, double thread, fine and coarse. The type of canvas required will depend upon the thickness of embroidery thread to be used.

Petit Point is the stitch used on a fine, single thread canvas, while Gros Point is suitable for the slightly heavier double thread canvas. Both come under the general name of Tent Stitch.

Embroidery Materials and Techniques

The effective combination of fabric, thread, design and stitch, all carefully chosen for their suitability in relation to each other, produce work of real beauty. To achieve this one must use the best materials. The chart on page 19 will help you to select the correct type and size of needle and thread to be used on a variety of fabrics.

Threads

Anchor Stranded Cotton has six separate strands which are loosely twisted together. Six strands may be used at one time, or they may be separated and used singly or in groups of two, three or four. The thread is lustrous and is suitable for most types of embroidery. Anchor Pearl Cotton No. 5 and No. 8 is a smooth corded thread, most suitable for Hardanger work and other types of Counted Thread work. Pearl Cotton No. 8 is widely used for Cut-work embroidery. It is also suitable for all medium fine embroidery – both Free Style and Counted. Anchor Soft Embroidery is a thread with a thick matt finish, for bold embroidery in either Free Style or Counted Thread; it is also suitable for tapestries. Anchor Tapisserie Wool is a firm, well twisted woollen yarn, excellent for canvas embroidery and the working of tapestries, as well as Free Style and Counted Thread. It is moth-resistant and colour fast and can be washed as well as the other threads without any danger of the colour running.

Needles

In Free Style embroidery, Milward 'Gold Seal' crewel and chenille needles are used; the former for fine and medium weight threads and fabrics, the latter for heavier threads and fabrics. For Counted Thread embroidery, Milward 'Gold Seal' round pointed tapestry needles are always used.

Scissors

These should be sharp with pointed blades suitable for trimming away the surplus fabric in Cut-work, as well as for snipping the threads in Hardanger and Drawn Thread embroideries.

Thimbles

A thimble is essential for embroidery, to protect the middle finger when pushing the needle through the fabric. Buy a good quality one in metal (preferably silver) or plastic and make sure that it fits well.

Embroidery Frames

Some embroideries with areas of closely worked stitches are apt to pucker. In this case, an embroidery frame is recommended to help keep the work flat and even. There are several types of frames. An embroidery ring is most commonly used for small pieces of work. The ring usually consists of two wooden or metal rings, fitting closely one within the other, so that the fabric may be stretched tightly. These rings can be obtained in various sizes, the most useful type having a small screw on the larger ring for loosening or tightening it. This allows any thickness of fabric to be used. The section of embroidery to be worked is placed over the smaller of the rings, the other ring being pressed down over the fabric on the smaller ring to hold the work taut. If a screw is attached, this should be tightened. The warp and weft threads of the fabric must be straight in the ring.

For large pieces of embroidery, especially tapestries, the work should be mounted on a square or rectangular frame. These frames generally consist of two rollers, each with a piece of tape firmly nailed along its length (ie top and bottom) and two side laths which fit into holes or slots on each roller. The fabric or canvas to be worked is stitched to the tape on each roller. The side laths are then secured with the four screws to make the fabric taut and even. The sides of the canvas are securely laced round the laths with double cotton; if fine fabric is used, stitch tape to the free sides then lace.

Embroidery rings and frames can be supplied with a stand, which leaves the embroideresses' hands free.

Tracing Methods

An embroideress who has created her own design will require to trace it on to a selected fabric. Many embroidery designs are produced in such a way that the embroideress either has to follow a large tracing sheet or make a tracing from an actual size reproduction of the design. We give four methods and the embroideress may select the one she prefers.

1. The simplest method is with the use of carbon paper. Yellow or light blue carbon paper may be used on dark coloured fabric, black or dark blue carbon on light coloured fabric. Place the carbon paper in position face downwards on the fabric, then place the drawing or tracing of the design on top. Draw over all the lines with a sharp-pointed pencil. Care must be taken to press only on the lines of the design, otherwise the carbon may smudge the fabric.

2. Trace the design on to firm tracing paper then, with a needle, prick small holes over all the lines, spacing the holes evenly about 2 mm ($\frac{1}{16}$ in) apart. Rub the back of the pricked design with fine sandpaper to remove the roughness. Place the pricked design on the fabric and keep in position with weights. Rub

powdered charcoal (for light coloured fabric) or powdered chalk (for dark coloured fabric) through the holes. Remove the tracing paper and blow off the surplus powder from the fabric. Paint over the dotted lines of powder with water colour paint, using a fine brush and not too much water. Use dark or light coloured paint depending upon the colour of the fabric.

3. The design can be traced directly on to fine transparent fabric such as organdie, nylon or fine silk, by placing the design underneath the fabric and painting over the lines with water colour paint or tracing with a soft pencil.

4. On very coarse or textured fabric, the pile makes it difficult to trace or paint a design. In this case, trace the drawing on to fine tracing paper, baste the paper in position on the fabric, then carefully mark over all the lines of the design with small Running Stitches. The drawing can be torn away before the embroidery is commenced. Remove all basting stitches after the completion of the embroidery.

General Washing Instructions

Use warm water and pure soap flakes. Wash by squeezing gently. Rinse thoroughly in warm water, squeeze by hand and leave until half dry. Iron on reverse side while still damp, using a moderately hot iron. An article worked on canvas *must* be dry cleaned.

Embroidery Threads, Needles and Fabrics

Fabric	Clark's Anchor Embroidery Threads	Thickness	Milward Needle Sizes	Remarks
Fine linen, lawn, organdie, sheer silk or fine synthetics	Stranded Cotton Pearl Cotton No. 8	1, 2 or 3 strands	Crewel Needles (sharp points) No. Strands 8 1 and 2	These fabrics, threads and needles are for working designs traced or transferred on to the fabric.
Medium weight linen, rayon, sailcloth, satin, etc.	Stranded Cotton Pearl Cotton No. 8	2, 3 or 4 strands	7 3 strands 6 4 strands and Pearl Cotton No. 8 5 6 strands and Pearl Cotton No. 5	The number of strands of Stranded Cotton may be varied on any article according to the requirements of the design.
Heavy linen, crash or furnishing fabric	Stranded Cotton Pearl Cotton No. 5	6 strands		
Fine evenweave linen	Stranded Cotton Pearl Cotton No. 8, 5	1–6 strands	Tapestry Needles (rounded point) No. Strands 1 and 2	These threads and needles are used when working over counted threads of canvas or fabric.
Medium weight evenweave linen, medium mesh canvas, etc.	Stranded Cotton Pearl Cotton No. 8, 5 or Tapisserie Wool	3, 4 or 6 strands	24 ⎰ 3 ⎱ 4 and Pearl Cotton No. 8 20 6 and Pearl Cotton No. 5 18 Soft Embroidery, Tapisserie Wool	
Coarse evenweave linen and fabric, heavy mesh canvas	Stranded Cotton Pearl Cotton No. 5 Soft Embroidery Tapisserie Wool	4 or 6 strands		
Medium weight square weave canvas	Stranded Cotton Pearl Cotton No. 5 Soft Embroidery Tapisserie Wool	3, 4 or 6 strands	Tapestry Needles (rounded point) No. Thickness 20 6 strands and Pearl Cotton No. 5 18 Soft Embroidery, Tapisserie Wool	These threads and needles are used for working over counted threads of fabric or canvas.
Heavy square weave canvas	Stranded Cotton Soft Embroidery Tapisserie Wool	6 strands		
Heavy linen, crash or furnishing fabric, etc.	Soft Embroidery Tapisserie Wool		Chenille Needle (sharp point) No. Thickness 18 Soft Embroidery, Tapisserie Wool	These threads and needle are used for traced or transferred design.

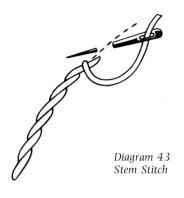

Diagram 43
Stem Stitch

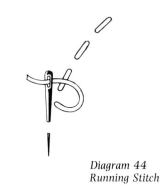

Diagram 44
Running Stitch

Diagram 45
Laced Running Stitch

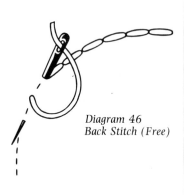

Diagram 46
Back Stitch (Free)

Diagram 47
Back Stitch (Counted)

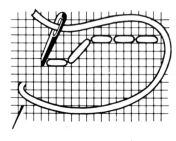

Outline Stitches

Stem Stitch

Work from left to right, taking regular, slightly slanting stitches along the line of the design. The thread always emerges on the left side of the previous stitch. This stitch is used for flower stems, outlines, etc. It can also be used as a filling, by working rows of Stem Stitch closely together within a shape until it is completely filled.

Running Stitch

Pass the needle over and under the fabric, making the upper stitches of equal length. The under stitches should also be of equal length, but half the size or less of the upper stitches.

Laced Running Stitch

Running Stitch can be laced with a contrasting colour to form a decorative border. Use a round-pointed needle for lacing, and do not pick up any of the fabric.

Back Stitch (Free)

Bring the thread through on the stitch line, then take a small backward stitch through the fabric. Bring the needle through again a little in front of the first stitch, and take another stitch, inserting the needle at the point where it first came through.

Back Stitch (Counted)

Bring the thread out at the right-hand side. Take a backward stitch over three threads, bringing the needle out three threads in front of the place where the threads first emerged. Continue in this way, working from right to left in the required direction.

Overcast Stitch (or Trailing)

Bring the laid threads through at A and hold with left thumb, then bring through the working thread at A and work small Satin Stitches (see page 21) closely over the laid threads, following the line of the design. The laid threads are taken through to the back of the fabric to finish. This stitch resembles a fine cord and is useful for embroidering delicate stems and outlines.

Flat Stitches

Straight Stitch

This is shown as single spaced stitches worked either in a regular or irregular manner. Sometimes the stitches are of varying size. The stitches should be neither too long nor too loose. This stitch may also be worked on evenweave fabric.

Straight Stitch Star

Work a number of Straight Stitches of varying lengths, all radiating from a central point.

Diagram 48
Overcast Stitch (or Trailing)

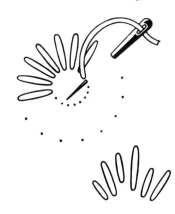

Diagram 49
Straight Stitch

Diagram 50
Straight Stitch Star

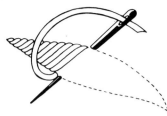

Diagram 51
Satin Stitch (Free)

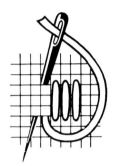

Diagram 52
Satin Stitch (Counted)

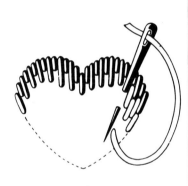

Diagram 53
Long and Short Stitch

Diagram 54
Roumanian Stitch

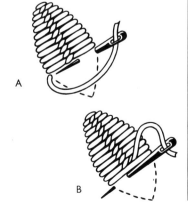

Satin Stitch (Free)

Proceed with Straight Stitches worked closely together across the shape, as shown in the diagram. If desired, Running Stitch or Chain Stitch may be worked first to form a padding underneath, giving a raised effect. Care must be taken to keep a good edge. Do not make the stitches too long, as they would then be liable to be pulled out of position.

Satin Stitch (Counted)

This stitch may be worked from right to left or left to right. The number of threads over which the stitches are worked may vary, depending upon the effect desired.

Long and Short Stitch

This form of Satin Stitch is so named as all the stitches are of varying lengths. It is often used to fill a shape which is too large or too irregular to be covered by Satin Stitch. It is also used to achieve a shaded effect. In the first row, the stitches are alternately long and short and closely follow the outline of the shape. The stitches in the following rows are worked to achieve a smooth appearance. The diagram shows how a shaded effect may be obtained.

Roumanian Stitch

A – Bring the thread through at the top left of the shape, carry the thread across and take a stitch on the right side of the shape with the thread below the needle. B – Take a stitch at left side, thread above needle. These two movements are worked until the shape is filled. Keep the stitches close together. The size of the centre crossing stitch can be varied to make a longer oblique stitch or a small straight stitch.

Herringbone Stitch

Bring the needle out on the lower line at the left side and insert on the upper line a little to the right, taking a small stitch to the left with the thread below the needle. Next, insert thé needle on the lower line a little to the right and take a small stitch to the left with the thread above the needle.

These two movements are worked throughout. For the best effect, the fabric lifted by the needle and the spaces between the stitches should be of equal size. This stitch can be laced with a matching or contrasting thread. Use a round-pointed needle for lacing and do not pick up any of the fabric. Herringbone Stitch may also be worked on evenweave fabric.

Double Back Stitch or Closed Herringbone Stitch

This stitch is used for Shadow-work on fine transparent fabric and can be worked on the right side of the fabric as at A – a small Back Stitch worked alternately on each side of the traced double lines (the dotted lines on the diagram show the formation of the thread on

Diagram 55
Herringbone Stitch

Diagram 56
Double Back Stitch or
Closed Herringbone Stitch

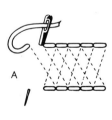

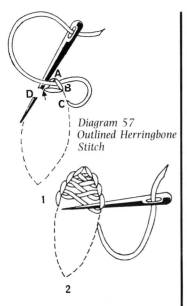

Diagram 57
Outlined Herringbone
Stitch

1

2

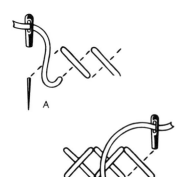

Diagram 58
Cross Stitch (Free)

A

B

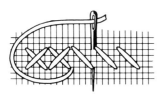

Diagram 59
Cross Stitch (Counted)

Diagram 60
Eyelet Holes

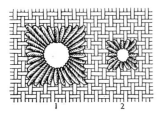

the wrong side of the fabric). The colour of the thread appears delicately through the fabric. B shows the stitch worked on the wrong side of the fabric as a Closed Herringbone Stitch, with no spaces left between stitches. Both methods achieve the same result.

Outlined Herringbone Stitch

1 – Bring the thread out at the arrow; insert the needle at A; bring out at B; insert at A; bring out at arrow; insert at B; and bring out at C. Pass the needle under the back stitch as shown and insert the needle at the arrow; bring out at D. Pass the needle under the first stitch made and insert at C. 2 – Continue working from side to side until the shape has been filled.

Cross Stitch (Free)

A – Bring the needle through on the lower right line of the cross and insert at the top of the same line, taking a stitch through the fabric to lower left line. Continue to the end of the row in this way.
B – Complete the other half of the cross. It is important that the upper half of each stitch lies in one direction.

Cross Stitch (Counted)

Bring the needle out at the lower right-hand side, insert the needle four threads up and four threads to the left and bring out four threads down, thus forming a half Cross Stitch. Continue in this way to the end of the row. Complete the other half of the cross as shown. Cross Stitch may be worked either from left to right, as shown, or from right to left. It is important that the upper half of all the stitches lies in one direction.

Eyelet Holes

1 – Large Eyelet Hole composed of thirty-two stitches worked over a square of eight fabric threads, one stitch between each of the fabric threads in the square and all stitches into the same central hole. No fabric threads are cut to make the hole, but each stitch being pulled firmly, draws the threads from the centre.
2 – Small Eyelet Hole composed of sixteen stitches worked over a square of four fabric threads.

Looped Stitches

Blanket Stitch and Buttonhole Stitch

These stitches are worked in the same way, the difference being that in Buttonhole Stitch the stitches are close together. Bring the thread out on the lower line, insert the needle in position in the upper line, taking a straight downward stitch with the thread under the needle point. Pull up the stitch to form a loop and repeat. This stitch may also be worked on evenweave fabric.

Up and Down Buttonhole Stitch

A – Commence as for ordinary Buttonhole Stitch and

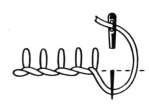

Diagram 61
Blanket Stitch and
Buttonhole Stitch

Diagram 62
Up and Down Buttonhole Stitch

A

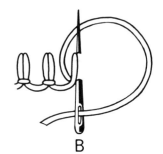

B

22

Diagram 63
Buttonhole Stitch Bars

Diagram 64
Feather Stitch

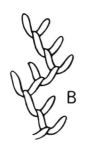

Diagram 65
Fly Stitch

pull thread through. B — Insert the needle on the bottom line and take a straight upward stitch with the thread under the needle point. Pull thread through first in an upward movement, then downwards to continue. This stitch may also be worked on evenweave fabric.

Buttonhole Stitch Bars and Double Buttonhole Stitch Bars

These bars are used in Cut-work and Richelieu work. Make a row of Running Stitch between the double lines of the design as a padding for the Buttonhole Stitch. Where a single line bar occurs, take a thread across the space and back, securing with a small stitch, and Buttonhole Stitch closely over the loose threads without picking up any of the fabric (A). Buttonhole Stitch round the shape, keeping the looped edge of the stitch to the inside, then cut away the fabric from behind the bar and round the inside of the shape. Where a double line or a broad bar is required between shapes or sometimes for stems of flowers, when the fabric is to be cut away on each side, make a row of Running Stitch along the centre, then Buttonhole Stitch along one side, spacing the stitches slightly. Buttonhole Stitch along the other side into the spaces left by the first row. The fabric is then cut away close to the Buttonhole Stitch, leaving a strong, broad bar.

Feather Stitch

A — Bring the needle out at the top centre, hold the thread down with the left thumb, insert the needle a little to the right on the same level and take a small stitch down to the centre, keeping the thread under the needle point. Next, insert the needle a little to the left on the same level and take a stitch to centre, keeping the thread under the needle point. Work these two movements alternately. B — Shows Double Feather Stitch, in which two stitches are taken to the right and left alternately.

Fly Stitch

Bring the thread through at the top left and hold it down with the left thumb. Insert the needle to the right on the same level, a little distance from where the thread first emerged, and take a small stitch downwards to the centre with the thread below the needle. Pull through and insert the needle again below the stitch at the centre (A) and bring it through in position for the next stitch. This stitch may be worked singly or in horizontal rows (A), or vertical rows (B).

Chain Stitches

Chain Stitch

Bring the thread out at top of line and hold with left thumb. Insert the needle where it last emerged and bring the point out a short distance away. Pull the

Diagram 66
Chain Stitch

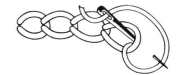

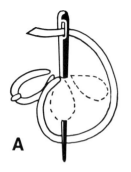

Diagram 67
Daisy Stitch or
Detached Chain Stitch

A

thread through, keeping the working thread under the needle point.

Daisy Stitch or Detached Chain Stitch

Work in the same way as Chain Stitch (A), but fasten each loop at the foot with a small stitch (B). This may be worked singly or in groups to form flower petals. Two Daisy Stitches, one worked within the other, form a Double Daisy Stitch (C).

Twisted Chain Stitch

Commence as for ordinary Chain Stitch, but instead of inserting the needle into the place from where it emerged, insert it close to the last loop and take a small slanting stitch, coming out on the line of the design. Pull the thread through. The loops of this stitch should be worked closely together to give the right effect.

Cable Chain Stitch

Bring the thread through at A and hold it down with the left thumb. Pass the needle from right to left under the working thread, then twist the needle back over the working thread to the right and, still keeping the thread under the thumb, take a stitch of the required length. Pull thread through.

Knotted Stitches

French Knots

Bring the thread out at the required position, hold the thread down with the left thumb and encircle the thread twice with the needle as at A. Still holding the thread firmly, twist the needle back to the starting point and insert it close to where the thread first emerged (see arrow). Pull thread through to the back and secure for a single French Knot or pass to the position of the next stitch as at B.

Double Knot Stitch

Bring the thread through at A. Take a small stitch across the line at B. Pass the needle downwards under the surface stitch just made, without piercing the fabric, as at C. With the thread under the needle, pass the needle again under the first stitch as at D. Pull the thread through to form a knot. The knots should be spaced evenly and closely to obtain a beaded effect.

Spanish Knotted Feather Stitch

Bring the thread through and hold down to the left with the left thumb. Take a slanting stitch to the left through the fabric under the laid thread and pull through with the needle point over the working thread as shown at A. Pass the thread over to the right and back to the left to form a loop and hold down, then take a slanting stitch to the right under the laid thread and pull through with the needle over the

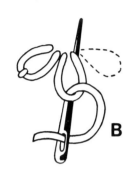

B

C

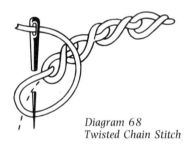

Diagram 68
Twisted Chain Stitch

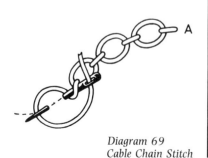

A

Diagram 69
Cable Chain Stitch

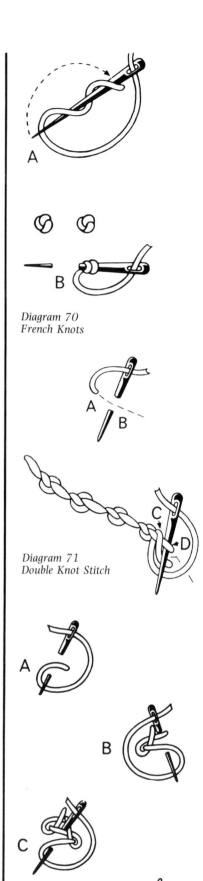

A

B

Diagram 70
French Knots

A **B**

C **D**

Diagram 71
Double Knot Stitch

A

B

C

Diagram 72
Spanish Knotted
Feather Stitch

D

Diagram 73
Couching

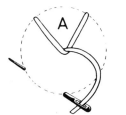

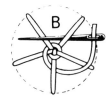

Diagram 74
Spider's Web Filling

working thread B. Take a stitch in the same way to the left C. Repeat B and C to the end of the line, then fasten off with a small stitch as shown at D.

Couching and Filling Stitches

Couching

Lay a thread along the line of the design and, with another thread, tie it down at even intervals with a small stitch into the fabric. The tying stitch can be of contrasting colour to the laid thread if desired.

Spider's Web Filling

Commence with a Fly Stitch to the centre of the circle as shown in A, then work two Straight Stitches, one on each side of the Fly Stitch tail, into the centre of the circle. This divides the circle into five equal sections and the 'spokes' form the foundation of the web. Weave over and under the 'spokes' until the circle is filled in as at B. In Drawn Thread embroidery the 'spokes' are not completely covered by the weaving; only half the circle is filled, which gives the filling an open, lacy appearance.

Double Faggot Filling Stitch

Bring the thread out at A, insert at B twice; bring out at C, insert at A twice; bring out at D; continue in this way required number of times. Insert needle as shown in 1, turn fabric and work second row in same way. In 2, the second row is shown without shading.

Composite Stitches

Raised Chain Band

Work the required number of foundation bars, which are fairly closely spaced horizontal Straight Stitches. Bring the thread through at A, then pass the needle upwards under the centre of the first bar and to the left of A. With the thread under the needle, pass the needle downwards to the right of A and pull up the chain loop thus formed.

Drawn Thread Embroidery

Hemstitch

Measure required depth of hem, plus turnings, and withdraw required number of threads. Do not withdraw the threads right across the fabric, but only to form a square or rectangle. Cut threads at the centre and withdraw gradually outwards on each side to within the hem measurement, leaving a sufficient length of thread at corners in order to darn the ends invisibly. Turn back the hem to the space of the drawn threads, mitre corners and baste. Bring the working thread out two fabric threads down from the drawn threads and through the folded hem at the right-hand side. Pass the needle behind four loose threads, then insert the needle behind the same four threads, bringing the needle out two threads down

Diagram 75
Double Faggot Filling Stitch

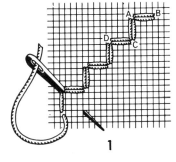

1

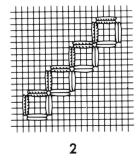

2

Diagram 76
Raised Chain Band

Diagram 77
Hemstitch

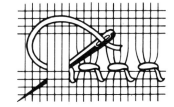

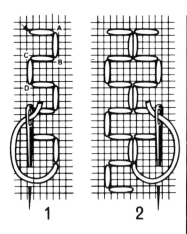

Diagram 78
Honeycomb Filling Stitch

Diagram 79
Four-Sided Stitch

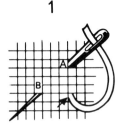

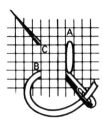

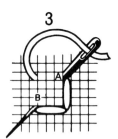

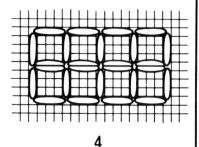

through all the folds of the hem in readiness for the next stitch. The number of threads may be varied to suit the fabric or design.

Drawn Fabric Stitches

Honeycomb Filling Stitch

This filling stitch is worked from the top downwards. 1 – Bring the thread through at the arrow; insert the needle at A (four threads to the right), bring through at B (four threads down), insert again at A, bring through at B; insert at C (four threads to the left), bring through at D (four threads down); insert again at C and bring through at D. Continue in this way for the required length. Turn the fabric round for next and each following row and work in the same way. Where rows connect, the vertical stitches are worked into the same holes. All stitches should be pulled firmly. 2 – Shows two rows of stitching and how they form a filling.

Four-Sided Stitch

This stitch is worked from right to left and can be used as a border or a filling. 1 – Bring the thread through at the arrow; insert the needle at A (four threads up), bring it through at B (four threads down and four to the left). 2 – Insert at the arrow, bring out at C (four threads up and four threads to the left of A). 3 – Insert again at A and bring out at B. Continue in this way to the end of the row or close the end for a single Four-Sided Stitch. For Filling Stitch: 4 – Turn the fabric round for next and all following rows and work in the same way. Pull all stitches firmly.

Pin Stitch

This stitch is mainly a Drawn Fabric stitch, but can be used in Drawn Thread embroidery and for outlining appliqué work. 1 – For a hem edge, bring the thread through the folded hem at A, insert the needle at B and bring out at C; insert once more at B and bring out again at C. 2 – Insert again at B, bring out through the folded hem at D. Continue in this way to end of row. Pull all stitches firmly.

Hardanger Stitches

Overcast Bars

These bars can also be used in Drawn Thread embroidery. To work the bars, withdraw the number of threads required from the fabric and separate the loose threads into bars by overcasting firmly over these threads as many times as required to cover the group of threads completely.

Woven Bars

These bars can also be used in Drawn Thread embroidery. To work them, withdraw an even number of threads from the fabric and separate the loose

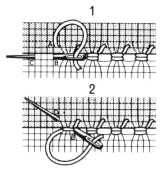

Diagram 80
Pin Stitch

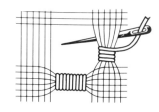

Diagram 81
Overcast Bars

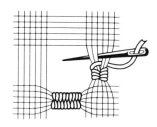

Diagram 82
Woven Bars

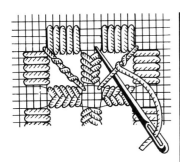

*Diagram 83
Twisted Bars*

threads into bars by weaving over and under an even number of threads until the threads are completely covered.

Twisted Bars

Carry the thread diagonally across the space and twist the thread over as many times as required back to the starting point.

Canvas Stitches

Trammed Gros Point Stitch

1 — Work a Trammed Stitch from left to right, then pull the needle through and insert again up and over the crossed threads. 2 — Pull the needle through on the lower line two double threads (vertical) to the left in readiness for the next stitch.

To work Gros Point Stitch using both hands — with right hand on top of canvas, insert the needle downwards through the canvas and pull the needle through with the left hand. With left hand, push the needle upwards through the canvas and pull out with the right hand.

Petit Point Stitch

1 — Bring the thread out on the left-hand side of the fabric on the top part of the first stitch; pass the needle down diagonally over the crossed threads, then under two threads. Continue in this way to complete the row. 2 — The second row is worked from right to left, the needle passing the crossed threads up and over, then under two threads. Work backwards and forwards in this way until the design is complete. All stitches should slope in the same direction. The stitches on the reverse side are longer and slope more than on the correct side.

General Counted Thread Stitches

Florentine Stitch

This stitch is used for working zig-zag patterns known as Florentine work. It is generally used to fill a large area and is then worked in two or more rows of different colours forming an all-over wave pattern. The size of the wave may be varied, depending upon the number of stitches or the number of threads over which the stitches are worked. The diagram shows the method of working the stitch.

Patchwork

Patchwork is fun to do and you can use lots of odd pieces of fabric that are in your workbox. Although it is easy to make, patchwork has to be carefully planned so that it forms an interesting and colourful design. Mix different types of patterned and plain fabrics, but have all the patches the same fabric weight. Also, never mix washable and unwashable fabrics. Various shapes may be used to form the design, eg octagons,

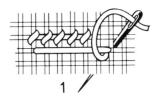

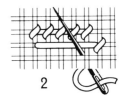

*Diagram 84
Trammed Gros Point Stitch*

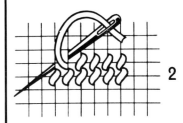

*Diagram 85
Petit Point Stitch*

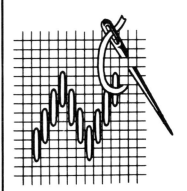

*Diagram 86
Florentine Stitch*

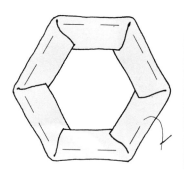

Diagram 87
Patchwork

hexagons, pentagons, squares, triangles and diamonds.

First of all cut the shape you want from stiff paper. The shape must be cut accurately as each section has to be joined together neatly. Cut out this shape from paper for each patchwork section required to form the complete article, then cut out the fabric from the pattern, allowing 6 mm ($\frac{1}{4}$ in) seam allowance. Place one paper shape to wrong side of fabric, turn in fabric edges over paper and baste (diagram 87). Repeat with all sections. Place two sections right sides together and oversew two sides. Repeat with remaining sections to form the design. Remove the paper and make up the article.

Patchwork can also be made using the sewing machine. The simplest shape to use for this is a square. Place two sections, right sides together and join two sides. Repeat to form a strip. Press seams open; baste and stitch strips, right sides together (diagram 88).

Quilting

English quilting was traditionally used for warmth, but it can be used today to decorate a wide variety of articles, both for household and personal wear. Italian quilting, however, was used for decoration much as it is today.

English Quilting

The simplest form of English quilting is done with straight lines. Geometric shapes may be marked lightly on to the fabric with a soft pencil. Place wadding to the wrong side of fabric and place muslin over wadding. Baste diagonally all over (diagram 89). Work the design with small Running Stitches, using Drima, or with Back Stitch or Chain Stitch, using Anchor Stranded Cotton. An all-over design formed by lines of stitching is worked in a similar way, but it is unnecessary to mark the lines as they can be worked very quickly using the sewing machine, Drima thread and the quilting guide (diagram 90).

Motif and curved designs may be made using a cardboard shape or a hot iron transfer. The wadding and muslin are then placed to the wrong side of design as before and the design quilted.

Italian Quilting

In this type of quilting the design is outlined and

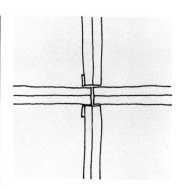

Diagram 88
Machine Patchwork

Diagram 89

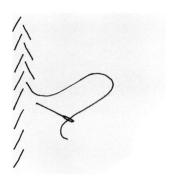

Diagram 90

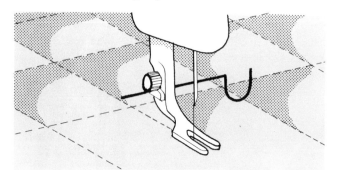

28

quilting wool is drawn through the channel between two layers of fabric, working on the wrong side and piercing the muslin with a bodkin, then drawing the quilting wool through fairly loosely. Where the design makes it necessary to bring the needle out, at a corner, it is inserted into the same hole, leaving a small loop as shown, then the wool is drawn through to avoid puckering the fabric.

Back Stitch

This stitch must be worked through all layers of fabric in two distinct movements, one downwards (from the front) and one upwards (from the back). This ensures that all layers are kept even.

Running Stitch

Worked similarly to Back Stitch through all layers of fabric in one downward and one upward movement to ensure that all layers are kept even.

Crochet

Crochet Stitch Diagrams

The shading on each stitch diagram denotes the foundation chain stitches and the number of turning chain stitches used at the end of the row.

Abbreviations

chain — ch; slip stitch — ss; double crochet — dc; half treble — hlf tr; treble — tr; double treble — dbl tr; triple treble — trip tr; quadruple treble — quad tr; space(s) — sp(s); block(s) — blk(s); picot — p; cluster(s) — cl(s); stitch(es) — st(s).
* (Asterisk). Repeat the instructions following the asterisk as many more times as specified, in addition to the original.
Repeat the instructions in parenthesis as many times as specified. For example, '(5 ch, 1 dc into next dc) 5 times,' means to make all that is in parenthesis 5 times in all.

Position of Thread and Hook

Diagram 91

91 — Grasp yarn near one end of ball between thumb and forefinger of left hand. With right hand form yarn into loop. Hold loop in place between thumb and forefinger of left hand.

92 — With right hand take hold of broad bar of hook as you would a pencil. Insert hook through loop and under yarn. With right hand, catch long end of yarn.

Diagram 92

93 — Draw loop through but do not remove hook from yarn. Pull short end in opposite direction to bring loop close round the end of the hook.

94 — Loop yarn round little finger, across palm and behind forefinger of left hand. Grasp hook and loop between thumb and forefinger of left hand. Pull yarn

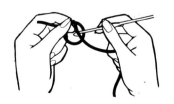

Diagram 93

Diagram 94

Diagram 95

Diagram 96

Diagram 97

Diagram 98

Diagram 99

gently so that it lies round the fingers firmly.

95 – Catch knot of loop between thumb and forefinger. Hold broad bar of hook with right hand as described in diagram 92.

96 – Pass your hook under yarn and catch yarn with hook. This is called 'yarn over'. Draw yarn through loop on hook. This makes one chain.

Chain – ch

97 – This is the foundation of crochet work. With yarn in position and the loop on the hook as shown in diagram 95, pass the hook under the yarn held in left hand and catch yarn with hook. Draw yarn through loop on hook, repeat this movement until chain is desired length (diagram 98).

Slip Stitch – ss

99 – Insert hook into stitch to left of hook, catch yarn with hook and draw through stitch and loop on hook.

Double Crochet – dc

100 – Insert hook into 2nd stitch to left of hook, then catch yarn with hook. Draw through stitch (2 loops on hook) (diagram 101), yarn over hook and draw through 2 loops on hook (1 loop remains on hook) (diagram 102). Continue working into each stitch to left of hook.

Half Treble – hlf tr

103 – Pass hook under the yarn held in left hand then insert hook into 3rd stitch to left of hook, yarn over hook and draw through stitch (3 loops on hook), yarn over hook (diagram 104), draw yarn through all loops on hook (1 loop remains on hook) (diagram 105). Continue working into each stitch to left of hook.

Treble – tr

106 – Pass hook under the yarn of left hand, insert hook into 4th stitch to left of hook, yarn over hook and draw through stitch (3 loops on hook), yarn over hook (diagram 107), and draw through 2 loops on hook, yarn over hook (diagram 108), and draw through remaining 2 loops (1 loop remains on hook) (diagram 109). Continue working into each stitch to left of hook.

Double Treble – dbl tr

110 – Pass hook under the yarn of left hand twice, insert hook into 5th stitch to left of hook, yarn over hook and draw through stitch (4 loops on hook) yarn over hook and draw through 2 loops on hook, yarn over hook and draw through other 2 loops on hook, yarn over hook and draw through remaining 2 loops (1 loop remains on hook).

Diagram 100

Diagram 101

Diagram 102

Diagram 103

Diagram 104

Diagram 105

Diagram 106

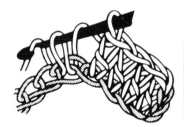

Diagram 107

Diagram 108

Diagram 109

Continue working into each stitch to left of hook.

Triple Treble — trip tr

111 — Pass hook under the yarn of left hand 3 times, insert hook into 6th stitch to left of hook, yarn over hook and draw through stitch (5 loops on hook), yarn over hook and draw through 2 loops on hook, (yarn over hook and draw through other 2 loops on hook) 3 times (1 loop remains on hook). Continue working into each stitch to left of hook.

Quadruple Treble — quad tr

112 — Pass hook under the yarn of left hand 4 times, insert hook into 7th stitch to left of hook and complete in same manner as trip tr until only 1 loop remains.

Space(s) — sp(s)

113 — Filet Crochet
The following four stitches are used mostly in Filet Crochet and are referred to as spaces and blocks, lacets and bars.
Spaces may be made with 2 ch, miss 2 stitches, 1 tr into next stitch.

Block(s) — blk(s) and Space (sp)

114 — 1 tr into 4th stitch to left of hook, 1 tr into each of next 2 stitches, 2 ch, miss 2 stitches, 1 tr into next stitch, 1 tr into each of next 3 stitches.

Bar and Lacet

115 — (a) A bar consists of 5 ch, miss 5 stitches or a lacet, 1 tr into next stitch.
(b) A lacet consists of 3 ch, miss 2 stitches, 1 dc into next stitch, 3 ch, miss 2 stitches, 1 tr into next stitch.

Picot — p

116 — Make a ch of 3, 4 or 5 stitches according to length of picot desired, then join ch to form a ring by working 1 dc into first ch.

Cluster(s) — cl(s)

117 — Leaving the last loop of each on hook, work 2, 3 or more tr or dbl tr into same stitch, yarn over hook and draw through all loops on hook.

Cluster worked into Loop

118 — Leaving the last loop of each on hook, work 3 or more stitches into space or loop on previous row, yarn over and draw through all loops on hook.

Cluster worked over 4 or more Stitches

119 — Leaving the last loop of each on hook, work 1 dbl tr into each of next 4 stitches, yarn over hook and draw through all loops on hook (4 dbl tr cluster).

Diagram 110

Diagram 111

Diagram 112

Diagram 113

Diagram 114

Diagram 115

Joining Circle with a Slip Stitch

120 – Make a ch of 6 stitches. Join with a ss into first ch to form a ring.

Popcorn Stitch

121 – 1 ch, 5 tr into next stitch, remove loop from hook, insert hook into 1 ch before group of treble then into dropped loop and draw it through.

Solomon's Knot

122 – Draw a loop on hook out 6 mm ($\frac{1}{4}$ in), yarn over hook and draw through loop on hook. Insert hook between loop and single thread of this ch and make a dc. Work another knot in same manner (1 Solomon's Knot made), miss 4 stitches, 1 dc into next stitch. Repeat from beginning to end of row. Make $1\frac{1}{2}$ Solomon's Knot to turn, 1 dc over double loop at right of first centre knot of preceding row, 1 dc over double loop at left of same knot, 1 Solomon's Knot. Repeat to end of row.

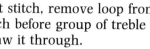

Puff Stitch

123 – Commence with a length of ch having a multiple of 2 ch plus 1. 1st Row: 1 tr into 4th ch from hook, * yarn over hook, insert hook into next ch and draw yarn up 1 cm ($\frac{3}{8}$ in) (yarn over hook, insert hook into same ch and draw yarn up as before) 3 times, yarn over and draw through all loops on hook (A Puff St made), 1 ch, miss 1 ch; repeat from * to last 3 ch, a Puff St into next ch, 1 tr into each of next 2 ch, 3 ch, turn.

Crossed Treble

124 – Commence with a length of ch, having a multiple of 4 ch plus 2. 1st Row: 1 dbl tr into 5th ch from hook, * yarn over hook twice, insert hook into next ch and draw yarn through, yarn over hook and draw through 2 loops, yarn over hook, miss 1 ch, insert hook into next ch and draw yarn through, (yarn over hook and draw through 2 loops) 4 times, 1 ch, 1 tr into centre point of cross (cross completed), 1 ch, miss 1 ch; repeat from * to last 2 ch, 1 dbl tr into each of next 2 ch, 4 ch, turn.

How to 'Turn your Work'

In rows of crochet a certain number of chain stitches are added at the end of each row to bring the work into position for the next row. Then the work is turned so that the reverse side is facing the worker. The number of turning chain depends upon the stitch with which you intend to begin the next row.

The list opposite gives the number of turning ch for each type of stitch which would be used when the following row is to be commenced with the same stitch. When applied to any of the stitches bracketed, the turning ch also stands as the first stitch of the next row.

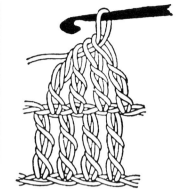

Diagram 119

Diagram 120

Diagram 121

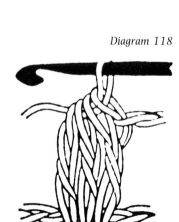

Diagram 116

Diagram 117

Diagram 118

Turning Chain

	dc	1 ch
hlf	tr	2 ch
	tr	3 ch
dbl	tr	4 ch
trip	tr	5 ch
quad	tr	6 ch
quin	tr	7 ch

Diagram 122

Diagram 123

Diagram 124

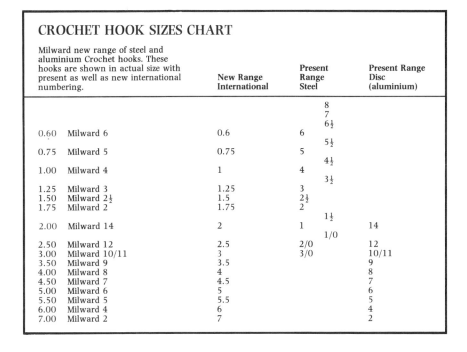

CROCHET HOOK SIZES CHART

Milward new range of steel and aluminium Crochet hooks. These hooks are shown in actual size with present as well as new international numbering.

		New Range International	Present Range Steel	Present Range Disc (aluminium)
			8	
			7	
			6½	
0.60	Milward 6	0.6	6	
			5½	
0.75	Milward 5	0.75	5	
			4½	
1.00	Milward 4	1	4	
			3½	
1.25	Milward 3	1.25	3	
1.50	Milward 2½	1.5	2½	
1.75	Milward 2	1.75	2	
			1½	
2.00	Milward 14	2	1	14
			1/0	
2.50	Milward 12	2.5	2/0	12
3.00	Milward 10/11	3	3/0	10/11
3.50	Milward 9	3.5		9
4.00	Milward 8	4		8
4.50	Milward 7	4.5		7
5.00	Milward 6	5		6
5.50	Milward 5	5.5		5
6.00	Milward 4	6		4
7.00	Milward 2	7		2

Tension

Important: Crochet workers should observe one basic rule: this is to adhere to the tension stated in instructions as only the correct tension will ensure the best result. It is desirable to work with the size of crochet hook quoted as this has been selected as the most suitable size for the thickness of yarn being used. If your tension is loose use a size finer hook, if tight use a size larger hook. By reference to Crochet Hook Sizes chart above, it will be seen that the new range provides an adequate number of sizes to work all patterns and to obtain the tension required.

Laundering Crochet

Mercer-Crochet colours are fast dyed and are highly resistant to even the most severe washing treatments, but these colours may be adversely affected when washed in certain commercial washing preparations which contain high levels of fluorescent brightening (whitening) agents. To maintain the true tones of Mercer-Crochet colours it is recommended that pure soap flakes or mild washing agents be used as these generally contain only low concentrations of fluorescent brightening (whitening) agents.

Crochet items should not be washed when work is still in progress. The assembled article should be washed on completion. Use a warm lather of pure soap flakes and wash in the usual way, either by hand or washing machine. If desired, the article may be spin-dried until it is damp, or left until it is half dry. Place a piece of paper, either plain white or squared, on top of a clean, flat board. Following the correct measurements, draw the shape of the finished article on to the paper, using ruler and set square for squares and rectangles and a pair of compasses for circles. Using rustless pins, pin the crochet out to the pencilled shape, taking care not to strain the crochet. Pin out the general shape first, then finish by pinning each picot, loop or space into position. Special points to note carefully when pinning out are:

a) When pinning loops, make sure the pin is in the centre of each loop to form balanced lines.

b) When pinning scallops, make all the scallops the same size and regularly curved.

c) Pull out all picots.

d) Where there are flowers, pull out each petal in position.

e) When pinning Filet Crochet, make sure that the spaces and blocks are square and that all edges are even and straight.

If the crochet requires to be slightly stiffened, use a solution of starch – 1 dessertspoonful to ½ litre (1 pint) hot water, and dab lightly over the article. Raise the crochet up off the paper, to prevent it sticking as it dries. When dry, remove the pins and press lightly.

Chapter 2

Bed Covers
&
Bed Linen

The bed is the focal point of a bedroom, so take care to choose a pattern and fabric for your bed cover which suits and complements the room. A fitted cover or duvet is in keeping with the simple, unfussy lines of a modern bedroom, while a crochet or throwover cover looks pretty in a more traditional setting. Covers should be easy to care for, and fabrics hard wearing, especially if the bed is in a bedsitter and is used as extra seating accommodation when entertaining friends. A great variety of fabrics is available, so your choice is wide. Use plain or patterned materials, or a combination of both for added interest. Add a touch of luxury with quilting, piping, scalloping, embroidery, or trimmings of braid or ribbon.

The following pages contain a selection of all types of covers — fitted covers to give a neat finish to divans, bunk bed covers, throwover covers, crochet bedspreads, and the increasingly popular duvet sets, which virtually do away with bed making, and are always fresh and attractive looking. Instructions for making all your bed linen are included, so you can quickly and easily make matching linen, in the sizes you need.

Measurements for all bed covers are taken over the made-up bed.

Fitted Divan Cover

To fit a divan 90 × 190 cm (3 ft × 6 ft 3 in), with a depth from top of mattress to floor of 48 cm (19 in).

Materials Required

These amounts are for a self coloured divan cover. Allow extra for matching a patterned fabric.
5.80 m ($6\frac{1}{4}$ yd) furnishing fabric 120 cm (approx. 48 in) wide.
5.80 m ($6\frac{1}{4}$ yd) piping cord, approximately 6 mm ($\frac{1}{4}$ in) thick.
Coats Drima (polyester) thread.

Cutting Out

2.5 cm (1 in) has been allowed for seams; 5 cm (2 in) for hems.
Top section — Cut 1 piece measuring 196 × 96 cm (77 × 38 in).
Side sections — Cut 2 pieces measuring 372 × 57 cm (146 × $22\frac{1}{2}$ in).
Piping — Cut sufficient straight strips of fabric 7 cm ($2\frac{3}{4}$ in) wide to go round top section. Join as required to make the desired length.

Fitted Divan Cover

Making Up

Cover piping cord (page 79). Place piping round top section, raw edges even, and clip piping at corners to lie flat. Baste. Baste and stitch the short ends of side sections right sides together. Baste and stitch hem on one long edge. Place remaining long edge to main section right sides together, raw edges even; with seams at diagonally opposite corners make 10 cm (4 in) pleats at each corner clipping corners to lie flat. Baste and stitch.

Throwover Divan Cover

Most furnishing fabrics will have to be joined to make the width necessary for this cover. The seams are generally made on the top section or at the sides of the top section depending on the width of the bed. A flat seam is used for heavier types of fabric and a machine fell or French seam for finer fabrics. When cutting, allow 2–2.5 cm ($\frac{3}{4}$–1 in) for seams and 5–10 cm (2–4 in) for hems.

Length

Length of bed plus added allowance at lower end is

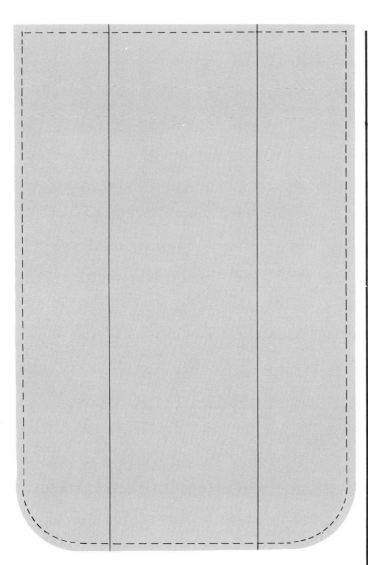

Diagram 1 Making up Throwover Divan Cover

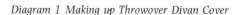

required so that the cover reaches the floor. A 30 cm (12 in) tuck-in under the pillow may be allowed if desired.

Breadth

Breadth of bed plus length to the floor on each side. The corners of the divan cover should be rounded to give a better line. To do this, measure an equal

Sketch of Throwover Divan Cover

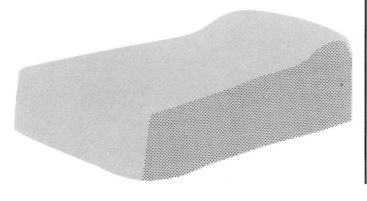

distance from corner on both sides; mark a gentle curve between the two points and cut away the surplus.

Making Up

Join the seams of cover. Turn in hems and slipstitch or machine stitch in position (diagram 1).

Patchwork Bunk Covers

Finished size is 152 × 216 cm (60 × 85 in).

Materials Required

The amounts given below make one cover.
1 m ($1\frac{1}{8}$ yd) each of six co-ordinated fabrics 90 cm (approx. 36 in) wide.
2.30 m ($2\frac{1}{2}$ yd) backing fabric (eg sheeting) 175 cm (approx. 70 in) wide.
Coats Drima (polyester) thread.

Cutting Out

The pattern on page 38 gives one third of the design. Each background square in the pattern represents a 15 cm (6 in) square.

	32
	36
	34
	34
	34
	34

Patchwork – Cut out sections, following pattern.
Repeat twice more to complete design.
Backing – Cut a piece of fabric 155 × 218 cm
(61 × 86 in).

Making Up

1.5 cm ($\frac{1}{2}$ in) has been allowed for seams. Baste and
stitch squares into strips. Baste and stitch strips
together to form the cover. Baste and stitch backing to
patchwork, right sides together, leaving an opening for
turning to the right side. Turn to the right side; turn in
open edges and slipstitch together. Make a line of
machine stitching 6 mm ($\frac{1}{4}$ in) from edges of cover.

Fitted Bedspread

Materials Required

As a rough guide, 6–7 m ($6\frac{1}{2}$–$7\frac{1}{2}$ yd) fabric 120/
140 cm (approx. 48/54 in) wide will be required for a
double bed, and 5–6 m ($5\frac{1}{2}$–$6\frac{1}{2}$ yd) for a single bed.

Measuring

The bed should be made up with the usual number of
pillows, blankets and eiderdown before taking
measurements. If making a fitted bedspread for the
first time, it is a good idea to draw a cutting chart to
scale, marking all the various pieces to be cut out of
the chosen width of fabric. Start with the length and
width necessary for the top of the bed, add depth and
length of frills (which should be $1\frac{1}{2}$–2 times the length
of the bed for each side, and $1\frac{1}{2}$–2 times the width at
lower end), gussets for pillows (diagram 2) and tuck-in
behind pillows, including 2–2.5 cm ($\frac{3}{4}$–1 in) for seams
and 5–10 cm (2–4 in) for hems. If replacing an old,
well-fitting bedspread it can be measured instead of the
bed itself.

The aim is to achieve a neat tailored look without
being skimpy. Once the exact measurements have
been made it is worth looking for a fabric in the most
economical width to avoid waste. If a patterned fabric

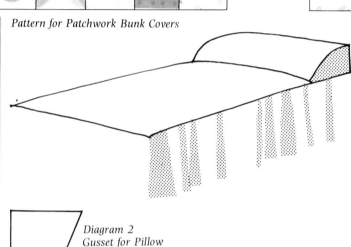

Pattern for Patchwork Bunk Covers

Diagram 2
Gusset for Pillow

Diagram 3
Tuck-in behind Pillow Section

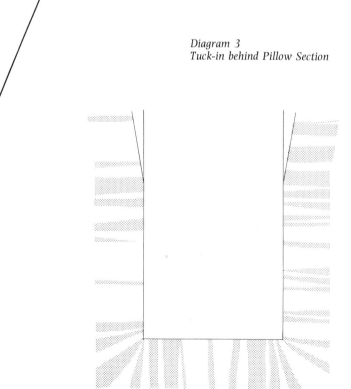

Patchwork Bunk Covers

of 120 cm (approx. 48 in) width is chosen for a double bed, it will be necessary to join two side sections to the centre piece to obtain the required width and, to allow for matching, a complete pattern-length extra will be needed. When these joins are necessary in a self coloured fabric it is best to make them a feature by using piping cord or other decoration. A textured fabric, such as candlewick, may be joined by a simple flat seam which will be almost invisible, and if this fabric is 140 cm (approx. 54 in) wide the joins will come where the frills are stitched to the top at both sides.

Cutting Out and Making Up

Cut fabric sections to measurements. Join frill sections together. Make a hem at two short ends and one long edge. Gather the other long edge to fit top section. Hem short end of gusset sections. With right sides together, baste and stitch straight sides of pillow gussets to top edges of frills at both sides. Baste and stitch the other side of gussets to main fabric section, right sides together, leaving tuck-in behind pillows free. With right sides together baste and stitch frill in position to top section. Make hems round tuck-in behind pillow section (diagram 3).

Crochet Bedspread

Materials Required

Coats Chain Mercer-Crochet Cotton No. 20 (20 g). 23 balls Parrot Green 463, 58 balls Apple Green 942, 20 balls Emerald Green 776. This model is worked in these 3 shades, but any other shades of Mercer-Crochet may be used.
Milward steel crochet hook 1.00 (no. 4). (If your crochet is loose use a size finer hook, if tight use a size larger hook.)

Tension

Size of Motif — 14 cm ($5\frac{1}{2}$ in) square.

Measurements

196 × 251 cm (77 × 99 in).

Close-up of Motif

41

Abbreviations

ch – chain; ss – slip stitch; sp – space; dc – double crochet; hlf tr – half treble; tr – treble; dbl tr – double treble; st(s) – stitch(es).

First Motif (Rose)

Using Parrot Green commence with 6 ch, join with a ss to form a ring.

1st Row: 8 ch, (1 dbl tr into ring, 4 ch) 7 times, 1 ss into 4th of 8 ch.

2nd Row: Into each 4 ch sp work 1 dc 1 hlf tr 3 tr 1 hlf tr and 1 dc, 1 ss into same ch as ss of previous row. (8 petals)

3rd Row: (5 ch, inserting hook from behind petals work 1 dc into dbl tr of 1st row) 7 times, 5 ch.

4th Row: Into each sp work 1 dc 1 hlf tr 5 tr 1 hlf tr and 1 dc.

5th Row: (6 ch, inserting hook from behind petals work 1 dc into dc of 3rd row) 7 times, 6 ch.

6th Row: Into each sp work 1 dc 1 hlf tr 7 tr 1 hlf tr and 1 dc.

7th Row: (7 ch, inserting hook from behind petals work 1 dc into dc of 5th row) 7 times, 7 ch.

8th Row: Into each sp work 1 dc 1 hlf tr 2 tr 5 dbl tr 2 tr 1 hlf tr and 1 dc, 1 ss into first dc. Fasten off.

9th Row: Attach Apple Green to centre dbl tr of any petal, 1 dc into same place as join, (11 ch, 1 dc into centre dbl tr of next petal) 7 times, 11 ch, 1 ss into first dc.

10th Row: 1 dc into same place as last ss, * 13 dc into next 11 ch loop, 1 dc into next dc; repeat from * omitting 1 dc at end of last repeat, 1 ss into first dc. (112 dc)

11th and 12th Rows: 1 dc into same place as ss, 1 dc into each dc, 1 ss into first dc.

13th Row: 3 ch, 3 tr into same place as ss, remove loop from hook insert hook into 3rd of 3 ch then into dropped loop and draw it through (popcorn st made), * 1 dc into each of next 27 dc, 4 tr into next dc, remove loop from hook insert hook into first tr of tr group then into dropped loop and draw it through; repeat from * ending with 1 dc into each of next 27 dc, 1 ss into first popcorn st.

14th Row: 1 ss into first dc, 3 ch, 1 tr into same place as last ss, 2 tr into next dc, remove loop from hook insert hook into 3rd of 3 ch then into dropped loop and draw it through (a popcorn st made), * miss 1 dc, 1 dc into each of next 23 dc, 2 tr into each of next 2 sts, remove loop from hook insert hook into first tr of tr group then into dropped loop and draw it through (another popcorn st made), 6 ch, a popcorn st over next 2 dc; repeat from * omitting a popcorn st at end of last repeat, 1 ss into first popcorn st.

15th Row: 1 ss into next dc, 3 ch and complete as popcorn st, * miss 1 dc, 1 dc into each of next 19 dc, a popcorn st over next 2 sts, 6 ch, into next loop work 1 dc 3 ch and 1 dc, 6 ch, miss next popcorn st, a popcorn st over next 2 sts; repeat from * omitting popcorn st at end of last repeat, 1 ss into first popcorn st.

16th Row: 1 ss into next dc, 3 ch and complete as popcorn st, * 1 dc into each of next 15 dc, miss 1 dc, a popcorn st over next 2 sts, (6 ch, into next 6 ch loop work 1 dc 3 ch and 1 dc) twice, 6 ch, miss next popcorn st, a popcorn st over next 2 dc; repeat from * omitting a popcorn st at end of last repeat, 1 ss into first popcorn st.

17th Row: 1 ss into next dc, 3 ch and complete as popcorn st, * 1 dc into each of next 11 dc, miss 1 dc, a popcorn st over next 2 sts, (7 ch, into next 6 ch loop work 1 dc 3 ch and 1 dc) 3 times, 7 ch, miss next popcorn st, a popcorn st over next 2 dc; repeat from * omitting a popcorn st at end of last repeat, 1 ss into first popcorn st.

18th Row: 1 ss into next dc, 3 ch and complete as popcorn st, * 1 dc into each of next 7 dc, miss 1 dc, a popcorn st over next 2 sts, (7 ch, into next 7 ch loop work 1 dc 3 ch and 1 dc) 4 times, 7 ch, miss next popcorn st, a popcorn st over next 2 dc; repeat from * omitting a popcorn st at end of last repeat, 1 ss into first popcorn st.

19th Row: 1 ss into next dc, 3 ch and complete as popcorn st, * 1 dc into each of next 3 dc, miss 1 dc, a popcorn st over next 2 sts, (7 ch, into next 7 ch loop work 1 dc 3 ch and 1 dc) 5 times, 7 ch, miss next popcorn st, a popcorn st over next 2 dc; repeat from * omitting a popcorn st at end of last repeat, 1 ss into first popcorn st.

20th Row: 1 ss into next dc, 3 ch, 1 tr into each of next 3 sts and complete as popcorn st, * (7 ch, into next 7 ch loop work 1 dc 3 ch and 1 dc) 6 times, 7 ch, 1 tr into each of next 4 sts and complete as popcorn st; repeat from * omitting a popcorn st at end of last repeat, 1 ss into first popcorn st. Fasten off.

21st Row: Attach Emerald Green to first 7 ch loop, 1 dc into same place as join, * (8 ch, into next 7 ch loop work 1 dc 3 ch and 1 dc) twice, 4 ch, miss 3 ch loop, 1 dbl tr into each of next 4 ch and complete as popcorn st, 12 ch, 1 dbl tr into same ch as last dbl tr and into each of next 3 ch and complete as popcorn st (corner made), 4 ch, (into next 7 ch loop work 1 dc 3 ch and 1 dc, 8 ch) twice, 1 dc into next 7 ch loop, 3 ch, 1 dc into next 7 ch loop; repeat from * omitting 1 dc at end of last repeat, 1 ss into first dc.

22nd Row: 1 ss into each of first 2 ch, into same loop work 1 dc 3 ch and 1 dc, * 9 ch, into next 8 ch loop work 1 dc 3 ch and 1 dc, 6 ch, miss 3 ch loop, a dbl tr popcorn st over next 4 ch, 2 ch, 1 dbl tr into each of next 6 ch, 7 ch, 1 dbl tr into each of next 6 ch (corner made), 2 ch, a dbl tr popcorn st over next 4 ch, 6 ch, into next 8 ch loop work 1 dc 3 ch and 1 dc, (9 ch, into next 8 ch loop work 1 dc 3 ch and 1 dc) twice; repeat from * omitting 1 dc 3 ch and 1 dc at end of last repeat, 1 ss into first dc. Fasten off.

Second Motif

Work as first motif for 21 rows.

22nd Row: 1 ss into each of first 2 ch, into same loop work 1 dc 3 ch and 1 dc, 9 ch, into next 8 ch loop work 1 dc 3 ch and 1 dc, 6 ch, miss 3 ch loop, a dbl tr popcorn st over next 4 ch, 2 ch, 1 dbl tr into each of next 6 ch, 3 ch, 1 ss into any corner loop on first motif, 3 ch, 1 dbl tr into each of next 6 ch on second motif, 2 ch, a dbl tr popcorn st over next 4 ch, 3 ch, 1 ss into corresponding loop on first motif, 3 ch, (into next 8 ch loop on second motif work 1 dc 3 ch and 1 dc, 4 ch, 1 ss into next loop on first motif, 4 ch) 3 times, into next 8 ch loop on second motif work 1 dc 3 ch and 1 dc, 3 ch, 1 ss into next loop on first motif, 3 ch, miss 3 ch loop on second motif, 1 dbl tr popcorn st over next 4 ch, 2 ch, 1 dbl tr into each of next 6 ch, 3 ch, 1 ss into next corner loop on first motif, 3 ch, 1 dbl tr into each of next 6 ch on second motif and complete as first motif.

Make 14 rows of 18 motifs joining adjacent sides as second motif was joined to first motif. Where 4 corners meet, join 3rd and 4th motifs to ss at joining of first 2 motifs.

Damp and pin out to measurements.

Alternative Colour Schemes

No. 1   23 balls   579 (Brown)
        58 balls 8918 (Lt. Coral Pink)
        20 balls   538 (Marigold)
No. 2   23 balls   439 (Rose Madder)
        58 balls   402 (Lt. Rose Pink)
        20 balls   854 (Petunia)

Daisy Motif Bedspread

Materials Required

Coats Musica Health Vest Cotton, 2 oz ready wound balls, 68 balls. 2 motifs can be worked from 1 ball. Milward Disc (aluminium) crochet hook 4.00 (no. 8). The above quantity is sufficient for 1 single size bedspread.

Tension

Size of Motif – 20 cm (8 in) square.
Depth of Edging – 2 cm ($\frac{3}{4}$ in).

Measurements

Finished size – 207 × 268 cm ($81\frac{1}{2}$ × $105\frac{1}{2}$ in) approximately.

Abbreviations

ch – chain; dc – double crochet; tr – treble; dbl tr – double treble; st(s) – stitch(es); ss – slip stitch; sp – space.

First Motif

Commence with 6 ch, join with a ss to form a ring.
1st Row: 6 ch, into ring work (1 tr, 3 ch) 7 times, 1 ss into 3rd of 6 ch.
2nd Row: 1 ss into each of next 2 sts, 3 ch, 4 tr into same place as last ss, * miss next 3 sts, 5 tr into next

Below:
Daisy Motif Bedspread

43

st; repeat from * ending with 1 ss into 3rd of 3 ch.
3rd Row: 3 ch, leaving the last loop of each on hook work 1 tr into each of next 4 tr, yarn over and draw through all loops on hook – a 4 tr cluster made –, * 6 ch, a 5 tr cluster over next 5 tr; repeat from * ending with 6 ch, 1 ss into first cluster.
4th Row: 1 dc into same place as ss, * 9 dc into next loop, 1 dc into next cluster; repeat from * ending with 9 dc into next loop, 1 ss into first dc.
5th Row: 1 dc into same place as ss, 1 dc into each dc, 1 ss into first dc.
6th Row: 6 ch, 1 tr into same place as ss, * miss 4 dc, into next dc work 1 tr 3 ch and 1 tr; repeat from * ending with 1 ss into 3rd of 3 ch.
7th Row: 1 ss into next loop, 3 ch, into same loop work 2 tr 3 ch and 3 tr, * (3 ch, 3 tr into next loop) 3 times, 3 ch, into next loop work 3 tr 3 ch and 3 tr; repeat from * omitting 3 tr 3 ch and 3 tr at end of last repeat, 1 ss into 3rd of 3 ch.
8th Row: 1 ss into each of next 2 tr and into next loop, 4 ch, into same loop work 2 dbl tr 3 ch and 3 dbl tr, * (3 ch, 3 tr into next loop) 4 times, 3 ch, into next loop work 3 dbl tr 3 ch and 3 dbl tr; repeat from * omitting 3 dbl tr 3 ch and 3 dbl tr at end of last repeat, 1 ss into 4th of 4 ch. Fasten off.

Second Motif

Work as first motif for 7 rows.
8th Row: 1 ss into each of next 2 tr and into next loop, 4 ch, 2 dbl tr into same loop, 1 ch, 1 ss into corresponding loop on first motif, 1 ch, 3 dbl tr into same loop on second motif, (1 ch, 1 ss into next loop on first motif, 1 ch, 3 tr into next loop on second motif) 4 times, 1 ch, 1 ss into next loop on first motif, 1 ch, 3 dbl tr into next loop, 1 ch, 1 ss into next loop on first motif, 1 ch, 3 dbl tr into same loop on second motif, 3 ch and complete as first motif.
Make 10 rows of 13 motifs joining adjacent sides as second motif was joined to first. Where four corners meet join 3rd and 4th motifs to previous joining.

Edging

1st Row: Attach yarn to sp at any corner, ** 5 dc into corner sp, * (1 dc into each of next 3 sts, 3 dc into next sp) 5 times, 1 dc into each of next 3 sts, 1 dc into next sp, 1 dc into ss at join of motifs, 1 dc into next sp; repeat from * along side omitting 3 dc at end of last repeat; repeat from ** ending with 1 ss into first dc.
2nd Row: 1 dc into same place as ss, ** 3 ch, 1 ss into last dc – a picot made –, (1 dc into each of next 2 dc, a picot) 3 times, * 1 dc into each of next 3 dc, a picot; repeat from * along side ending with 1 dc into each of next 2 dc; repeat from ** omitting 1 dc at end of last repeat, 1 ss into first dc. Fasten off.

Damp and press.

It is easy to make your own bed linen. Choose your favourite colours, add contrasting trim, or decorate

sheets and pillowcases with embroidered motifs or a simple crochet edging.

Mattresses are made in a variety of sizes and this of course determines the size of the bed linen. Below is a list of mattress sizes with the corresponding sizes for bed linen.

Small Single Bed

Dimensions 90 × 190 cm (3 ft × 6 ft 3 in); sheet size 175 × 260 cm (70 × 100 in).

Small Double Bed

Dimension 135 × 190 cm (4 ft 6 in × 6 ft 3 in); sheet size 230 × 260 cm (90 × 100 in).

Bunk Beds

Dimensions 70 × 175 cm (2 ft 3 in × 5 ft 9 in), or 75 × 190 cm (2 ft 6 in × 6 ft 3 in); single bed sheets would fit.

Sheets and Valances

Sheeting is available in most large stores in two widths, 175 cm (approx. 70 in) for single bed, 230 cm (approx. 90 in) for small double bed, in a variety of colours and patterns.

To work out the amount of fabric required for 1 plain sheet, subtract the width of the mattress from the width of fabric, and add this difference to the length of the mattress.

If the whole width of the fabric is not required, measure the sheet from the top left hand corner so as to leave a selvedge strip of fabric at the right hand side. The strip may then be used for some form of decoration – say frills for matching pillowcases.

Plain Sheet

Finish a plain sheet with narrow hems along the sides (if necessary) and lower edge, and 5 cm (2 in) hem along the top.

Width of mattress –   90 cm (approx. 36 in).
Length of mattress– 190 cm (75 in).
Depth of mattress –   18 cm (7 in).
Tuck-in under mattress and hem 25 cm (10 in).

Width of sheeting – 175 cm (approx. 70 in).
Length of sheeting– 275 cm (109 in).

Width of mattress – 135 cm (approx. 54 in).
Length of mattress– 190 cm (75 in).
Depth of mattress –   18 cm (7 in).
Tuck-in under mattress and hem 28 cm (11 in).

Width of sheeting – 230 cm (approx. 90 in).
Length of sheeting– 285 cm (111 in).

Making Fitted Sheets from Plain Sheets

Fitted sheets are awkward to iron, so try to use a drip-dry fabric, such as a cotton/polyester mixture.

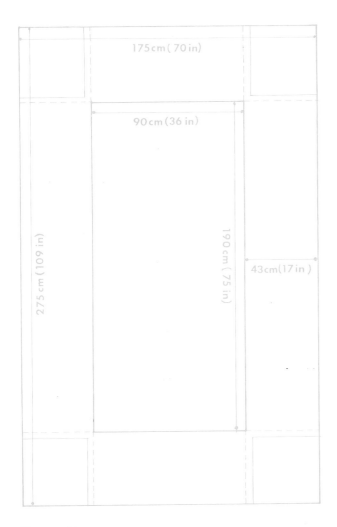

175 cm (70 in)

90 cm (36 in)

275 cm (109 in)

190 cm (75 in)

43 cm (17 in)

230 cm (90 in)

135 cm (54 in)

285 cm (111 in)

190 cm (75 in)

46 cm (18 in)

Diagram 4A
Fabric required for Single Sheet

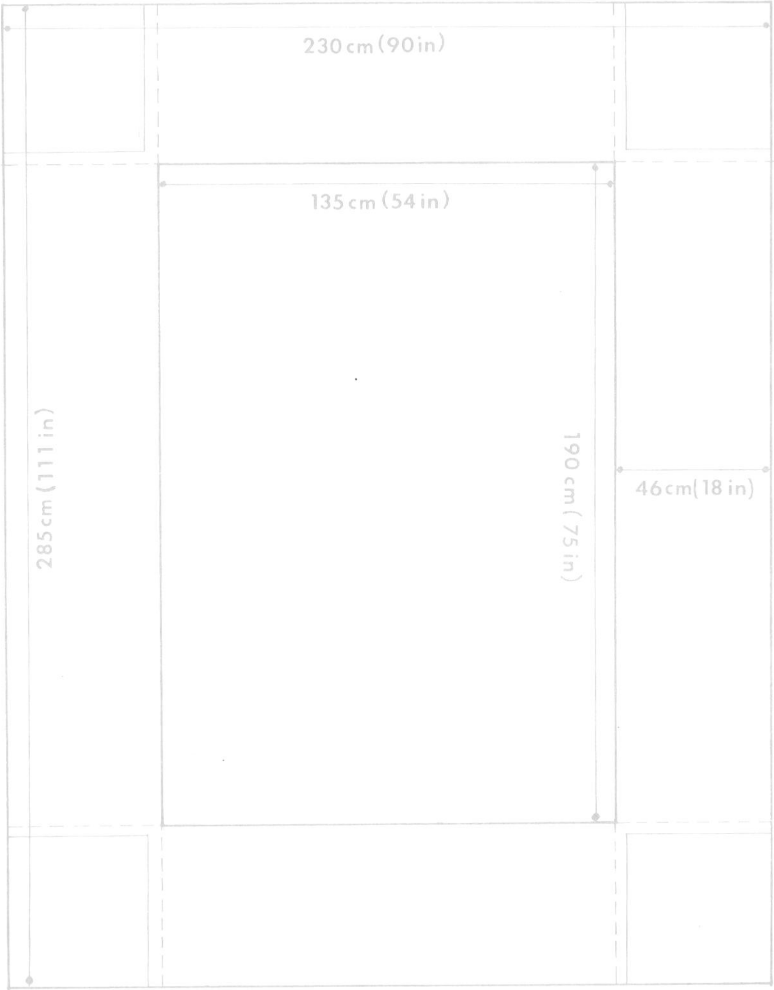

Diagram 4B
Fabric required for Double Sheet

These fabrics are often composed of 50% cotton and 50% polyester, but are softer and smoother if the percentage of polyester exceeds that of cotton up to 65% to 35%.

A fitted under sheet can be made from a plain sheet, by mitring the four corners. Make a casing and insert a 30 cm (12 in) length of elastic at each corner.

To make a fitted top sheet only 2 corners have to be mitred to fit the bottom of the bed or divan.

As the top sheet folds down over the bedclothes with the right side of fabric showing, the corner shaping is made by joining the 2 wrong sides together with the raw edges to the right side. The corners of the mattress are slightly rounded, so the sheet corners will fit better if stitching is curved slightly at this point.

Fitted sheets are subject to a considerable strain when putting on and taking off, and they have to withstand frequent washing, so the elastic must be stitched firmly with good quality thread at both ends of each casing.

Making Fitted Sheets from Sheeting

To make fitted sheets from sheeting, work out the quantity of fabric required for each sheet as given on page 44 and proceed as follows.

Making the Bottom Sheet

Measure and mark fabric as shown in diagram 4A or B, page 45.
Mitre each corner by folding the adjacent edges, right sides together, diagonally so that the lines match. Pin along straight grain of fabric and machine stitch, curving the stitching slightly to give extra ease when putting sheet on to mattress. (Diagram 5). Trim excess fabric to within 6 mm ($\frac{1}{4}$ in) from the stitching, press turnings to one side and overcast them together.

Fold 2.5 cm (1 in) to wrong side all round the edge of the sheet and make a 2 cm ($\frac{3}{4}$ in) hem leaving 2.5 cm (1 in) openings about 25 cm (10 in) from each corner seam for elastic insertion. Insert elastic. Sew firmly in place. Close openings.

Making the Top Sheet

Measure and mark top sheet to the same measurement as for bottom sheet but omitting 2 top mitres. Mitre lower corners placing fabric wrong sides together. Make up as bottom sheet but make an 8 cm (3 in) hem at top edge to the wrong side so that when bed is made up the right side of the fabric will be uppermost.

Bed Valances

These were made originally of white cotton or linen, starched and gathered or pleated on to a band which was tacked on to the wooden frame of the bed which stood about 51 cm (20 in) or more from the floor. Bedspreads were then throwover style and valances covered the unsightly space between bed springs and floor.

With the advent of low divan beds, and fitted bedspreads, valances were no longer necessary, but now the introduction of the duvet or continental quilt requires the space between bed base and floor to be covered.

Made of suitable fabric, a valance can also help to disguise a divan bed in a bed-sitting room.

To make, measure depth from edge of base to floor and add 10 cm (4 in), 5 cm (2 in) for hem and 5 cm (2 in) to cover edge of base under mattress. Cut the fabric into widthwise strips to the depth required. Join the side seams to make one long strip. Finish short ends with a 5 cm (2 in) hem. To make a satisfactory frill, the complete length should be $1\frac{1}{2}$–2 times the circumference of the bed – 2, 3, or 4 sides. Make a complete cover of cheap fabric, slightly smaller than the top of the base. Gather frill to fit. With right sides together baste and stitch frill to top section, machine zig-zag or oversew raw edges to neaten.

For pleated valances, pleat one width of fabric as desired. Measure how far this covers the circumference of the bed, then work out how much fabric will be needed to go round 2, 3 or 4 sides of the bed. Make up as for frilled valance.

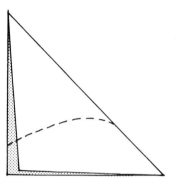

Diagram 5
Mitred Corner

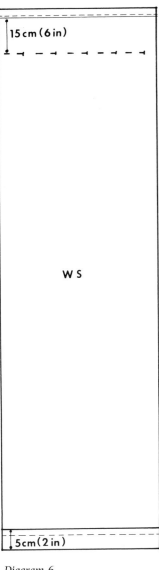

15 cm (6 in)

W S

5 cm (2 in)

Diagram 6
Making up Plain Pillowcase

Diagram 7
Making up Plain Pillowcase

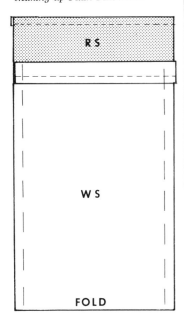

R S

W S

FOLD

Pillowcases

Plain Pillowcase

Materials Required

Amounts are for one pillowcase size 50 × 75 cm
(approx. 20 × 30 in).
60 cm ($\frac{5}{8}$ yd) sheeting, 175 cm (approx. 70 in) wide.
Coats Drima (polyester) thread.

Cutting Out

From fabric cut a piece 53 × 175 cm (21 × 69 in).

Making Up

1.5 cm ($\frac{1}{2}$ in) has been allowed for seams.
Make a 1.5 cm ($\frac{1}{2}$ in) hem to the wrong side at one
short end of fabric and a 5 cm (2 in) hem to the right
side at the other short end. With pins mark a line
15 cm (6 in) from end with 1.5 cm ($\frac{1}{2}$ in) hem
(diagram 6). With right sides together fold 5 cm (2 in)
hem edge up to pin line and baste raw edges together
at each side (diagram 7). Fold 15 cm (6 in) extension
down over 5 cm (2 in) hem and baste in place
(diagram 8). Stitch side seams. Neaten raw edges.
Turn to right side.

Frilled Pillowcase

Materials Required

Amounts are for one pillowcase size 50 × 75 cm
(approx. 20 × 30 in).
80 cm ($\frac{7}{8}$ yd) sheeting, 175 cm (approx. 70 in) wide.
Coats Drima (polyester) thread.

Cutting Out

From fabric cut two main sections 53 × 79 cm
(21 × 31 in) and one flap section 53 × 19 cm
(21 × 7$\frac{1}{2}$ in) for frills. Cut sufficient 8 cm (3 in) strips
to measure 1$\frac{1}{2}$–2 times the measurement round
outside edges of pillowcase.

Making Up

1.5 cm ($\frac{1}{2}$ in) has been allowed for seams. Join strips
for frills into one long length and make a 6 mm ($\frac{1}{4}$ in)
hem on one long edge. Gather to fit round one main
section. Baste frill right sides together and raw edges
even to one main section, spacing gathers evenly.
Make a 1.5 cm ($\frac{1}{2}$ in) hem to wrong side of one long
edge of flap section. Baste and stitch flap section, right
side down, over frills at one short end of main section,
raw edges even. Press flap section away from frills.
Make a 1.5 cm ($\frac{1}{2}$ in) hem at one short end of
remaining main section. Baste this section, right side
down, over frilled section at sides and lower end. Fold
flap section down over hemmed edge and baste at side
edges. Stitch side and lower end seams. Neaten raw
edges. Turn to right side.

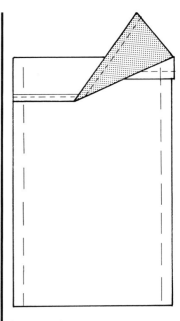

Diagram 8
Making up Plain Pillowcase

47

Duvet Cover

Diagram 9
Cutting out material for Duvet Cover

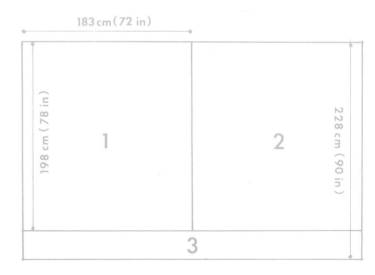

Duvet or Continental Quilt

A duvet reduces bed making to a minimum, eliminates the need for blankets and causes no dust under the bed. The use of a top sheet is optional, though this would mean less frequent washing of the cover.

There are four different types of filling for duvets:
Pure Duck Down contains at least 85% and probably 95% of duck down and is therefore light, soft and long lasting. Should be treated carefully.
Duck Down/Feather means more down than feathers – about 70% down overall. Provides luxury without the expense of pure down.
Feather/Down means more feathers than down – usually 30% down. Extremely suitable for children and people accustomed to heavy bed clothes.
Terylene P.3. The best of the synthetics – washable, non-matting, and very durable. Beware of unbranded 'Polyesters'.

Before deciding to change from eiderdown, blankets and bedspread, remember it is not just a question of changing the quilt, but of giving the bed – and bedroom – a new look.

A good deal of time and thought should be taken to study finished results in demonstration bedrooms in stores and in exhibitions, and to find out the availability of suitable fabrics for your own bedroom colour scheme.

Duvets are most effective on beds with no end board and where the space between mattress and floor can easily be covered by a ruffle or valance of matching or contrasting fabric – in other words, they look best on a modern, low, divan-type bed. A duvet does not cover the whole bed when made up, and matching or contrasting pillowcases are essential to lay at the top of the bed.

Even if initially a ready-made duvet cover, valance and pillowcases have been bought, you may want to make a second set yourself. Careful consideration must be given to how much fabric will be required, depending on size and height of bed and the width of fabric. If you wish to make your own duvet instead of buying one ready-made, duvet kits are obtainable.

Duvet Cover

Fabric requirements and making up instructions for duvet covers are given for a small double bed. For other bed sizes the fabric required is twice the bed width measurement plus 46 cm (18 in).

Materials Required

3.70 m (4 yd) sheeting 230 cm (approx. 90 in) wide.
1 zip fastener 66 cm (26 in) in length.
Coats Drima (polyester) thread.

Cutting Out

Cut fabric into three pieces as shown in diagram 9. The 30 cm (12 in) strip can be used to make frills around pillowcases.

Making Up

Place sections 1 and 2 right sides together. Baste and stitch one long side leaving a 66 cm (26 in) opening at the centre for zip insertion. Insert zip. Place closed zip behind opening and pin top and bottom, working on the right side. Tack and stitch 6 mm ($\frac{1}{4}$ in) from centre, along both sides, working a double row for extra strength at both ends. Open zip, baste and stitch remaining long side and the two shorter ends. Neaten raw edges. Turn cover to the right side.

Sheet and Pillowcase Trimming

Materials Required

Coats Chain Mercer-Crochet Cotton No. 20 (20 g).
5 balls. This model is worked in shade 439 (Rose Madder), but any other shade of Mercer-Crochet may be used.
Milward steel crochet hook 1.25 (no. 3).
The above quantity is sufficient to trim 1 sheet and 2 pillowcases.

Tension

Size of Motif – 4 cm ($1\frac{1}{2}$ in) square.

Measurements

Width of Sheet – 180 cm (approx. 70 in) adjustable.
Width of Pillowcase – 47 cm ($18\frac{1}{2}$ in) adjustable.
Depth of Trimming – 4.5 cm ($1\frac{3}{4}$ in).

Abbreviations

ch – chain; dc – double crochet; tr – treble; sp – space; st – stitch; ss – slip stitch.

Sheet

First Motif

Commence with 10 ch, join with a ss to form a ring.
1st Row: 3 ch, 5 tr into ring, remove loop from hook, insert hook into 3rd of 3 ch then into dropped loop and draw it through (a popcorn st made), * 10 ch, 6 tr into ring, remove loop from hook, insert hook into first tr of group then into dropped loop and draw it through (another popcorn st made); repeat from * twice more, 10 ch, 1 ss into first popcorn st.
2nd Row: 12 dc into each 10 ch loop, 1 ss into first dc.
3rd Row: 1 dc into same place as ss, * 7 ch, miss 5 dc, into next dc work a popcorn st 5 ch and a popcorn st, 7 ch, miss 5 dc, 1 dc into next dc; repeat from * omitting 1 dc at end of last repeat, 1 ss into first dc. Fasten off.

Second Motif

Work as first motif for 2 rows.
3rd Row: 1 dc into same place as ss, 7 ch, miss 5 dc, into next dc work a popcorn st and 2 ch, 1 tr into any

Sheet and Pillowcase Trimming

5 ch sp on first motif, 2 ch, a popcorn st into same dc on second motif, 2 ch, 1 tr into next 7 ch loop on first motif, 4 ch, miss 5 dc, 1 dc into next dc on second motif, 4 ch, 1 tr into next 7 ch loop on first motif, 2 ch, miss 5 dc, into next dc on second motif work a popcorn st and 2 ch, 1 tr into corresponding loop on first motif, 2 ch and a popcorn st into same dc, * 7 ch, miss 5 dc, 1 dc into next dc, 7 ch, miss 5 dc, into next dc work a popcorn st 5 ch and a popcorn st; repeat from * once more ending with 7 ch, 1 ss into first dc. Fasten off.

Make 38 more motifs (or number required) joining each as second motif was joined to first to form a strip.

Edging

With right side facing, attach thread to first corner sp on edge of strip, 3 ch, into same sp work 5 tr, remove loop from hook, insert hook into 3rd of 3 ch then into dropped loop and draw it through, 5 ch and a popcorn st, * 7 ch, 1 dc into next loop, 6 ch, 1 dc into 4th ch from hook, 2 ch (a picot loop made), 1 dc into next loop, 7 ch, into next sp at next joining of 2 motifs work a popcorn st a picot loop and a popcorn st; repeat from * to within last motif, (7 ch, 1 dc into next loop, a picot loop, 1 dc into next loop, 7 ch, into next corner work a popcorn st 5 ch and a popcorn st) twice and complete other 2 sides to correspond ending with 1 ss into first popcorn st. Fasten off.

Pillowcase

Make 21 motifs (or number required) joining as before and joining last motif to first motif to correspond.

Edging

With right side facing, attach thread to sp at joining of any 2 motifs, 3 ch, into same sp work a popcorn st a picot loop and a popcorn st, * 7 ch, 1 dc into next loop, a picot loop, 1 dc into next loop, 7 ch, into next sp at joining of motifs work a popcorn st a picot loop and a popcorn st; repeat from * omitting a popcorn st a picot loop and a popcorn st at end of last repeat, 1 ss into first popcorn st. Fasten off.

Attach thread to opposite side and complete to correspond.

Damp and pin out to measurements. Sew in position as shown in illustration.

Chapter 3

BEDHEADS

The bedhead can make or mar the appearance of a bed. If the headboard is badly marked or in discord with the colour scheme, the simplest way to smarten it up or co-ordinate it is to make a padded bedhead cover to slip over the headboard. This will add a touch of luxury to your bedroom, at very low cost.

For a completely new look, make your own comfortable foam-padded bedhead, and attach it to the wall with suitable rings or rod.

There are two bedhead covers and two complete bedheads to choose from in this chapter. Matching items (mats, cushion and pouffe), are also included, and a beautifully embroidered Mirror Surround and Cheval Runner complete the decoration.

Remember that any design can be adapted to suit other articles. For example, the design shown on the Mirror Surround and Cheval Runner would make a most attractive bedhead.

Simple Slip Cover Padded Bedhead

This is made to cover the bedhead and give it a luxurious finish. Make a paper pattern large enough to slip over the headboard easily.

Materials Required

Sufficient fabric and lining to cover headboard front and back.
Wadding and muslin to cover front only.
Button moulds as required.
Coats Drima (polyester) thread.

Cutting Out

Allow 2.5 cm (1 in) for seams.
Front — Cut 4 pieces by pattern (1 from fabric, 1 from lining, 1 from wadding and 1 from muslin).
Back — Cut 2 pieces (1 from fabric, 1 from lining).

Making Up

Place the wadding, then the muslin, to wrong side of front fabric section and baste securely all over. Cover button moulds and sew in place as desired through all thicknesses. Place front and back fabric sections right

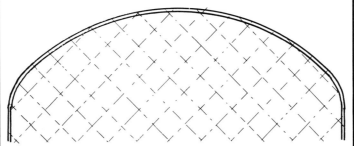

sides together. Baste and stitch, leaving lower edges open. Trim seams. If the bedhead cover has square corners, the top corners should be fitted. To do this, on wrong side of bedhead cover place side seam and top seam together at corner and stitch across corner (diagram 1).

Lining sections should be treated in the same way. The thickness of the bedhead is the measurement to be stitched across corner. Place lining sections right sides together. Baste and stitch as fabric sections. Turn lining right side out. Pull lining section over fabric and catch-stitch at intervals to top and side seams to hold in place. Turn bedhead to right side. Turn in seam allowance on lower edges at front and back and sew neatly. Ties may be sewn to lower edges to hold bedhead cover in position if desired. A quilted bedhead is made in the same way by quilting the front section before making up (see quilting page 28).

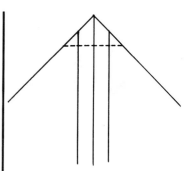

Diagram 1

Padded Bedhead Cover with Gusset and Piping

Make a paper pattern the size and shape of the bedhead, and a gusset strip the length and width required.

Materials Required

Sufficient fabric and lining to cover bedhead, including gusset. Allow extra fabric to cut bias strips for piping. Piping cord twice the length of top and sides of headboard.
Wadding and muslin to cover front only.
Button moulds as required.
Coats Drima (polyester) thread.

Cutting Out

Allow 2.5 cm (1 in) for seams.
Front – Cut 4 pieces by pattern (1 from fabric, 1 from lining, 1 from wadding and 1 from muslin).
Back – Cut 2 pieces by pattern (1 from fabric, 1 from lining).
Gusset – Cut 2 pieces (1 from fabric, 1 from lining) joining where necessary.
Cut sufficient bias strips from fabric 4–5 cm (1½-2 in) wide, joining where necessary, to cover piping cord (diagrams 2 and 3 page 79).
Cut piping cord in half.

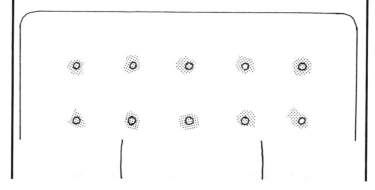

Padded Bedhead Cover with Gusset and Piping

Making Up

Fabric sections – Cover piping cord with bias strips (page 79).

Front – Place the wadding then the muslin to wrong side of front section and baste securely all over. Cover buttons and sew in place where desired through all thicknesses. Baste one length of piping to top and sides of front section, right sides together and seam lines matching. Baste gusset right side down over piping and stitch close to cord (diagram 4 page 79). Attach piping and other edge of gusset to back section in the same way.

Lining sections – Baste and sew gusset between back and front sections. Turn lining to right side and pull over fabric section. Catch-stitch at intervals to seams to hold in place. Turn bedhead cover to right side. Turn in and baste seam allowance round lower edge and sew lining to fabric neatly. Ties may be sewn to lower edges to hold bedhead in place. A quilted bedhead is made in a similar way by quilting the front section before making up (see quilting page 28).

Bedhead Cushion, Bedside Mats and Cushion

Bedhead Cushion

Materials Required

Clark's Anchor Stranded Cotton: 13 skeins Gorse Yellow 0300; 12 skeins Forest Green 0218; 9 skeins Lilac 0105; 7 skeins each Petunia 094, tapestry shade 0856; 6 skeins Jade 0189. Use 6 strands throughout.
1.40 m ($1\frac{1}{2}$ yd) mid green medium weight fabric, as in illustration, with approximately 13 threads to 2.5 cm (1 in), 140 cm (approx. 54 in) wide.
Foam pad approx. 100 × 50 × 8 cm (40 × 20 × 3 in).
7 curtain rings 4 cm ($1\frac{1}{2}$ in) in diameter.
Decorative rod, the required length.
1 Milward 'Gold Seal tapestry needle No. 20.

Suitable fabric brand is Munrospun Hopsac Tweed (Green H 840).
The finished size of the cushion is approximately 100 × 50 × 8 cm (40 × 20 × 3 in).

Instructions

Cut a piece from fabric 122 × 71 cm (48 × 28 in) for front section and a piece 107 × 56 cm (42 × 22 in) for back section. 2.5 cm (1 in) has been allowed for seams. Mark the centre of front piece both ways with a line of basting stitches. The pattern gives a little more than one quarter of the design, centre indicated by the large blank arrows which should coincide with the basting stitches. Each background square on the pattern represents two threads of fabric. The design is worked throughout in Cross Stitch, each stitch over two threads. It is important that the upper half of each

cross should lie in the same direction. With long side of fabric facing, commence the embroidery at large black arrow to the right of pattern, 107 threads down from crossed basting stitches and 1 thread to the right, and work quarter as given following pattern and Key for the design and colours used. Work other three quarters to correspond. Press the embroidery on the wrong side.

Making Up

Place embroidered front piece of fabric centrally right side down on foam pad. Pin corners to fit, baste and stitch. Trim seams. Turn to right side and place over pad. Turn under seam allowance on back section and stitch in place. Attach rings, spacing evenly, and insert rod.

Bedside Mats

Materials Required

Clark's Anchor Stranded Cotton: 3 skeins Forest Green 0218 ; 2 skeins Gorse Yellow 0300 ; skein each Lilac 0105 and Jade 0189. Use 3 strands throughout.
50 cm ($\frac{1}{2}$ yd) pale green evenweave embroidery linen, as in illustration, 21 threads to 2.5 cm (1 in), 150 cm (approx. 60 in) wide.
1 Milward 'Gold Seal' crewel needle No. 7.

The finished size of each mat is approximately 32 cm ($12\frac{1}{2}$ in) square.

Instructions

Cut two pieces from fabric 35 cm (14 in) square. Mark the centre of each piece both ways with a line of basting stitches. Only the border section within bracket A on the pattern is used for the mats, and this gives one quarter of the design. Each background square on the pattern represents two threads of fabric. The design is worked throughout in Cross Stitch, each stitch over two threads. It is important that the upper half of each cross should lie in the same direction. Commence the embroidery on each mat at the small black arrow on pattern, 107 threads down from crossed basting stitches and 1 thread to the right, and work quarter within bracket A, following pattern for the design and colours used. Work other three quarters to correspond. Press the embroidery on the wrong side.

Making Up

Baste 1.5 cm ($\frac{1}{2}$ in) hems on all edges, mitre corners and slipstitch.

Cushion

Materials Required

Clark's Anchor Stranded Cotton: 8 skeins Gorse Yellow 0300; 6 skeins tapestry shade 0856; 5 skeins

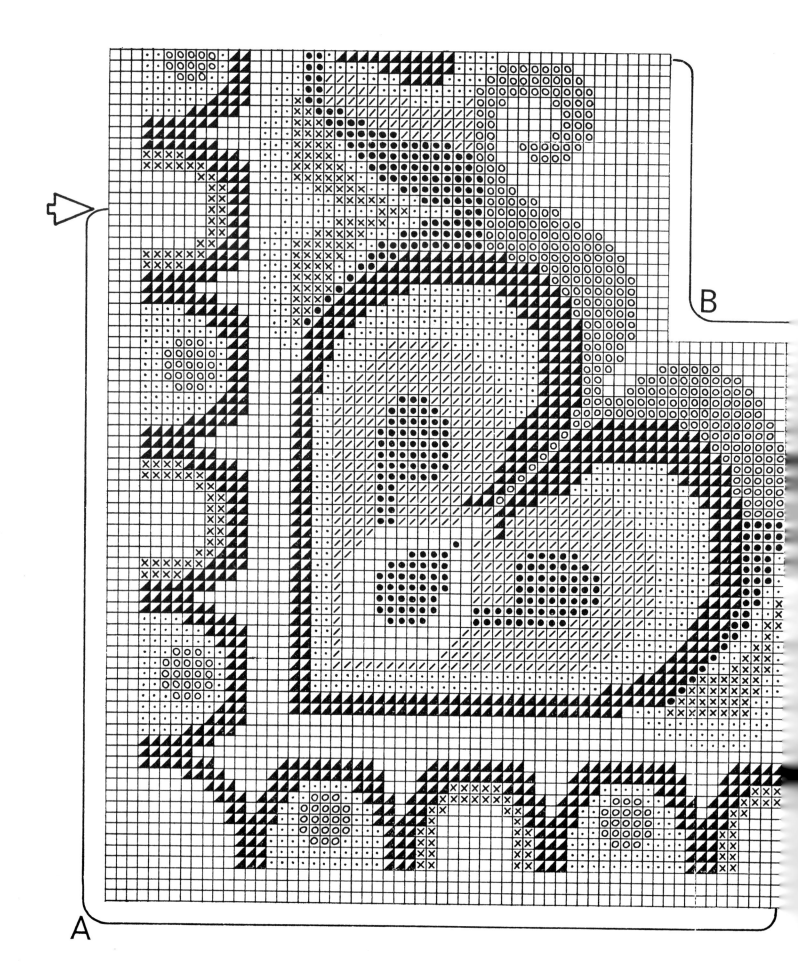

A

B

each Petunia 094, Lilac 0105, Forest Green 0218;
1 skein Jade 0189. Use 6 strands throughout.
70 cm (¾ yd) mid green medium weight fabric, as in
illustration, with approximately 13 threads to 2.5 cm
(1 in), 140 cm (approx. 54 in) wide.
Cushion pad to fit.
1 Milward 'Gold Seal' tapestry needle No. 20.

Suitable fabric brand is Munrospun Hopsac Tweed
(Green H840).
The finished size of the cushion is approximately 53 cm
(21 in) square.

Instructions

Cut two pieces from fabric 58 cm (23 in) square.
Mark one piece across the centre both ways with a line

Pattern for Bedhead Cushion, Bedside Mats and Cushion

of basting stitches. Only the section within bracket B
(excluding the border) on pattern is used for the
cushion, and this gives one quarter of the design. Each
background square on the pattern represents two
threads of fabric. The design is worked throughout in
Cross Stitch, each stitch over two threads. It is
important that the upper half of each cross should lie
in the same direction. Commence the embroidery at
the small blank arrow on pattern, 77 threads down
from crossed basting stitches and 15 threads to the
left and work quarter within bracket B, following
pattern and key for the design and colours used.
Work other three quarters to correspond. Press
embroidery on the wrong side.

Making Up

Make up cushion, taking 2.5 cm (1 in) seams.

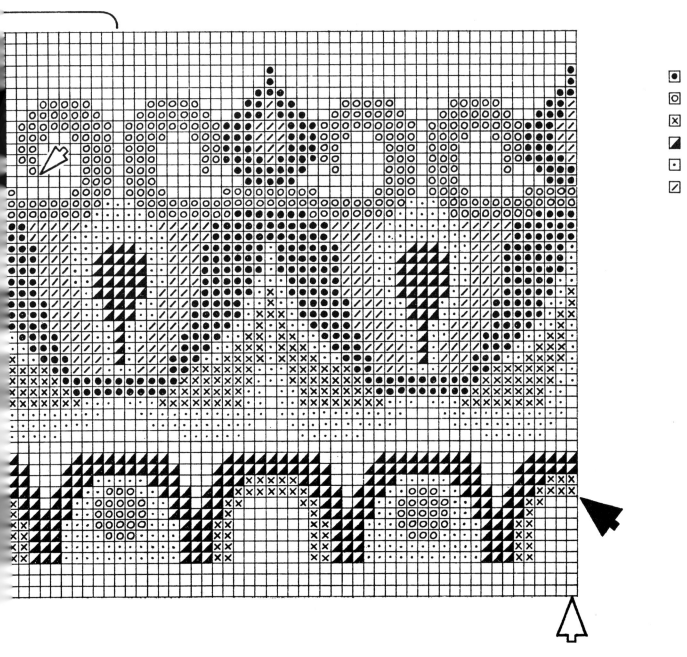

⊙	–	094
⊡	–	0105
⊠	–	0189
◢	–	0218
⊡	–	0300
◪	–	0856

Bedhead Cushion, Bedside Mats and Cushion

Pouffe and Matching Bedhead

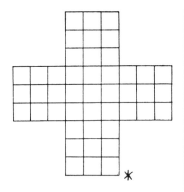

POUFFE

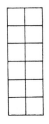

BEDHEAD

Pouffe and Matching Bedhead

Materials Required

Coats Chain Mercer-Crochet Cotton No. 20 (20 g).
12 balls Brown 579 and 12 balls Lt. Beige 625.
This model is worked in these two shades, but any
other shades of Mercer-Crochet may be used.
Milward steel crochet hook 1.25 (no. 3).
Pouffe pad 46 × 46 × 46 cm (18 × 18 × 18 in).
Piece of foam padding 30 × 90 × 8 cm (12 ×
36 × 3 in).
Metal or bamboo rod required length.
7 rings approx. 4 cm (1½ in) in diameter or required
size (use as alternative fabric tabs).
2.20 m (2⅓ yd) fabric 115 cm (approx. 45 in) wide in
contrasting colour. 5 motifs may be worked from
1 ball of each colour.

Tension

Size of Motif − 15 cm (6 in) square.

Measurements

Pouffe − 46 × 46 × 46 cm (18 × 18 × 18 in).
Bedhead − 30 × 90 cm (12 × 36 in).

Abbreviations

ch − chain; dc − double crochet; hlf tr − half treble;
tr − treble; dbl tr − double treble; st(s) − stitch(es);
ss − slip stitch.

First Motif

Using Brown, commence with 12 ch, join with a ss to
form a ring.
1st Row: 24 dc into ring, 1 ss into first dc.
2nd Row: 1 dc into each dc, 1 ss into first dc.
3rd Row: 1 dc into same place as ss, 14 ch, 1 dbl tr
into 5th ch from hook, over remaining 9 ch work
7 dbl tr * 2 tr 1 hlf tr and 1 dc, 1 dc into next dc on
ring, turn, miss first st, 1 dc into each of next 13 sts,
5 ch, turn, miss first 2 dc, ** (1 dc into next dc, 5 ch,
miss next dc) 5 times, 1 dc into next dc, 1 dc into
next dc on ring (a spoke made), 9 ch, turn, 1 dc into
3rd loop from tip of spoke, 4 ch, turn, over 9 ch work
8 dbl tr; repeat from * 11 times more ending last
repeat at **, 1 dc into next dc, 5 ch, miss next dc, 1 dc
into next dc, 2 ch, 1 dc into base of first dbl tr on first
spoke, 2 ch, miss next dc on last spoke, 1 dc into next
dc and complete last spoke as before, 1 ss into first dc
on ring. Fasten off.
4th Row: Attach Brown to 5 ch loop at tip of any
spoke, 1 dc into same place as join, * 15 ch, 1 dc into
next 5 ch loop at tip of next spoke, (9 ch, 1 dc into
next 5 ch loop at tip of next spoke) twice; repeat from
* omitting 1 dc at end of last repeat, 1 ss into first dc.
5th Row: 3 ch, 1 tr into each of next 7 ch, * into next ch
work 1 tr 5 ch and 1 tr, 1 tr into each of next 35 sts;
repeat from * omitting 8 tr at end of last repeat, 1 ss
into 3rd of 3 ch.

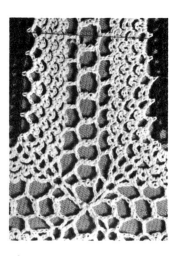

*Close-up of Motif, Pouffe
and Matching Bedhead*

6th Row: 4 ch, * (miss 1 tr, 1 tr into next tr, 1 ch) 4 times, miss 2 ch, into next ch work 1 tr 5 ch and 1 tr, 1 ch, (1 tr into next tr, 1 ch, miss 1 tr) 14 times, 1 tr into next tr, 1 ch; repeat from * omitting 1 tr and 1 ch at end of last repeat, 1 ss into 3rd of 4 ch. Fasten off.

7th Row: Using Lt. Beige, attach thread to centre ch at any corner, into same ch work 1 dc 3 ch and 1 dc (a picot loop made), * 5 ch, miss next 4 sts, 1 dc into next st, (5 ch, miss next 3 sts, 1 dc into next st) 9 times, 5 ch, miss next 4 sts, a picot loop into next st; repeat from * omitting a picot loop at end of last repeat, 1 ss into first dc.

8th Row: 1 ss into next loop, a picot loop into same loop, * 3 ch, a picot loop into next loop; repeat from * omitting a picot loop at end of last repeat, 1 ss into first dc.

9th Row: 1 ss into next loop, into same loop work 1 dc 5 ch and 1 dc, * 3 ch, 1 dc into next loop, (3 ch, miss next picot loop, a picot loop into next loop) 10 times, 3 ch, miss next picot loop, 1 dc into next loop, 3 ch, into next picot loop work 1 dc 5 ch and 1 dc; repeat from * omitting 1 dc 5 ch and 1 dc at end of last repeat, 1 ss into first dc.

10th Row: 1 ss into next loop, into same loop work 1 dc 5 ch and 1 dc, * 3 ch, miss next loop, (a picot loop into next loop, 3 ch, miss next picot loop) 10 times, a picot loop into next loop, 3 ch, miss next loop, into next loop work 1 dc 5 ch and 1 dc; repeat from * omitting 1 dc 5 ch and 1 dc at end of last repeat, 1 ss into first dc.

11th Row: 1 ss into next loop, into same loop work 1 dc 5 ch and 1 dc, * 3 ch, (a picot loop into next loop, 3 ch, miss next picot loop) 11 times, a picot loop into next loop, 3 ch, into next loop work 1 dc 5 ch and 1 dc; repeat from * omitting 1 dc 5 ch and 1 dc at end of last repeat, 1 ss into first dc.

12th Row: 1 ss into next loop, into same loop work 1 dc 5 ch and 1 dc, * 3 ch, 1 dc into next loop, (3 ch, miss next picot loop, a picot loop into next loop) 11 times, 3 ch, miss next picot loop, 1 dc into next loop, 3 ch, into next loop work 1 dc 5 ch and 1 dc; repeat from * omitting 1 dc 5 ch and 1 dc at end of last repeat, 1 ss into first dc.

13th Row: 1 ss into next loop, 8 ch, 1 ss into 4th ch from hook, 2 ch, into same loop as ss work (1 tr, 5 ch, 1 ss into 4th ch from hook – a picot made, 2 ch) twice and 1 tr, * (a picot, 2 ch, miss next loop, 1 tr into next loop) 12 times, a picot, 2 ch, into next 5 ch loop work (1 tr, a picot, 2 ch) 3 times and 1 tr; repeat from * omitting (1 tr, a picot, 2 ch) 3 times and 1 tr at end of last repeat, 1 ss into 3rd of 8 ch. Fasten off.

Second Motif

Work as first motif for 12 rows.
13th Row: 1 ss into next loop, 8 ch, 1 ss into 4th ch from hook, 2 ch, into same loop work (1 tr, 3 ch, 1 ss into corresponding picot on first motif, 2 ch, 1 ss into

2nd of 3 ch – a joining picot made – 2 ch) twice and 1 tr, (a joining picot into next picot on first motif, 2 ch, miss next loop on second motif, 1 tr into next loop) 13 times, (into same loop as last tr work a joining picot 2 ch 1 tr) twice a picot 2 ch and 1 tr and complete to correspond with first motif.

Make 43 more motifs joining each as shown in layout, then damp and pin out to measurements.

With right side facing, attach thread to corner picot on first section – marked by * on layout – 2 ch, 1 dc into corresponding picot on second section, * (2 ch, 1 dc into next picot on first section, 2 ch, 1 dc into next picot on second section) 15 times, 2 ch, 1 dc into next joining picot on first section, 2 ch, 1 dc into joining picot on second section; repeat from * twice more omitting 2 ch and 1 dc at end of last repeat, working last dc into next joining picot. Fasten off.

Join other 3 sides to correspond.

For the bedhead, make 12 motifs joining as before and placing as shown on layout.

Making Up

1.5 cm (½ in) seam allowance has been given on all pieces.

Pouffe

Cut 1 piece 48 × 185 cm (19 × 73 in) for sides, and 2 pieces 48 cm (19 in) square for top and base. Fold side piece right sides together and machine stitch short ends.

Place square for top to side piece, right sides together and machine stitch all round.

Trim seams, turn to right side and slip over pad.

Turn in seam allowance all round base piece and slipstitch in position to sides round lower edge.

Slip crochet over pad and stitch in place.

Bedhead

Cut 2 pieces 33 × 94 cm (13 × 37 in) for front and back.

Cut 2 pieces 10 × 94 cm (4 × 37 in) and 2 pieces 10 × 33 cm (4 × 13 in) for gussets.

Join 1 long gusset piece to 1 short gusset piece by machine stitching short ends. Join 2 remaining gusset pieces in same manner.

Join 2 sections together to form rectangle, machine stitching across free short ends. Place front section to gussets, right sides together, and machine stitch all round.

Trim seams, turn to right side, and slip over pad.

Turn in seam allowance all round back section and slipstitch to gussets. Sew motifs in place to front of pad.

Tabs

Cut 7 pieces 8 × 17 cm (3 × 6¾ in). With right sides together stitch across one short and one long edge. Turn to right side. Turn in remaining short end and slipstitch.

Complete other 6 tabs in same manner.
Sew rings or tabs in place as shown in illustration.

Alternative Suggestions

Cushion – 2 motifs × 3 motifs.
Runner – 2 motifs × 7 motifs.

Mirror Surround and Cheval Runner

Materials Required

Clark's Anchor Stranded Cotton: 5 skeins Peacock
Blue 0168: 4 skeins Jade 0187; 3 skeins Jade 0185;
1 skein each Cyclamen 086, Chestnut 0351 and
Beige 0378. Use 2 strands for Double Knot Stitch,
3 strands for Satin Stitch and French Knots, 4 strands
for rest of embroidery.
1.40 m (1½ yd) fine, light brown embroidery fabric, as
in illustration, 90 cm (approx. 36 in) wide.
1 packet each small glass beads, champagne and dark
brown.
Mirror, approximately 76 × 44 × 2 cm (30 ×
17¼ × ¾ in) as in illustration.
2 rings and chain for hanging.
1 each Milward 'Gold Seal' crewel needles Nos. 6, 7
and 8 for 4, 3 and 2 strands respectively.
1 Milward 'Gold Seal' beading needle.

The finished size of the illustrated cheval runner is
approximately 84 × 29 cm (33 × 11½ in) and each
mirror panel is approximately 44 × 17 cm
(17¼ × 6¾ in).

Cutting Out

Cut the following pieces from fabric:
Cheval Runner – 1 piece 88 × 33 cm (34½ × 13 in).
Mirror Panels – 2 pieces 68 × 52 cm (27 × 20½ in).

Cheval Runner

Fold fabric in half both ways and crease lightly. These
folds act as a guide when placing the pattern. With
short end of fabric facing, trace the pattern centrally
on to lower and upper halves, spacing 3 mm (⅛ in)
apart at widthwise fold (see Tracing Instructions on
page 19). Follow Key on page 65 for the embroidery.
NB for numbers 16 and 17 use French Knots only. All
parts similar to numbered parts are worked in the
same colour and stitch. Press embroidery on the wrong
side. To make up, turn back 1.5 cm (½ in) hems on all
sides, mitre corners and slipstitch.

Mirror Panels

Fold both pieces of fabric in half lengthwise and crease
lightly. This fold acts as a guide when placing the
design. Left-hand panel (diagram 2) – with long side
of fabric facing trace the pattern centrally on to fold
6.5 cm (2½ in) from right-hand edge (see Tracing

Instructions on page 19). Right-hand panel – motifs
are in reverse position. With long side of fabric facing,
trace motif B on to upper half 6.5 cm (2½ in) from
left-hand edge and motif A on to lower half in the
corresponding position, spacing 3 mm (⅛ in) apart at
lengthwise fold. Follow the Key on page 65 for the
embroidery. NB for numbers 16 and 17 use glass beads
only. All parts similar to numbered parts are worked in
the same colour, stitch and bead. Press embroidery on
the wrong side, being extra careful with glass beads.

Making Up

The embroidered panels are joined at the back of the
mirror for easy removal for cleaning. On left-hand
piece mark with basting stitches the position of
embroidered section (shaded section on diagram 2).
Neaten the short raw edge at embroidered end. Turn
up 5 cm (2 in) hem to the wrong side on the basting
line and sew in position. Place embroidery right side
down, centred over mirror, having left-hand row of
basting in line with edge of mirror. Pin sides and end

Motif, Mirror Surround and Cheval Runner

Diagram 2

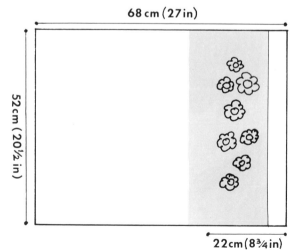

Mirror Surround and Cheval Runner

B

A

in position as in diagram 3. Remove from mirror; baste, stitch and trim. Turn to the right side. Replace over mirror and turn in excess fabric along top and lower edges to the wrong side; also mark position where ring screws on to mirror. Remove fabric, baste and stitch narrow hems along the top and lower edges. Makc an eyelet at marked position. Repeat with remaining right-hand embroidered piece. Remove ring screws from mirror. Place fabric over ends of mirror, pull taut, trim short ends at centre back as necessary and oversew. Replace ring screws in position through eyelets.

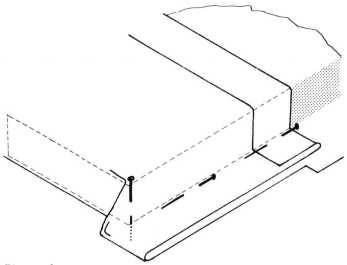

Diagram 3

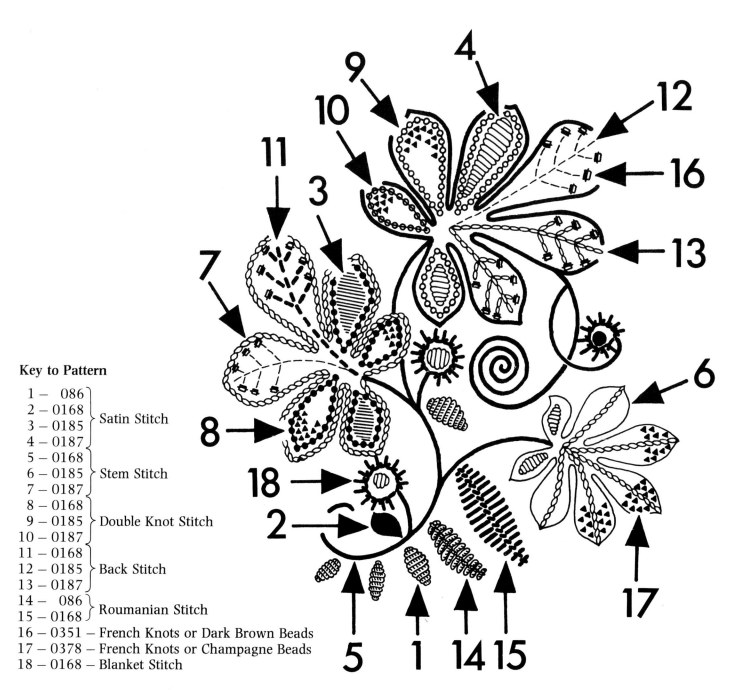

Key to Pattern

1 – 086 ⎫
2 – 0168 ⎪ Satin Stitch
3 – 0185 ⎬
4 – 0187 ⎭

5 – 0168 ⎫
6 – 0185 ⎬ Stem Stitch
7 – 0187 ⎭

8 – 0168 ⎫
9 – 0185 ⎬ Double Knot Stitch
10 – 0187 ⎭

11 – 0168 ⎫
12 – 0185 ⎬ Back Stitch
13 – 0187 ⎭

14 – 086 ⎫ Roumanian Stitch
15 – 0168 ⎭

16 – 0351 – French Knots or Dark Brown Beads
17 – 0378 – French Knots or Champagne Beads
18 – 0168 – Blanket Stitch

Chapter 4

What's the first thing you notice when you go into a room? Ten to one it's the curtains. So often the curtains set the mood for the whole room, with various combinations of style, fabric, and colour creating quite different atmospheres. There are so many materials to choose from today that anyone can try their hand at interior designing: and with the extensive range of aids now available, curtain making has become a simple and rewarding way of giving your home a face-lift and yourself and your family lasting pleasure.

Among the 'musts' for the modern curtain maker are the many 'Rufflette' products – their wide and versatile selection of tapes, hooks, and tracks have made it easy for those at home to produce professional-looking curtains of all types, suitable for every room in the house.

General Tips

1. Always allow plenty of fabric to be sure your curtains will look their best. However lovely the material, you will be disappointed with the results if you skimp on the width. Decide whether full-length or sill-length curtains will best suit the effect you wish to create. It is better not to have an 'in-between' length.
2. Patterns will have to be matched up so that they run at the same level on all curtains, and this will mean buying extra fabric. As a general rule, allow one pattern repeat per width after the first, eg four widths would require the equivalent of three pattern repeats. Remember that colour depends on light so it is worthwhile buying or borrowing a 50 cm ($\frac{1}{2}$ yd) sample so that you can see the effect in the actual room it is intended for, both in daylight and artificial light.
3. Linings will help your curtains to drape more attractively and lengthen their life by protecting the fabric from damaging effects of sun and dirt. You can now add detachable linings to your curtains very easily with 'Rufflette' Lining Tape. This method has the extra advantage of allowing the lining to be hooked on and off for washing separately. Detachable lining tape can be used with all styles of tape.
4. Allow for shrinkage. Unless the fabric is guaranteed non-shrink, allow at least 2.5 cm (1 in) per 1 m (1 yd) extra on your curtain length. (Your shop assistant should be able to help you.)
5. Selvedge: to prevent fabric puckering cut off the selvedge, or snip at intervals of 5–8 cm (2–3 in).
6. Points to check when buying curtain fabric: can it be washed by machine; should you iron it – and on which side; is dry-cleaning best; is it shrink-and

crease-resistant; will it fade? Ask the name of the manufacturers and if the retailer is unable to help, it is worth the effort of writing direct to the maker.

7. Never let your curtains get too dirty — wash frequently or dry clean but tell your cleaners if the material contains any of the synthetic fibres.

8. For 'Terylene' — use soap or detergent powder in hand-hot water. Nets, especially in town, should be washed very frequently. If they have been allowed to get really dirty, soak in cold water for 15 minutes before washing.

9. Glass Fibre Fabrics — should be washed gently in warm water with a mild detergent, rinsed and drip-dried. Don't scrub, rub or wring. Never dry-clean. To avoid damaging the fibres, hang over a smooth rod or line without pegging. Never iron. Glass fibre fabrics drip-dry perfectly crease-free. Make sure the bottom hem does not chafe against the window sill or floor as this may cause fraying. 'Rufflette' Nylon 2.5 cm (1 in) curtain tape is recommended for glass fibre curtains.

10. To pleat your curtains — be sure to knot the cords before sewing on tape. Pleat the fabric along the cords until all the fabric is packed to one end. Pull out again to the required width, and knot the cords to hold the width. This method preforms the pleats, makes even distribution of fullness easier, and gives a better finish to the heading. Insert curtain hooks at each end and every 8 cm (3 in) between.

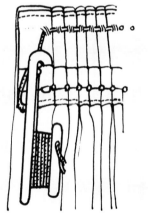

Diagram 1

11. Do not cut off surplus cord as this allows the curtain to be pulled flat for washing and ironing. After pleating the curtains, wind the surplus cord on to a 'Rufflette' Cord Tidy (diagram 1) and suspend neatly out of sight from a 'Rufflette' hook inserted in the curtain tape.

12. Hem — always sew hems by hand. This gives a better finish and allows easy alteration later if necessary. For nets, make double hems (page 12) and headings to prevent raw edges showing against the light. With other fabrics, extra length allowed for shrinkage can be taken up as a deep or double hem. Allow your curtains to hang for a few days before finishing the bottom hem, as some fabrics may stretch after hanging. The chart on page 76 gives information on hems and seams to use with various weights of fabric.

13. The Final Touch — There is no doubt that a cord control on your curtain track will double the life of your curtains. Just think of all the handling curtains get — drawn to and fro at least twice a day, pulled at from behind furniture (and even the cleanest fingers have a certain amount of natural oil on them!) More important still, by avoiding continual handling you will also avoid pulling the curtains out of shape. The modest cost of a cord control is more than offset by the saving on curtain replacement. Cording sets are very easy to fix to most curtain tracks and certainly add that final touch of luxury and care your beautiful, thoughtfully-planned curtains deserve.

Measuring

See chart on page 77 for details regarding fabric measurements for individual styles.

As a general rule, your curtain width should always be calculated from the width of your curtain track (diagram 2). Be sure to allow ample material for generous draping. Always add at least 4 cm (1½ in) for each side hem, 3 cm (1¼ in) for each join that may be required, and an allowance for any overlap required. Measure your curtain length from the curtain track and add on allowances for hem and heading, pattern matching and possible shrinkage (page 76). Full-length curtains should finish 2.5 cm (1 in) above the floor or carpet to allow the curtains to hang properly and prevent the fabric wearing through constant chafing against the floor. Similarly, sill-length curtains should just clear the window sill.

Where central heating radiators are placed under windows, do not drop the curtains to the floor in front of the radiator. This causes heat loss and obstructs the free run of the curtains.

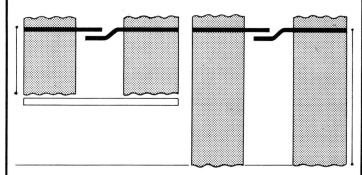

Diagram 2

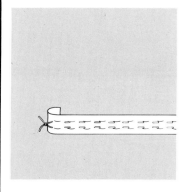

Diagram 3

Cutting of Fabric

It is important to prepare the fabric carefully before cutting ; ie the cut edge must be at right angles to the selvedge.

Conventional Heading

'Rufflette' Standard Tape — (see chart for fabric requirements.) For even gathering on all types of curtain fabrics, use 'Rufflette' Standard Tape. Available in a choice of 21 colours, it is completely reversible — no right or wrong side to worry about — and the curtains are easily pulled flat for washing and ironing. With man-made fabrics such as glass fibre, use 'Rufflette' Nylon Tape 2.5 cm (1 in) wide, which is drip-dry and non-shrink.

After joining widths where necessary and making side hems, turn over the top raw edge of the curtain about 4 cm (1½ in) and baste. Pull out about 4 cm (1½ in) of the cords at one end of the Standard Tape and knot them together. Trim off the surplus tape. Turn under this prepared end so that the knotted cords are enclosed under the tape. At the other end of the tape, pull out 2.5–5 cm (1–2 in) of the cords and leave free

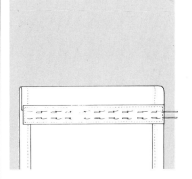

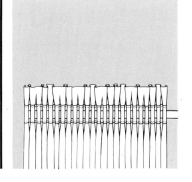

69

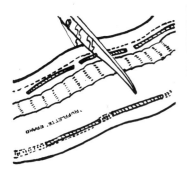

Diagram 4A

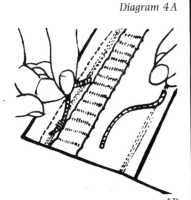

4B

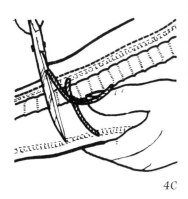

4C

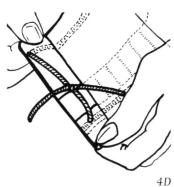

4D

4E

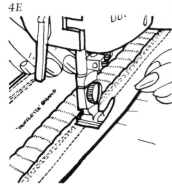

for pleating up. Turn under the end of the tape to make a neat finish. Pin or baste the tape to the curtain, covering the raw edge and leaving not more than 2.5 cm (1 in) between the top edge of the curtain and the top edge of the tape. Stitch all round the outer edge of the tape, outside the cords (diagram 3). Pleat your curtain as described on page 71 and insert hooks.

Hooks

Use 'Rufflette' curtain hooks. (See chart on page 76.)

Track

Curtains made with 'Rufflette' Standard Tape may be hung on any 'Rufflette' curtain track. For a final touch of luxury – and to save wear and tear on your curtains – easily-fitted Cording Sets are available, which can be used on most curtain tracks.

'Rufflette' Autopleat and Sheerpleat

These tapes are used for beautiful fanned pinch pleating. Once upon a time you needed complicated hooks, and lots of patience to make pinch pleats. Nowadays you simply use a tape called Autopleat for 9 cm ($3\frac{1}{2}$ in) deep fanned pinch pleats, or Sheerpleat if you want a narrow 4 cm ($1\frac{1}{2}$ in) pinch pleat effect.
Autopleat and Sheerpleat may be used on both curtain fabric or nets.

Formula for Material Required

A minimum of double the width of the track for the finished curtain.

There are two versions of Autopleat Styling Tape :
a) Conventional Autopleat – for curtains which are to conceal the track. (The pockets have been woven at the bottom of the tape.)
b) Autopleat Underslung for use on curtains which are to be suspended below a decorative pole or alternatively where the curtain track is fixed to the ceiling. (The pockets have been woven at the top of the tape.)

Making up your Curtains (diagram 4)

A. Ensure that the tape is the correct way up (check the 'Rufflette' brand printed on the tape). Taking the end of the tape which will come to the centre of the track, cut in the middle of the first group of pleats.
B. Pull out and knot together the ends of the cord. After joining widths where necessary and making side hems, turn under and baste 1.5 cm ($\frac{1}{2}$ in) at top of curtain.
C. Trim off the surplus tape 1.5 cm ($\frac{1}{2}$ in) from the knotted cord.
D. Turn under 2.5 cm (1 in) at the end of the tape, including the knotted ends of the cords. At the other end of the tape take out an inch or two of the cords and leave free for pleating the curtain. Turn under the

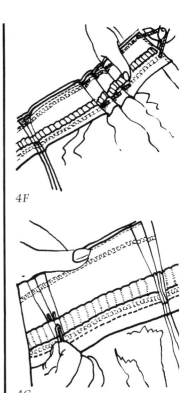

4F

4G

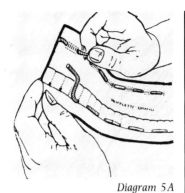

Diagram 5A

5B

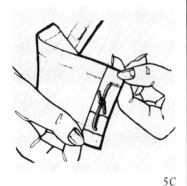

5C

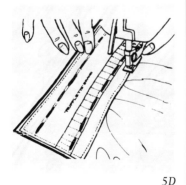

5D

5E

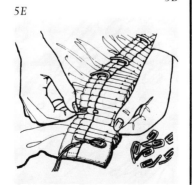

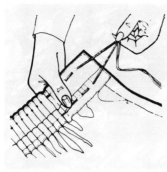

5F

edge of the tape to neaten.

E. Turn and tack a 1.5 cm (½ in) hem at the top of the curtain. Lay the tape over the top of the curtain with the folded ends level with the side edge of the curtain. The top edge of the tape should be 3 mm (⅛ in) from the top edge of the curtain.

Machine across one folded edge and along the top edge of the tape. The bottom row of stitching should be machined along the line which has been woven into the tape for guidance. Ensure that both rows of stitching follow the same direction. Machine across the final folded edge of the tape.

Avoid stitching over cords at the top and bottom of the tape.

F. It is very important to pull the curtain up correctly. Holding the free ends of the cord firmly with one hand, position the fingers as indicated. By pleating in this way you will avoid puckering the flat area between the pleats.

Push the first set of pleats into position along the cords. Advance to the second set of pleats and push into position. Return to the first set of pleats and push into position. Advance and return in similar fashion until all the pleats are in position along the heading.

Do not pleat up tightly to begin with; this will enable you to tighten up the pleats should the curtain be too wide when offered to the curtain track.

G. The special R10 hooks should now be inserted by slipping the two prongs into the two pockets formed at the back of each group of pleats. A hook should be inserted at each end of the curtain, by inserting the two prongs into adjacent pockets.

'Rufflette' Regis and Tervoil 60

These tapes are for pencil pleats on curtains and nets. Regis pencil pleat tape with its built-in stiffener is ideal for all types of curtain material. Tervoil 60 also has been woven by a unique process to give your heading a permanent upright appearance on nets.

Formula for Material Required

'Rufflette' Regis — $2\frac{1}{4}$–$2\frac{1}{2}$ times the track width.
'Rufflette' Tervoil 60 — $2\frac{1}{2}$–3 times the wire or track width.

Position of Pockets on Tape

If your curtain track is fixed to the wall with 8 cm (3 in) or more space between the track and the ceiling, sew the tape on with the pockets at the bottom. Where curtains are suspended below the curtain track (as with decorative poles or ceiling fixed track) sew the tape on with the pockets at the top.

After joining widths where necessary and making side hems, turn under and baste 1.5 cm (½ in) at top of curtain.

Sewing the Tape on to the Curtain (diagram 5)

A. From one end of the tape pull out about 4 cm

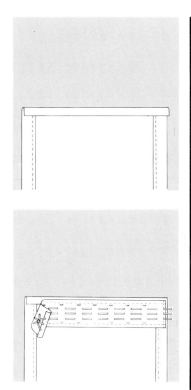

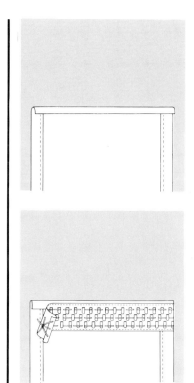

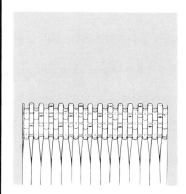

($1\frac{1}{2}$ in) of each cord.

B. Knot the cords together and trim off surplus tape, 1.5 cm ($\frac{1}{2}$ in) from the knot.

C. Turn under the prepared end so that the knotted cords are enclosed under the tape. At the other end of the tape take out an inch or two of the cords and leave free for pleating up the curtain. Turn under the edge of the tape to neaten.

D. Turn and tack a 1.5 cm ($\frac{1}{2}$ in) hem at the top of the curtain. Making sure that the hook pockets are facing you, tack the tape to the curtains leaving 3 mm ($\frac{1}{8}$ in) between the top of the tape and the curtain, and machine along the outer edge of the tape. Ensure that both rows of stitching follow the same direction.

E. To pleat up your curtains, hold the free cords in one hand and gently push the curtain along the cords until the fabric is packed to one end. Pull the curtain out again to the required width and then tie a slip knot to hold.

By pleating up using this method, the pleats are preformed. Do not cut off surplus cord as this allows the curtain to be pulled flat again for washing.

F. Insert curtain hooks at each end of the curtain and approximately every 8 cm (3 in) along the curtain.

'Rufflette' Hi-Style Tape (see chart for fabric requirements)

'Rufflette' Hi-Style is an alternative method of pencil-pleating. The pleats are made simply by drawing up three cords, but in this case, the heading is held erect by the special Hi-Style hooks. This graceful curtain style does not need pelmets or valances. Long curtains falling in an unbroken line from this easily-pleated inexpensive heading will look charming in any type of fabric.

After joining widths where necessary and making side hems, turn and baste 1.5 cm ($\frac{1}{2}$ in) at top of curtain. Pull out about 4 cm ($1\frac{1}{2}$ in) of the cords at one end of the 'Rufflette' Hi-Style tape and knot them together. Trim off the surplus tape. Turn under this prepared end so that the knotted cords are enclosed under the tape. At the other end of the tape, pull out 2.5–5 cm (1–2 in) of cords and leave free for pleating up. Turn under the end of the tape to make a neat finish.

Baste the tape to the curtain flush with the top edge of the material. Stitch all round the outer edge of the tape, outside the cords (diagram 6). Pleat up your curtains as described on page 71 and insert hooks.

NOTE: To make sure the track is concealed by the heading when the curtains are closed, before making your curtains measure the distance from the bottom of the runner ring or glider to the top of the track (including any fitting which may be visible over the track). If this measurement is greater than 4 cm ($1\frac{1}{2}$ in) allow sufficient heading on the curtain above the top edge of the tape to close the gap, but this should not exceed 1.5 cm ($\frac{1}{2}$ in).

Diagram 6

Diagram 7

Hooks

With Hi-Style curtain tape, the special Hi-Style curtain hooks must be used. They have been designed to keep the heading crisply upright without drooping or sagging.

Track

Because this delightful curtain style does not need a pelmet, 'Rufflette' Trimtrack is ideal to use with 'Rufflette' Hi-Style. The choice of attractive finishes will ensure your track blends beautifully with your curtains and your room.

'Rufflette' Trident Tape (see chart for fabric requirements)

'Rufflette' Trident is an 8 cm (3 in) wide tape which gives tall pencil pleats. It has three draw cords and strong woven pockets which are staggered to offer three differing suspension points. The choice of pocket depends on the track and the circumstances under which it will be used, ie whether the track is fixed to the wall or ceiling.

After joining widths where necessary and making side hems turn and baste 1.5 cm ($\frac{1}{2}$ in) at top of curtain. Pull out about 4 cm ($1\frac{1}{2}$ in) of the cords at one end of the Trident tape and knot them together. Trim off the surplus tape. Turn under this prepared end so that the knotted cords are enclosed under the tape. At the other end of the tape, pull out 2.5–5 cm (1–2 in) of the cords and leave free for pleating up. Turn under the end of the tape to make a neat finish to the edge.

Baste the tape to the curtain flush with the top edge of the material and stitch all round the outer edge of the tape, outside the cords (diagram 7).

Pleat up your curtains as described on page 71 and insert hooks.

Hooks

Use 'Rufflette' curtain hooks. (See chart on page 76).

Track

'Rufflette' Trimtrack is ideal to use with this no pelmet curtain style.

Detachable Linings

These may be hooked on and removed easily for laundering. They can be added to your curtains very easily and help them to drape more effectively. They also protect curtains from the damaging effects of the sun and dirt, and help to insulate windows and prevent draughts.

Formula for Material Required

One and a half to twice the length of the curtain track.

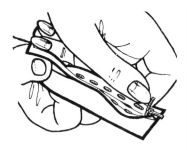

Diagram 8A

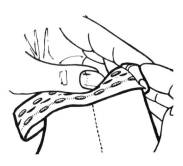

8B

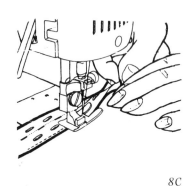

8C

Making Up

Make up the curtain lining with side and bottom hems, joining widths where necessary, but leave the top edge unfinished.

Taking the edge of the tape which will come to the centre of the track, pull free 4 cm (1½ in) of each draw cord and knot the ends (diagram 8A). Trim off the surplus tape to within 6 mm (¼ in) of the point where the cords enter the tape. Slip the lining in between the two skirts of the lining tape (diagram 8B). Turn under the end of the tape including the knotted cords and stitch across the folded edge to neaten. Machine over the knotted end of the tape and then proceed to machine one line of stitching to trap the lining in between the two skirts of the tape (diagram 8C). Finish the end of the tape in a similar manner to the commencing edge, but leave the ends of the cord free for pleating the lining.

Pleat up the lining by pulling all the fullness as far as it will go to one end of the curtain, as tightly as possible.

Pull out the pleating evenly to the required width to fit the curtain. The sides of the lining and the curtain can be anchored together with a few tacks or light stitches every 30 cm (12 in) if desired.

How to attach Lining to your Curtain

The following illustrations and hints will show you how to attach lining to your curtain.

Detachable Linings with Gathered Headings (diagram 9A)

Insert the hook through the small hole in the top of the lining tape.
Position the lining on your Standard headed curtain and insert the hook through the pocket of the Standard Tape and turn this over in the normal way.

Detachable Linings on Regis Headed Curtains (9B)

Insert the hook through the small hole in the top of the lining tape.
Position the lining on your Regis headed curtain and insert the prong of the hook through the Regis pocket and turn this over in the normal way.

Detachable Linings on Autopleat and Sheerpleat Headed Curtains (9C)

Insert a single prong of the R10 hook through the small hole in the top of the lining tape.
Position the lining on your curtain and insert each of the hook prongs into the two pockets which have been formed in the Autopleat or Sheerpleat curtains and turn the hook over in the normal way.

Nets and Sheer Fabric

'Rufflette' Tervoil 2.5 cm (1 in) Tape — see chart for

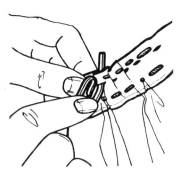

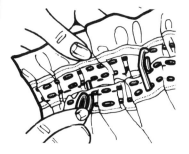

Diagram 9A Gathered Headings

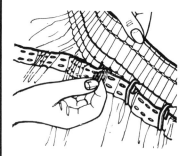

9B Regis Headed Curtains

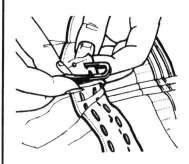

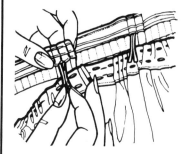

9C Autopleat and Sheerpleat Headed Curtains

fabric requirements.

Crispest ever Tervoil 2.5 cm (1 in) Heading for Nets was developed on the Continent, where the imaginative draping of nets has always been popular. Tervoil Tape is a new fabric which has an open weave to blend with the net, yet is stiffened to hold the curtain heading crisply upright and closely gathered. 2.5 cm (1 in) wide Tervoil Tape is as simple to use as Standard Tape to give a professional-looking, perfectly pleated finish to your net curtains.

After joining widths and making side hems, turn over the top edge of the material double to give a hem about 5 cm (2 in) deep, and baste. From one end of the Tervoil Tape pull out about 4 cm (1½ in) of each cord and knot the two together. Trim off surplus tape. Turn under this prepared end so that the knotted cords are enclosed under the tape. At the other end of the tape, pull out 2.5–5 cm (1–2 in) of the cords for pleating up, and turn under the edge of the tape to make a neat finish. Pin or baste the tape to the curtain, leaving not more than 2.5 cm (1 in) between the top edge of the curtain and top edge of the tape. Stitch all round the outer edge of the tape, taking care not to stitch over cords. Pleat your curtain as described on page 71 and insert hooks.

IMPORTANT NOTE: 'Rufflette' Tervoil Tape must NOT be ironed. It is drip-dry and specially made so that your net curtains can be washed without unpleating the curtain heading.

Hooks

Use 'Rufflette' hooks. (See chart on page 76).

Tracks

Net curtains may be suspended on all 'Rufflette' tracks. Alternatively, Tervoil pleated nets may be hung on rods or wires with 'Rufflette' curtain hooks and rings. 'Rufflette' Terylene 1.5 cm (½ in) Tape – see page 77 for fabric requirements. This tape may be used for conventional styles but is suitable for making crossover drapes and festoons.

Festoons

Fascinating festoons are surprisingly easy to make with 'Rufflette' Terylene Tape – and are very practical to launder too, as the tape drip-dries with the curtain. Your Terylene material should measure 2½ to 3 times the depth of the window (measuring from the track or wire) and 1½ times the width of the track or wire. Be sure to select the correct width of fabric for the width of window.

Hem each side but leave top and bottom edges unfinished until later. Measure the total width of your fabric and decide how wide each festoon must be – eg if your material is 182 cm (72 in) wide, leaving 2.5 cm (1 in) at either side you could get seven festoons each 25 cm (10 in) wide. Ensure that any joining seams will be hidden under the vertical tape.

Fold the fabric vertically accordion-wise to the festoon width, pressing the folded edges as you go. When unfolded the fabric will be marked evenly in vertical panels.

Sew lengths of Terylene Tape along each of these vertical fold lines from top to bottom, including one along each side hem, 2.5 cm (1 in) from the edge. Secure the drawcords by knotting ends at the bottom. Turn up and finish bottom hem, enclosing the knotted ends in the hem. Finish the top edge of the curtain with a double hem and Terylene Tape. Now pleat each length of Terylene Tape by drawing up cords until the curtain is the depth you require.

Hooks

Use 'Rufflette' hooks. (See chart on page 76).

Track

'Rufflette' Trimtrack may be used.

'Rufflette' Lead-Weighted Tape

'Rufflette' Lead-Weighted Tape is ideal for use with all fabrics and helps to give a graceful hang and professional finish to your curtains. The tape is available in three weights and has a neat slim finish because the lead-shot is elongated and enclosed in a tube of tough polyester fibre:

25 grammes per metre for net curtains.
70 grammes per metre for nets and lightweight fabric curtains.
150 grammes per metre for heavier fabric curtains. Amount needed is the same width as the finished curtain.

This tape is simplicity itself to use as it is only necessary to tie a piece of cotton to one end of the tape, which is then pulled through the hem of the curtain by means of a bodkin. When in place the ends of the tape are secured with basting stitches, which can easily be removed when the curtains need laundering; it is not necessary to remove the weighted tape for hand washing.

Tracks

'Rufflette' Trimtrack

'Rufflette' Trimtrack is produced in strong white plastic, and all you see is a slim straight band when the curtains are drawn back. There is also a range of easily applied self adhesive finishes designed to tone with your curtains and room schemes. As an extra, you can have long extension brackets on which can be mounted a second track (Sheerglide) for your net curtains. A smooth running cording set is also available to save wear and tear on your curtains from hand pulling.

Trimtrack can be fixed either to walls or ceilings with the same brackets. (The extension bracket is for wall fixing only.)

FABRICS, SEAMS AND HEMS

Type of Fabric	Type of Seam	Type of Hem
Fine	French Seam	Slipstitched, Hemmed, or blindstitched with the machine
Sheer	French Seam	Double Hem
Medium	French Seam, Flat Seam, Machine Fell Seam }	Catchstitched or Herringbone Stitched (if curtains are lined) otherwise slipstitched, hemmed or blindstitched with the machine
Heavy	Flat Seam Machine Fell Seam }	As for medium fabrics

'Rufflette' Sheerglide

'Rufflette' have produced this neat, strong plastic curtain track which uses the same gliders as Trimtrack. Two types of bracket have been produced for either ceiling or wall fixing. These should be requested when ordering the track for your particular purpose. For nets and sheers or used as a second curtain track Sheerglide is the ideal partner when used with Trimtrack.

'Rufflette' Classic

'Rufflette' Classic Decorative Curtain Track is a decorative pole that is fashioned in anodized aluminium with Classic lines to compliment your window décor. Will give a lifetime of beauty and dependable service.

'Rufflette' Royal

Royal curtain track incorporates a decorative wood facing to blend with any room décor. 'Rufflette' offer the most comprehensive selection of wood facings.

'RUFFLETTE' TAPES AND HOOKS

N.B. Allowances:	Allow 4 cm (1½ in) for each side hem, 3.5 cm (1¼ in) for each join, plus allowance for any overlap required.
Shrinkage:	Allow not less than 2.5 cm (1 in) per 1 m (1 yd), unless fabric is definitely non-shrink.
Pattern matching:	Allow 1 pattern repeat per width after the first, eg. if 4 widths are required allow 3 pattern repeats.

Rufflette Tapes	Rufflette Hooks		Type of Fabric	Allowance for Hems and Headings
Standard 2.5 cm (1 in)	Plastic Plastic Nylon Brass Zinc Chromate Solid Brass	−R40 −R4 −R5 −R7 −R67 −R77	Fine/Medium/Heavy	13–20 cm (5–8 in)
Nylon 2.5 cm (1 in) Terylene 1.5 cm (½ in)	Plastic Plastic Zinc Chromate	−R40 −R4 −R67	All Types	13–20 cm (5–8 in)
Tervoil 2.5 cm (1 in)	Plastic Plastic Nylon Rings: Split Zinc Chromate	−R40 −R4 −R5 −R21	Nets	15 cm (6 in) for Double Hem 20 cm (8 in) for Double Heading
Regis 8 cm (3 in)	Plastic Brass Solid Brass Zinc Chromate	−R40 −R7 −R77 −R67	Heavy/Medium	20 cm (8 in)
Hi-Style 8 cm (3 in)	Hi-Style	−HS1	Fine/Medium	20 cm (8 in)
Trident 8 cm (3 in)	Plastic Zinc Chromate Plastic	−R40 −R60 −R4	Fine/Medium/Heavy	20 cm (8 in)
Tervoil 60, 7 cm (2¾ in)	Plastic Zinc Chromate Plastic Rings	−R40 −R60 −R4 −R21	Nets	Single Heading 15–20 cm (6–8 in) for Double Hem
Tervoil 60, 7 cm (2¾ in)	Plastic Zinc Chromate Plastic Rings	−R40 −R60 −R4 −R21	Fine Fabric	Single Heading 15–20 cm (6–8 in) for Double Hem
Autopleat 9 cm (3½ in) Sheerpleat 4 cm (1½ in)	Zinc Chromate Zinc Chromate	−R10 −R10	Medium/Heavy Fine	20 cm (8 in) 20 cm (8 in)
Lining Tape	All Types		All Types	Depends on Curtain Style

Right:
Curtains headed with Regis Tape

Far right:
Curtains headed with Trident Tape

Imperial

TABLE 1. GATHERED HEADING

Track Width		5′	6′	7′	8′	9′	10′	11′	12′	13′	14′
No. of 48″ fabric widths		2	3	3	3	4	4	4	5	5	6
Yds of tape per pair		3	4¼	4¼	4¼	5½	5½	5½	7	7	8¼
Curtain Drop	4′	3¼	4⅔	4⅔	4⅔	6¼	6¼	6¼	8	8	9⅓
	4′6″	3½	5¼	5¼	5¼	7	7	7	8⅔	8⅔	10⅓
	5′	4	5⅔	5⅔	5⅔	7⅔	7⅔	7⅔	9½	9½	11⅓
	5′6″	4¼	6¼	6¼	6¼	8¼	8¼	8¼	10⅓	10⅓	12⅓
	6′	4½	6⅔	6⅔	6⅔	9	9	9	11¼	11¼	13⅓
	6′6″	5	7¼	7¼	7¼	9⅔	9⅔	9⅔	12	12	14⅓
	7′	5¼	7⅔	7⅔	7⅔	10¼	10¼	10¼	12¾	12¾	15⅓

TABLE 2. PENCIL PLEAT HEADING

Track Width		5′	6′	7′	8′	9′	10′	11′	12′	13′	14′
No. of 48″ fabric widths		3	4	5	5	6	6	7	8	8	9
Yds of tape per pair		4	5½	7	7	8	8	9½	11	11	12
Curtain Drop	4′	4⅔	6¼	8	8	9⅓	9⅓	11	12½	12½	14
	4′6″	5¼	7	8⅔	8⅔	10⅓	10⅓	12	13¾	13¾	15½
	5′	5⅔	7⅔	9½	9½	11⅓	11⅓	13¼	15¼	15¼	17
	5′6″	6¼	8¼	10⅓	10⅓	12⅓	12⅓	14⅓	16½	16½	18½
	6′	6⅔	9	11¼	11¼	13⅓	13⅓	15½	17¾	17¾	20
	6′6″	7¼	9⅔	12	12	14⅓	14⅓	16¾	19¼	19¼	21½
	7′	7⅔	10¼	12¾	12¾	15⅓	15⅓	18	20½	20½	23

TABLE 3. FANNED PINCH PLEAT HEADING

Track Width		5′	6′	7′	8′	9′	10′	11′	12′	13′	14′
No. of 48″ fabric widths		3	3	4	4	5	5	6	6	7	7
Yds of tape per pair		4⅔	4⅔	6	6	7⅓	7⅓	8⅔	8⅔	10	10
Curtain Drop	4′	4⅔	4⅔	6¼	6¼	8	8	9⅓	9⅓	11	11
	4′6″	5¼	5¼	7	7	8⅔	8⅔	10⅓	10⅓	12	12
	5′	5⅔	5⅔	7⅔	7⅔	9½	9½	11⅓	11⅓	13¼	13¼
	5′6″	6¼	6¼	8¼	8¼	10⅓	10⅓	12⅓	12⅓	14⅓	14⅓
	6′	6⅔	6⅔	9	9	11¼	11¼	13⅓	13⅓	15½	15½
	6′6″	7¼	7¼	9⅔	9⅔	12	12	14⅓	14⅓	16¾	16¾
	7′	7⅔	7⅔	10¼	10¼	12¾	12¾	15⅓	15⅓	18	18

The Rufflette calculator will tell you:
A. The number of (full) 48″ widths of fabric required.
B. The amount of curtain heading tape required.
C. The total yardage of 48″ fabric required for a pair of plain coloured curtains. Additional material will be required for pattern matching or possible shrinkage. An allowance has been included for top and bottom hems.

Metric

TABLE 1. GATHERED HEADING

Track Width/cm		150	175	200	225	250	275	300	325	350	375	400	425
No. of 120 cm/48″ fabric widths		2	3	3	3	3	4	4	4	5	5	5	6
Metres of tape per pair		2.5	3.7	3.7	3.7	3.7	4.9	4.9	4.9	6.1	6.1	6.1	7.3
Curtain Drop	1.2 m	2.8	4.2	4.2	4.2	4.2	5.6	5.6	5.6	7.0	7.0	7.0	8.4
	1.4 m	3.2	4.8	4.8	4.8	4.8	6.4	6.4	6.4	8.0	8.0	8.0	9.6
	1.5 m	3.4	5.1	5.1	5.1	5.1	6.8	6.8	6.8	8.5	8.5	8.5	10.2
	1.7 m	3.8	5.7	5.7	5.7	5.7	7.6	7.6	7.6	9.5	9.5	9.5	11.4
	1.8 m	4.0	6.0	6.0	6.0	6.0	8.0	8.0	8.0	10.0	10.0	10.0	12.0
	2.0 m	4.4	6.6	6.6	6.6	6.6	8.8	8.8	8.8	11.0	11.0	11.0	13.2
	2.2 m	4.8	7.2	7.2	7.2	7.2	9.6	9.6	9.6	12.0	12.0	12.0	14.4

TABLE 2. PENCIL PLEAT HEADING

Track Width/cm		150	175	200	225	250	275	300	325	350	375	400	425
No. of 120 cm/48″ fabric widths		3	4	4	5	5	6	6	7	7	8	8	9
Metres of tape per pair		3.7	4.9	4.9	6.1	6.1	7.3	7.3	8.5	8.5	9.7	9.7	10.9
Curtain Drop	1.2 m	4.2	5.6	5.6	7.0	7.0	8.4	8.4	9.8	9.8	11.2	11.2	12.6
	1.4 m	4.8	6.4	6.4	8.0	8.0	9.6	9.6	11.2	11.2	12.8	12.8	14.4
	1.5 m	5.1	6.8	6.8	8.5	8.5	10.2	10.2	11.9	11.9	13.6	13.6	15.3
	1.7 m	5.7	7.6	7.6	9.5	9.5	11.4	11.4	13.3	13.3	15.2	15.2	17.1
	1.8 m	6.0	8.0	8.0	10.0	10.0	12.0	12.0	14.0	14.0	16.0	16.0	18.0
	2.0 m	6.6	8.8	8.8	11.0	11.0	13.2	13.2	15.4	15.4	17.6	17.6	19.8
	2.2 m	7.2	9.6	9.6	12.0	12.0	14.4	14.4	16.8	16.8	19.2	19.2	21.6

TABLE 3. FANNED PINCH PLEAT HEADING

Track Width/cm		150	175	200	225	250	275	300	325	350	375	400	425
No. of 120 cm/48″ fabric widths		3	3	4	4	5	5	5	6	6	7	7	7
Metres of tape per pair		4.0	4.0	5.2	5.2	6.4	6.4	6.4	7.6	7.6	8.8	8.8	8.8
Curtain Drop	1.2 m	4.2	4.2	5.6	5.6	7.0	7.0	7.0	8.4	8.4	9.8	9.8	9.8
	1.4 m	4.8	4.8	6.4	6.4	8.0	8.0	8.0	9.6	9.6	11.2	11.2	11.2
	1.5 m	5.1	5.1	6.8	6.8	8.5	8.5	8.5	10.2	10.2	11.9	11.9	11.9
	1.7 m	5.7	5.7	7.6	7.6	9.5	9.5	9.5	11.4	11.4	13.3	13.3	13.3
	1.8 m	6.0	6.0	8.0	8.0	10.0	10.0	10.0	12.0	12.0	14.0	14.0	14.0
	2.0 m	6.0	6.6	8.8	8.8	11.0	11.0	11.0	13.2	13.2	15.4	15.4	15.4
	2.2 m	7.2	7.2	9.6	9.6	12.0	12.0	12.0	14.4	14.4	16.8	16.8	16.8

The Rufflette calculator will tell you:
A. The number of (full) 120 cm widths of fabric required.
B. The amount of curtain heading tape required.
C. The total length in metres of 120 cm fabric required for a pair of plain coloured curtains. Additional material will be required for pattern matching or possible shrinkage. An allowance has been included for top and bottom hems.

Chapter 5

Cushions

The trend for gay home furnishings has inspired this collection of cushions, with embroidery or crochet trim. Cushions can be made in a variety of interesting shapes and they can be used in unusual ways as decorative features in the bedroom as well as the lounge, and even as a sag bag on the floor. A design on a cushion may be adapted to suit another article or vice versa. The charming design of leaves shown on the chairback and TV runner would look very attractive on a matching cushion.

Whatever size, shape or type of cushion is being made it is best to make a paper pattern to the finished size. This ensures accuracy, and when laid out will indicate the amount of fabric required. If a piped cushion is required allow approximately 50 cm ($\frac{1}{2}$ yd) (depending on the size of the cushion) extra fabric to cut bias strips for covering piping cord.

Diagram 1

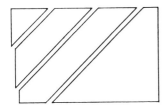

Diagram 2

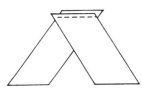

Diagram 3

Piping

This is made with bias cut strips covering piping cord. To cut strips on the bias, fold the fabric diagonally so that the lengthwise thread lies parallel to the widthwise thread (diagram 1). When the fabric is pulled on the true bias, it gives the maximum elasticity. Cut strips the desired width, usually 4–5 cm ($1\frac{1}{2}$–2 in) depending on the thickness of piping cord, and join to form the required length. Diagrams 2 and 3 show the correct method. Fold the strip in half lengthwise, wrong sides together, inserting the piping cord. Baste and stitch close to the cord (diagram 4). Place piping to the right side of cushion seam edge and baste. Lay gusset or other seam edge in position, baste and stitch close to cord (diagram 5). When the piping is round a curved edge, it is necessary to clip it so that it will lie flat (diagram 6).

Plain Square or Round Cushion

Materials Required

Make a paper pattern to the desired finished size of cushion.
Fabric as required.
1 cushion pad to fit.
Coats Drima (polyester) thread.

Cutting Out

From fabric cut two sections as pattern plus 1.5 cm ($\frac{1}{2}$ in) seam allowance all round.

Making Up

Place fabric right sides together. Baste and stitch,

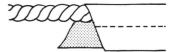

Diagram 4

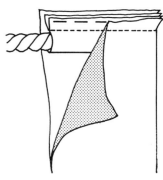

Diagram 5

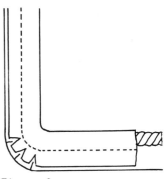

Diagram 6

79

Plain Round Cushion

leaving an opening at the centre of one side for pad insertion. Turn to right side and press. Insert pad and sew opening neatly.

Round Piped Cushion with Gusset

Materials Required

Make a paper pattern to the desired finished size of cushion main section, and a gusset section pattern to fit round outer edge of main section by the depth required, generally 5–10 cm (2–4 in) depending on size of circle.
Sufficient fabric to cut two main sections and gusset strip, plus extra fabric for bias strips for piping, plus seam allowance.
1 cushion pad with gusset to fit.
Piping cord, twice the circumference of main section, plus 5 cm (2 in) for ease.
Coats Drima (polyester) thread.

Cutting Out

From fabric cut two main sections and a gusset section length required, joining if necessary (diagram 3) and leaving seam allowance on all sections. Cut sufficient bias strips to cover piping. Cut piping cord in half.

Making Up

Cover cord with bias strips (diagram 4). Join gusset section at short ends to form a circle. Baste one piece of piping to right side of one main section, having raw edges even. Place gusset section right side down over piping, raw edges even. Baste and stitch close to piping. Repeat for the other main section, leaving an opening for inserting pad. Insert pad and sew opening neatly.

Piped Square Cushion with Gusset in Four Sections

Materials Required

Make a paper pattern to the desired finished size of cushion main section, and a gusset section the length of one side of the cushion by the depth of gusset required. The gusset should be in proportion to the main section, generally 5–10 cm (2–4 in).
Sufficient fabric for two main sections, four gusset sections and bias strips for piping plus seam allowances.
Piping cord sufficient to go twice round cushion plus 10 cm (4 in) for ease at corners.
1 cushion pad with gusset to fit.
Coats Drima (polyester) thread.

Cutting Out

From fabric cut two main sections, four gusset sections plus seam allowance on all sections. Cut sufficient bias strips, joining where necessary (diagrams 2 and 3,

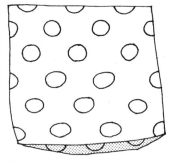

Plain Square Cushion

Round Piped Cushion with Gusset

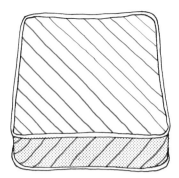

Piped Square Cushion with Gusset

page 79) to cover piping cord. Cut piping cord in half.

Making Up

Cover piping cord with bias strips (diagram 4, page 79). Join gusset sections at short ends. Baste one piece of piping to right side of one main section, having raw edges even. Place gusset right side down over piping with raw edges even and having joins in gusset at corners. Baste and stitch close to piping (diagram 5, page 79). Clip piping and gusset at the corners (diagram 6, page 79). Repeat with the other main section, leaving an opening at one side to insert pad. Insert pad and sew opening neatly.

Plain or Piped Bolster Cushion

Materials Required

Make a paper pattern to desired finished size of cushion.
To do this make a circle to diameter required for end of bolster and cut a straight strip the circumference of circle by length required.
Fabric as required. Extra fabric for a piped cushion.
1 bolster pad to fit.
1 Lightning zip fastener 10 cm (4 in) shorter than finished size of bolster.
Piping cord twice the circumference of bolster for a piped cushion.
Coats Drima (polyester) thread.

Cutting Out

From fabric cut two circular end sections and one main section, plus seam allowance on all sections. If making a piped bolster cut sufficient bias strips to cover piping cord (page 79). Cut piping cord in half.

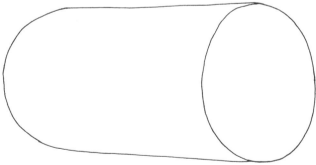

Bolster Cushion

Making Up

Fold main section in half with long edges even. Stitch seam at each end, leaving an opening in the centre the length of the zip. Baste and stitch zip in place. Open zip and turn to right side. With right sides together baste and sew one end circle in place. Clip seam at intervals so that seam will lie flat. Repeat with the other end circle. Turn to right side. The ends may

81

be finished by sewing a covered button or a tassel to the centre of the circles. For a piped bolster make up piping (page 79) and, with raw edges even, baste to circular sections before joining end sections to main section. Baste main section in place and stitch close to piping.

Piped Bolster Cushion with Gathered Ends

Materials Required

1 m (1⅛ yd) fabric 90 cm (approx. 36 in) wide.
46 cm (18 in) Lightning zip fastener.
1.40 m (1½ yd) piping cord, approximately 6 mm (¼ in) in diameter.
2 button moulds 4 cm (1½ in) in diameter.
Coats Drima (polyester) thread.

Cutting Out

Cut one piece of fabric 53 × 68 cm (21 × 27 in) for main section and two pieces 13 × 68 cm (5 × 27 in) for ends.
Cut piping cord in half.
Cut sufficient bias strips 4 cm (1½ in) wide to cover piping cord, joining as necessary to make required length.

Making Up

1.5 cm (½ in) has been allowed for seams.
Fold main section in half, right sides together, with 53 cm (21 in) edges meeting. Baste and sew 4 cm (1½ in) at each end leaving centre open for zip fastener insertion. Insert zip fastener. Fold each end section in half, right sides together and short ends meeting. Baste and sew short ends to form two circles. Gather one edge of each circle 6 mm (¼ in) from edge. Pull tightly and finish off ends securely. Cover piping cord with bias strips (page 79). Place piping to each end of main section, raw edges even, and baste. With right sides together, baste and sew an end section to each end of main section. Turn to the right side. Cover buttons and sew in position to cover gathers.

Sag Bag

Materials Required

3.70 m (4 yd) firm fabric, 120 cm (approx. 48 in) wide for sag bag.
3.70 m (4 yd) firm fabric, 120 cm (approx. 48 in) wide for inner pad.
0.34 cu m (12 cu ft) polystyrene beads.
1 Lightning zip fastener, 56 cm (22 in) long.
Coats Drima (polyester) thread.

Cutting Out

Make a paper copy of the pattern. 1 sq = 2.5 cm (1 in).
Allow 2 cm (¾ in) for seams when cutting.
Pattern A – Main Section: cut 6 pieces from outer

fabric. Cut 6 pieces from inner fabric.
Pattern B – Bottom (Broken Outline): cut 2 pieces from outer fabric. Cut 2 pieces from inner fabric.
Pattern C – Top (Solid Outline): cut 1 piece from outer fabric. Cut 1 piece from inner fabric.

Making Up

Baste and stitch main sections of inner fabric right sides together to within 2 cm (¾ in) from each end. Baste and stitch the two bottom sections to notches, leaving centre section open for the insertion of beads. Baste and stitch top and bottom sections to main sections. Insert beads and sew up open edges. Make up outer fabric in the same way, inserting zip between open edges of bottom section.

Norweave Cushion

Materials Required

Coats Anchor Tapisserie Wool: 8 skeins Tangerine 0314; 7 skeins Chestnut 0347; 3 skeins each Chestnut 0350, Peat Brown 0359; 2 skeins Olive Green 0423; 1 skein Buttercup 0298.
50 cm (½ yd) single thread tapestry canvas, 68 cm (approx. 27 in) wide. 18 threads to 2.5 cm (1 in).
50 cm (½ yd) matching tangerine medium weight furnishing fabric, 120 cm (approx. 48 in) wide, for backing.
Tapestry frame with 68 cm (27 in) tapes.
1 Milward 'Gold Seal' tapestry needle No. 18.

The finished size of the illustrated cushion is approximately 42 × 38 cm (16½ × 15 in).

Instructions

Mark the centre thread of canvas widthwise and the centre between two threads lengthwise with a line of basting stitches. Mount the canvas on the frame – fold down 1.5 cm (½ in) of the cut edges and sew securely to the tape on the rollers which lie at the top and bottom of frame; wind the surplus canvas round the rollers, assemble the frame and adjust the screws so that the canvas is stretched taut from top to bottom. The sides of the canvas are now laced round the laths with fine string or 4 strands of button thread. The pattern gives the complete design, centre marked by blank arrows which should coincide with the basting stitches. Each background square of the pattern represents one block of 4 Satin Stitches over 4 threads of canvas. Commence the design centrally, following the Key on page 84 for the embroidery.

Making Up

Trim canvas to within 2.5 cm (1 in) of embroidery. Cut a piece the same size from backing fabric. Place back and front pieces right sides together and sew close to the embroidery, leaving an opening on one side so that the pad may be inserted easily. Turn to

Norweave Cushion

Close-up of motif,
Norweave Cushion

Key to Pattern

⊡ — 0298

☐ — 0314

⊡ — 0347

⊙ — 0350

■ — 0359

☒ — 0423

Pattern for Norweave Cushion

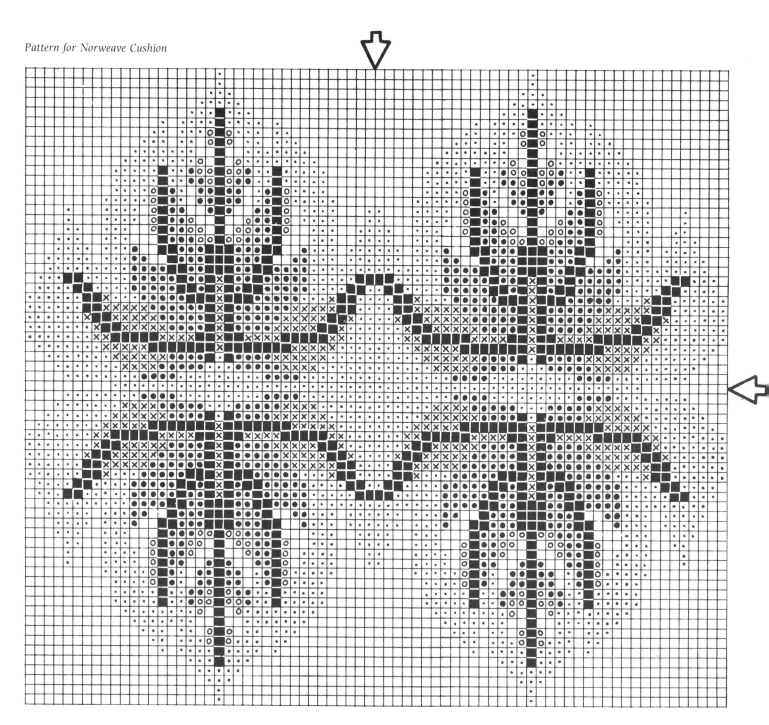

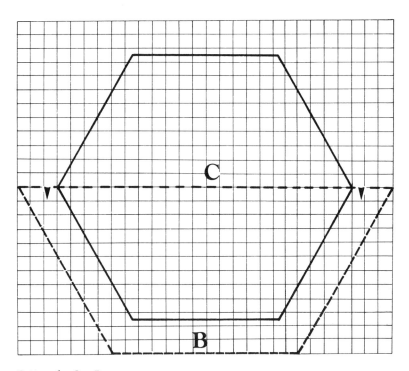

Pattern for Sag Bag

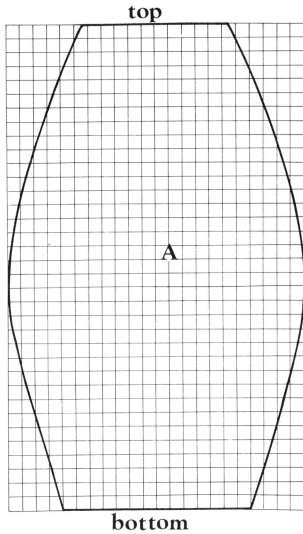

top

bottom

right side. Insert pad. Turn in seam allowance on the open edges and slipstitch together.

Florentine Cushion and Co-ordinating Articles

Cushion

Materials Required

Coats Anchor Tapisserie Wool: 2 skeins each Carnation 023, Raspberry 068, 069, 071, Cream 0386, Linen 0390, 0391, Sienna 0426, 0427, 0428, Spice Brown 0570, Smoke 0984, 0986.
60 cm ($\frac{5}{8}$ yd) single thread tapestry canvas 68 cm (approx. 27 in) wide, 7 threads to 1 cm (18 threads to 1 in).
Piece matching fabric for backing.
Pad to fit.
Tapestry frame with 68 cm (approx. 27 in) tapes.
Milward 'Gold Seal' tapestry needle No. 18.

Instructions

Draw a 40 cm (15$\frac{3}{4}$ in) square centrally on canvas and mark the centre both ways with a line of basting stitches. Mount canvas in frame, raw edges to tapes.
* The pattern gives a section of the design and shows the arrangement of the stitches on the threads of the canvas represented by the background lines. All stitches are worked over 6 threads. Work foundation row following the pattern for the design. Each numbered row is worked in the same way as foundation row. Following pattern, work each numbered section with appropriate colour as given in Key. When this colour sequence has been completed, commence embroidery again and continue as before. Part stitches may be necessary to complete the outlined shape. Commence the design centrally following the pattern for the design. Repeat section number of times required to marked edge. *

Making Up

Trim canvas to within 1.5 cm ($\frac{1}{2}$ in) of embroidery on all sides. Cut a piece from backing fabric the same size as canvas. Place both pieces right sides together and sew close to the embroidery, leaving an opening on one side to enable the pad to be easily inserted. Turn to right side. Insert pad. Turn in seam allowance and slipstitch.

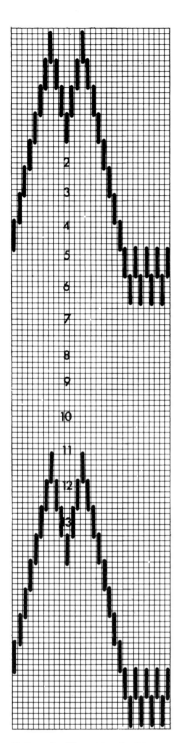

Pattern for Florentine Cushion etc

023 foundation row

2 — 068
3 — 069
4 — 071
5 — 0428
6 — 0427
7 — 0426
8 — 0570
9 — 0386
10 — 0390
11 — 0391
12 — 0984
13 — 0986

Waste Paper Bin

Materials Required

Coats Anchor Tapisserie Wool: 1 skein each
Carnation 023, Raspberry 068, 069, 071, Cream
0386, Linen 0390, 0391, Sienna 0426, 0427, 0428,
Spice Brown 0570, Smoke 0984, 0986.
40 cm ($\frac{3}{8}$ yd) single thread tapestry canvas, 68 cm
(approx. 27 in) wide, 7 threads to 1 cm (18 threads to
1 in).
Waste paper bin 23 × 59 × 18 cm (9 × 23$\frac{1}{4}$ × 7 in).
Tapestry frame with 68 cm (27 in) tapes.
Milward 'Gold Seal' tapestry needle No. 18.

Instructions

Draw a rectangle 23 × 59 cm (9 × 23$\frac{1}{4}$ in) centrally
on canvas and mark the centre both ways with a line
of basting stitches. Mount canvas in frame, raw edges
to tapes. Follow the instructions from * to * as given
for cushion.

Making Up

Trim canvas to within 2.5 cm (1 in) of embroidery on
all sides. Baste and stitch short ends together. Turn
down excess canvas to wrong side at top and lower
edges and Herringbone Stitch lightly in position. Slip
over bin.

Telephone Book Cover

Materials Required

Coats Anchor Tapisserie Wool: 2 skeins each
Carnation 023, Raspberry 068, 069, 071 ; 1 skein
each Cream 0386, Linen 0390, 0391, Sienna 0426,
0427, 0428, Spice Brown 0570, Smoke 0984, 0986.
40 cm ($\frac{3}{8}$ yd) single thread tapestry canvas, 68 cm
(approx. 27 in) wide, 7 threads to 1 cm (18 threads
to 1 in).
40 cm ($\frac{3}{8}$ yd) lining fabric, 90 cm (approx. 36 in)
wide.
Telephone book 46 × 27 cm (18 × 10$\frac{3}{4}$ in).
Tapestry frame with 68 cm (27 in) tapes.
Milward 'Gold Seal' tapestry needle No. 18.

Instructions

Draw centrally on to canvas an area same size as
telephone book and mark the centre both ways with a
line of basting stitches. Mount canvas in frame, raw
edges to tapes. Follow instructions from * to * as
given for cushion.

Making Up

Trim canvas to within 1.5 cm ($\frac{1}{2}$ in) of embroidery all
round. Cut one main lining section the same size as
embroidered section and two strips 13 cm (5 in) by
depth of embroidery for flaps. Make a narrow hem on
one long edge of each flap section. Baste flap sections,
one at each end, together over embroidered section.

Florentine Cushion and Co-ordinating Articles

87

Place main lining section right side down over flaps. Baste and stitch one long edge and two short ends, leaving remaining edge open for turning to right side. Turn to right side. Turn in 1.5 cm ($\frac{1}{2}$ in) seam allowance on open edges and sew. Place cover on telephone book.

Lamp Base

Materials Required

Coats Anchor Tapisserie Wool: 1 skein each Carnation 023, Raspberry 068, 069, 071, Cream 0386, Linen 0390, 0391, Sienna 0426, 0427, 0428, Spice Brown 0570, Smoke 0984, 0986.
40 cm ($\frac{3}{8}$ yd) single thread tapestry canvas, 68 cm (approx. 27 in) wide, 7 threads to 1 cm (18 threads to 1 in).
Lamp base 23 cm (9 in) in height, 9.5 cm ($3\frac{3}{4}$ in) in diameter.
Tapestry frame with 68 cm (27 in) tapes.
Milward 'Gold Seal' tapestry needle No. 18.

Instructions

Draw a rectangle 33 × 23.5 cm (13 × $9\frac{1}{4}$ in) centrally on canvas and mark the centre both ways with a line of basting stitches. Mount canvas in frame, raw edges to tapes. Follow the instructions from * to * as given for cushion.

Making Up

Trim canvas to within 2.5 cm (1 in) of embroidery. Turn short ends right sides together and sew close to embroidery. Fold down excess canvas at top and bottom edges and Herringbone Stitch in place. Turn to right side and slip over lamp base.

Chairseat

Materials Required

Coats Anchor Tapisserie Wool: 3 skeins each Carnation 023, Raspberry 068, 069, 071, Cream 0386, Sienna 0426, 0427, 0428; 2 skeins each Linen 0390, 0391, Spice Brown 0570, Smoke 0984, 0986.
70 cm ($\frac{3}{4}$ yd) single thread tapestry canvas, 68 cm (approx. 27 in) wide, 7 threads to 1 cm (18 threads to 1 in).
Tapestry frame with 68 cm (27 in) tapes.
Milward 'Gold Seal' tapestry needle No. 18.

The finished size of the illustrated chairseat is approximately:
Front edge – 49 cm ($19\frac{1}{4}$ in).
Back edge – 41 cm (16 in).
Length from front to back edge – 46.5 cm ($18\frac{1}{4}$ in).

Instructions

Using firm paper make a paper pattern of chairseat. Place the canvas over pattern, making sure that the straight of the pattern matches the straight weave of

canvas and mark with a pencil the shape of the chairseat. DO NOT CUT OUT. Mark the centre of outline both ways with a line of basting stitches. Mount canvas in frame, raw edges to tapes. Follow the instructions from * to * as given for cushion.

Making Up

Place the embroidery centrally on the chair pad. Fold the surplus canvas to the back and secure in position on the underside with upholstery tacks.

Spectacle Case

Materials Required

Coats Anchor Tapisserie Wool: 1 skein each Carnation 023, Raspberry 068, 069, 071, Cream 0386, Linen 0390, 0391, Sienna 0426, 0427, 0428, Spice Brown 0570, Smoke 0984, 0986.
30 cm ($\frac{1}{4}$ yd) single thread tapestry canvas, 68 cm (27 in) wide, 7 threads to 1 cm (18 threads to 1 in).
Piece matching felt for gusset and lining.
Milward 'Gold Seal' tapestry needle No. 18.

Instructions

Draw two rectangles on canvas 9.5 × 18 cm ($3\frac{3}{4}$ × 7 in), leaving a space of at least 7 cm ($2\frac{3}{4}$ in) between, and mark the centre of each both ways with a line of basting stitches. Follow the instructions from * to * as given for cushion for each rectangle.

Making Up

Trim canvas on both pieces to within 1.5 cm ($\frac{1}{2}$ in) of embroidery on all sides. Cut two pieces from felt same size as canvas and one strip of felt 2.5 × 46 cm (1 × 18 in). Place gusset between two main embroidered sections, leaving one short end open, and sew in position. Baste and stitch felt lining sections together taking 6 mm ($\frac{1}{4}$ in) seams, leaving one short end open. Place inside case. Turn in canvas at top edge. Trim felt to fit and sew together.

Alternative Patterns

Materials Required

Clark's Anchor Stranded Cotton: Carmine Rose 040, 042, 045, Rose Pink 048, 050, Jade 0185, 0187, 0189, Forest Green 0213, 0214, Snuff Brown 0372, 0373, 0375. Use 6 strands throughout.
Single thread petit point canvas, 7 threads to 1 cm (18 threads to 1 in).
Milward 'Gold Seal' tapestry needle No. 20.

Instructions

The pattern gives a section of the design and shows the arrangement of the stitches on the threads of the canvas represented by the background lines. All stitches are worked over 4 threads. Follow the pattern and work each numbered section with appropriate colour as given in Key.

Key to Pattern

1 – 048
2 – 050
3 – 040
4 – 042
5 – 045
6 – 0189
7 – 0187
8 – 0185
9 – 0214
10 – 0213
11 – 0375
12 – 0373
13 – 0372

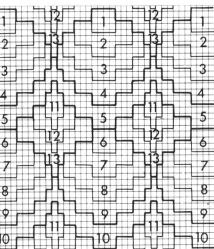

Pattern 1

Materials Required

Coats Anchor Tapisserie Wool: Carnation 024, 037, Kingfisher 0161, 0162, 0163, 0164, Beige 0376, 0378, 0379, Coffee 0381, Grey 0399, 0401, White 0402, Black 0403, Haze 0497, Carmine Rose 0503. Single thread petit point canvas, 7 threads to 1 cm (18 threads to 1 in).
Milward 'Gold Seal' tapestry needle No. 18.

Instructions

The pattern gives a section of the design and shows the arrangement of the stitches on the threads of the canvas represented by the background lines. There are two colour combinations and these repeat horizontally as shown in photograph. Follow the pattern and Key No. 1 for the embroidery. To complete the design repeat section immediately below, leaving no spaces between, following Key No. 2.

Pattern 2

Key to Pattern

	No. 1	No. 2			No. 1	No. 2
⌗	024	0497		⫴	0381	0164
⌾	037	0399		⌗	0402	0402
⌗	0376	0161		⬤	0403	0403
⌗	0378	0162		⯅	0503	0401
⌗	0379	0163				

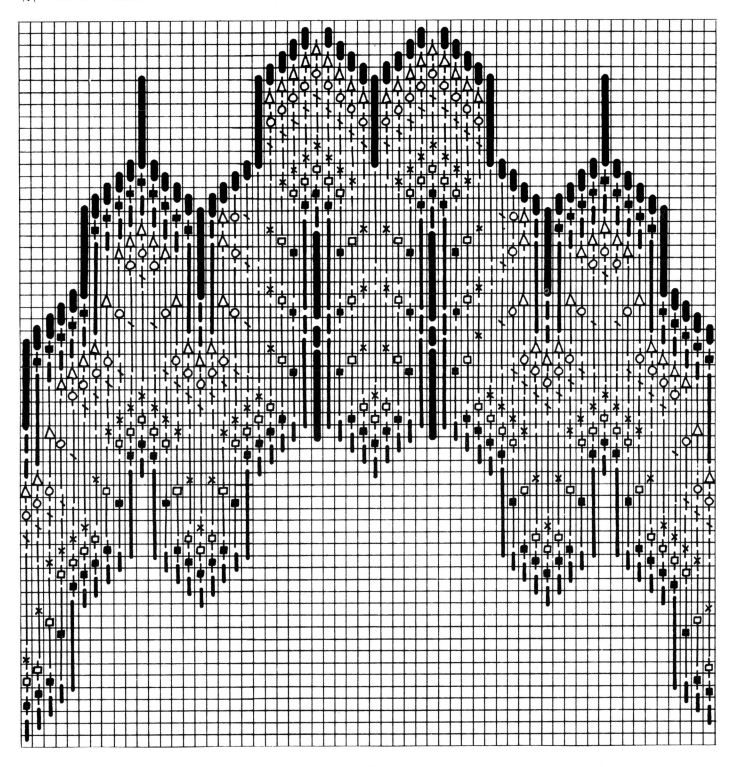

Materials Required

Coats Anchor Tapisserie Wool: Grey 0399, White 0402, Black 0403, Haze 0497.
Silver Metallic Cord.
Single thread petit point canvas, 7 threads to 1 cm (18 threads to 1 in).
Milward 'Gold Seal' tapestry needle No. 18.

Instructions

The pattern gives a section of the design and shows the arrangement of the stitches on the threads of the canvas represented by the background lines. All stitches are worked over 4 threads. The silver metallic cord is worked twice into each hole. Work foundation rows following the pattern for the design. Work outlined numbered sections with appropriate colour as given in Key, within each diamond shape.

Pattern 3

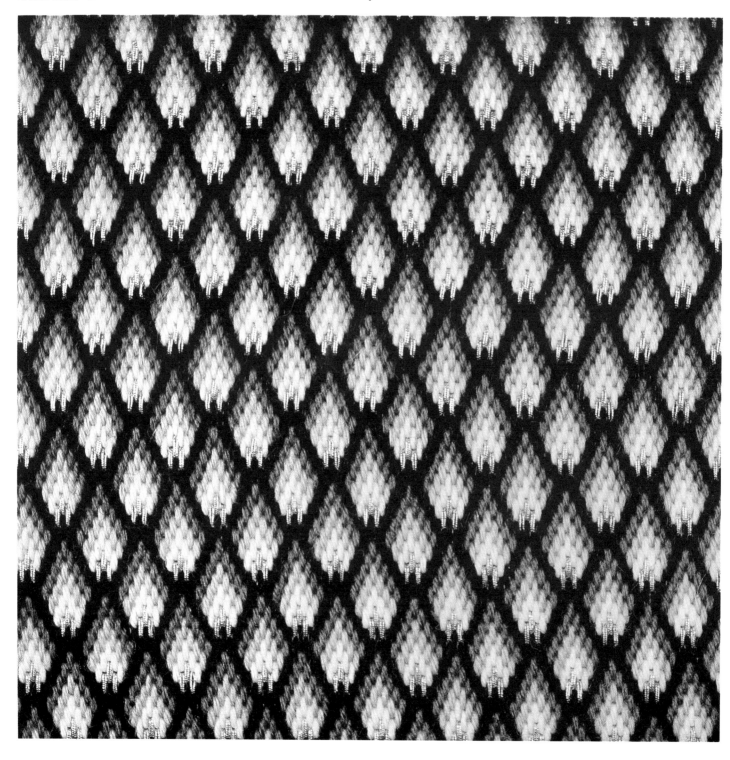

0403 foundation row

2 – 0399
3 – 0497
4 – 0402
5 – Silver Metallic Cord

0850 foundation row

2 – 0432
3 – 0848
4 – 0373
5 – 0388
6 – 0305
7 – 0213
8 – 0215
9 – 0218

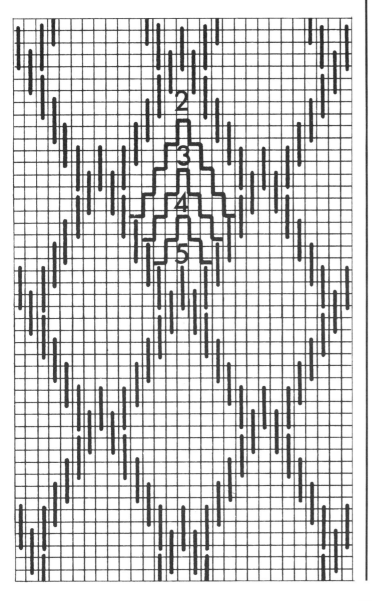

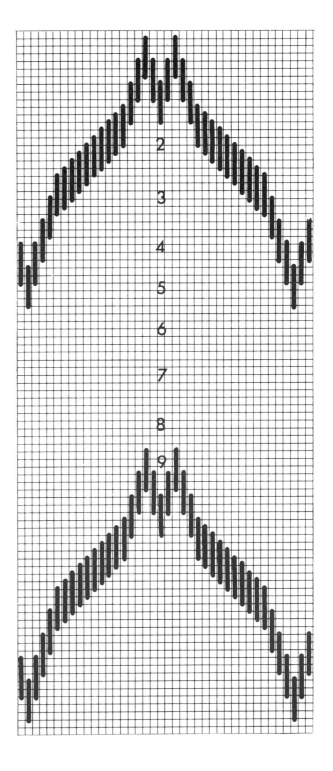

Materials Required

Coats Anchor Tapisserie Wool: Forest Green 0213, 0215, 0218, Amber Gold 0305, Snuff Brown 0373, Ecru 0388, Petrol Blue 0432, 0848, 0850.
Single thread petit point canvas, 7 threads to 1 cm (18 threads to 1 in).
Milward 'Gold Seal' tapestry needle No. 18.

Instructions

The pattern gives a section of the design and shows the arrangement of the stitches on the threads of the canvas represented by the background lines. All stitches are worked over 6 threads. Work foundation row following the pattern for the design. Each numbered row is worked in the same way as foundation row. Following pattern, work each numbered section with appropriate colour as given in Key. When this colour sequence has been completed commence embroidery again with foundation row and continue as before.

Pattern 4

Materials Required

Coats Anchor Tapisserie Wool: Buttercup 0297,
Amber Gold 0305, 0306, 0565, Peat Brown 0358,
0360, Snuff Brown 0375, Sea Green 0506, 0507.
Clark's Anchor Stranded Cotton: Jade 0185, Laurel
Green 0206. Use 6 strands.
Single thread petit point canvas, 7 threads to 1 cm
(18 threads to 1 in).
Milward 'Gold Seal' tapestry needle No. 18 for
Tapisserie Wool.
Milward 'Gold Seal' tapestry needle No. 20 for
Stranded Cotton.

Instructions

The pattern gives a section of the design and shows
the arrangement of the stitches on the threads of the
canvas represented by the background lines. All
stitches are worked over 4 threads. Work foundation
row following the pattern for the design. Work
numbered sections with appropriate colour as given
in Key, within each outlined shape.

Pattern 5

95

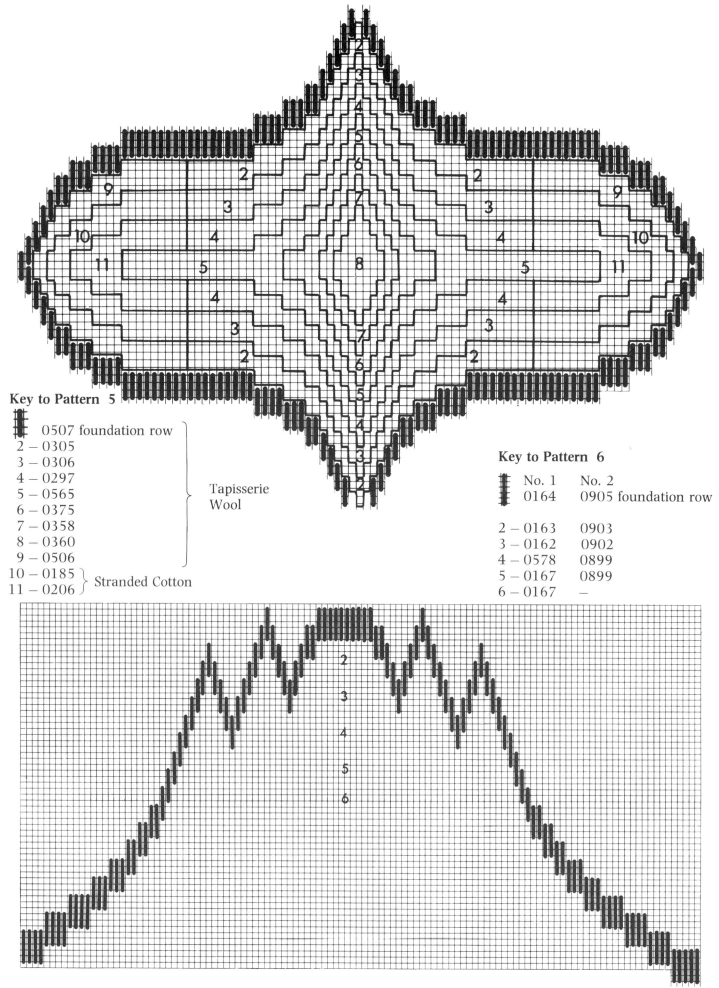

Key to Pattern 5

0507 foundation row
2 – 0305
3 – 0306
4 – 0297
5 – 0565   Tapisserie
6 – 0375   Wool
7 – 0358
8 – 0360
9 – 0506
10 – 0185 } Stranded Cotton
11 – 0206 }

Key to Pattern 6

	No. 1	No. 2
	0164	0905 foundation row
2 –	0163	0903
3 –	0162	0902
4 –	0578	0899
5 –	0167	0899
6 –	0167	–

Materials Required

Coats Anchor Tapisserie Wool: Kingfisher 0162, 0163, 0164, Peacock Blue 0167, Turquoise 0578, Biscuit 0899, 0902, 0903, 0905.
Single thread petit point canvas, 7 threads to 1 cm (18 threads to 1 in).
Milward 'Gold Seal' tapestry needle No. 18.

Instructions

The pattern gives a section of the design and shows the arrangement of the stitches on the threads of the canvas represented by the background lines. All stitches are worked over 6 threads. There are two colour combinations and these repeat horizontally as shown in photograph. Work foundation row following the pattern for the design. Each numbered row is worked in the same way as foundation row. Following pattern, work each numbered section with appropriate colour as given in Key No. 1. When colour sequence has been completed commence embroidery again with foundation row following Key No. 2 and continue as before. It should be noted that there are only five repeats in Key No. 2.

Pattern 6

97

Materials Required

Coats Anchor Tapisserie Wool: Tangerine 0311, Flame 0332, Snuff Brown 0373, Ecru 0388, Chocolate 0418, 0420, Gold 0500.
Single thread petit point canvas, 7 threads to 1 cm (18 threads to 1 in).
Milward 'Gold Seal' tapestry needle No. 18

Instructions

The pattern gives a section of the design and shows the arrangement of the stitches on the threads of the canvas represented by the background lines. All stitches are worked over 6 threads. Work foundation row following the pattern for the design. Each numbered row is worked in the same way as foundation row. Following pattern, work each numbered section with appropriate colour as given in Key. When this colour sequence has been completed commence again with foundation row and continue as before.

Pattern 7

Key to Pattern

0420 foundation row

2 – 0332
3 – 0500
4 – 0311
5 – 0388
6 – 0373
7 – 0418

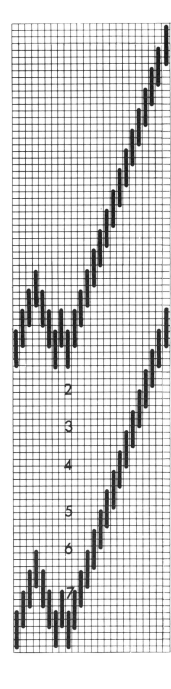

Cushion

Materials Required

Coats Chain Mercer-Crochet Cotton No. 20 (20 g).
2 balls. This model is worked in shade 508 (Lt. Marine Blue), but any other shade of Mercer-Crochet may be used.
Milward steel crochet hook 1.25 (no. 3).
2.30 m (2½ yd) piping cord.
1.20 m (1¼ yd) apricot furnishing fabric 120 cm (approx. 48 in) wide.
Cushion pad 51 × 51 × 10 cm (20 × 20 × 4 in).

Tension

3 sps and 3 rows – 2.5 cm (1 in).

Measurements

Size of Cushion – 51 cm (20 in) square.

Abbreviations

ch – chain; dc – double crochet; dbl tr – double treble; sp(s) – space(s); st(s) – stitch(es).

Suitable Types of Fabric – Moygashel or Repp.

Instructions

Commence with 52 ch.
1st Row (wrong side): 1 dbl tr into 7th ch from hook, 1 ch, inserting hook from behind last dbl tr work 1 dbl tr into 5th of 6 ch missed (a cross made), 1 dbl tr into next ch, (3 ch, miss 3 ch, 1 dbl tr into next ch) 10 times (10 sps made), miss 2 sts, 1 dbl tr into next st, 1 ch, inserting hook from behind last dbl tr work 1 dbl tr into first of 2 sts missed (another cross made), 1 dbl tr into next st, 7 ch, turn.
2nd Row: Miss first 4 sts, 1 dbl tr into next dbl tr (a sp made over a cross at beginning of row), 1 cross, 1 dbl tr into next dbl tr, 3 sps, 3 ch, leaving the last loop of each on hook work 3 dbl tr into next dbl tr, thread over and draw through all loops on hook (a 3 dbl tr cluster made), 4 sps, 1 cross, 1 dbl tr into next dbl tr, 3 ch, miss 3 sts, 1 dbl tr into next st (sp made at end of row), 7 ch, turn.
3rd Row: 2 sps, 1 cross, 1 dbl tr into next dbl tr, 1 sp, a 3 dbl tr cluster into next dbl tr, (4 ch, a 2 dbl tr cluster into 4th ch from hook) twice, a 3 dbl tr cluster into same place as last 3 dbl tr cluster (a diamond cluster made), 1 dbl tr into next cluster, a diamond cluster into next dbl tr, 1 dbl tr into next dbl tr, 1 sp, 1 cross, 1 dbl tr into next dbl tr, 2 sps, 7 ch, turn.
4th Row: 3 sps, 1 cross, (1 dbl tr into next dbl tr, 3 ch, 1 dc into centre of next diamond, 3 ch) twice, 1 dbl tr into next dbl tr, 1 cross, 1 dbl tr into next dbl tr, 3 sps, 7 ch, turn.
5th Row: 2 sps, a diamond cluster into next dbl tr, 1 dbl tr into next dbl tr, 1 cross, 1 dbl tr into next dc, 2 sps, 1 cross, 1 dbl tr into next dbl tr, a diamond

99

Cushion

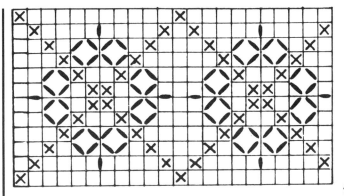

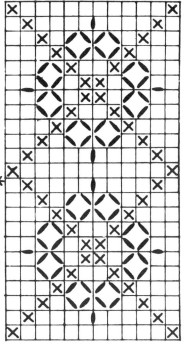

cluster into next dbl tr, 1 dbl tr into next dbl tr, 2 sps, 7 ch, turn.

6th Row: 1 sp, 4 ch, a 2 dbl tr cluster into 4th ch from hook, (a cluster bar made), 1 dbl tr into next dbl tr, 3 ch, 1 dc into centre of next diamond, continue to follow pattern to end of row.

7th to 11th Row: Follow pattern ending last row with 4 ch, turn.

12th Row: 1 cross, 10 sps, 1 cross, 7 ch, turn.
Repeat 2nd to 12th row twice more, ** then 2nd to 23rd row. Fasten off.
Turn pattern. With wrong side facing attach thread to top of dbl tr marked by * on pattern and working over row ends continue to follow pattern to end of row.
Follow pattern to end.
Repeat from ** twice more then 2nd to 11th row again. Fasten off.

Pattern for Cushion

Edgings

With right side facing attach thread to any sp and work a row of dc neatly all round ending with 1 ss into first dc. Fasten off.

Damp and pin out to measurements.

Making Up

1.5 cm ($\frac{1}{2}$ in) seam allowance has been given on all pieces.
From fabric, cut 2 pieces 53 cm (21 in) square.
Cut one strip 10 × 206 cm (4 × 81 in) for gusset.
Cut one strip 5 × 206 cm (2 × 81 in) for piping.
Cover piping cord and place in position to one square. Stitch short end of gusset, place in position and stitch gusset and piping to square. Stitch square for base in position to gusset leaving an opening to insert pad. Sew crochet centrally to top. Insert pad and sew opening.

Long Cushion

Materials Required

Coats Chain Mercer-Crochet Cotton No. 20 (20 g).
5 balls. This model is worked in shade 513 (Orange), but any other shade of Mercer-Crochet may be used.
Milward steel crochet hook 1.25 (no. 3).
40 cm ($\frac{3}{8}$ yd) fabric 120 cm (approx. 48 in) wide, in contrasting colour.

101

1 spool Drima (polyester) multi-purpose thread to match fabric.

Tension

First 6 rows – 2.5 cm (1 in).

Measurements

48 × 30 cm (19 × 12 in).

Abbreviations

ch – chain; dc – double crochet; tr – treble.

Back and Front (both alike)

Commence with 179 ch.
1st Row: 1 dc into 2nd ch from hook, * (5 ch, miss 4 ch, 1 dc into next ch) 5 times, 15 ch, miss 12 ch, 1 dc into next ch; repeat from * omitting 15 ch and 1 dc at end of last repeat, 5 ch, turn.
2nd Row (right side): 1 dc into first loop, * 5 tr into next dc (a shell made), (1 dc into next loop, 5 ch) 3 times, 1 dc into next loop, 2 ch, 1 tr into next dc, 13 ch, 1 tr into next dc, 2 ch, 1 dc into next loop; repeat from * omitting 13 ch 1 tr 2 ch and 1 dc at end of last repeat, 1 ch, turn.
3rd Row: 1 dc into first tr, * (5 ch, 1 dc into next 5 ch loop) 3 times, a shell into next dc, 1 dc into centre tr of next shell, 5 ch, 1 dc into next tr, 13 ch, 1 dc into next tr; repeat from * omitting 1 dc 13 ch and 1 dc at end of last repeat, 1 dc into 3rd of 5 ch, 5 ch, turn.
4th Row: 1 dc into first loop, * 5 ch, 1 dc into centre tr of next shell, a shell into next dc, (1 dc into next loop, 5 ch) twice, 1 dc into next loop, 2 ch, 1 tr into next dc, 7 ch, working over ch loops of previous 3 rows work 1 dc over next 3 loops, 7 ch, 1 tr into next dc, 2 ch, 1 dc into next loop; repeat from * omitting 7 ch 1 dc 7 ch 1 tr 2 ch and 1 dc at end of last repeat, 1 ch, turn.
5th Row: 1 dc into first tr, * (5 ch, 1 dc into next loop) twice, a shell into next dc, 1 dc into centre tr of next shell, 5 ch, 1 dc into next loop, 5 ch, 1 dc into next tr, 15 ch, 1 dc into next tr; repeat from * omitting 1 dc 15 ch and 1 dc at end of last repeat, 1 dc into 3rd of 5 ch, 5 ch, turn.
6th Row: 1 dc into first loop, * 5 ch, 1 dc into next loop, 5 ch, 1 dc into centre tr of next shell, a shell into next dc, 1 dc into next loop, 5 ch, 1 dc into next loop, 2 ch, 1 tr into next dc, 13 ch, 1 tr into next dc, 2 ch, 1 dc into next loop; repeat from * omitting 13 ch 1 tr 2 ch and 1 dc at end of last repeat, 1 ch, turn.
7th Row: 1 dc into first tr, * 5 ch, 1 dc into next loop, a shell into next dc, 1 dc into centre tr of next shell, (5 ch, 1 dc into next loop) twice, 5 ch, 1 dc into next tr, 13 ch, 1 dc into next tr; repeat from * omitting 1 dc 13 ch and 1 dc at end of last repeat, 1 dc into 3rd of 5 ch, 5 ch, turn.
8th Row: 1 dc into first loop, * (5 ch, 1 dc into next loop) twice, 5 ch, 1 dc into centre tr of next shell, a shell into next dc, 1 dc into next loop, 2 ch, 1 tr into

next dc, 7 ch, working over ch loops of previous 3 rows work 1 dc over next 3 loops, 7 ch, 1 tr into next dc, 2 ch, 1 dc into next loop; repeat from * omitting 7 ch 1 dc 7 ch 1 tr 2 ch and 1 dc at end of last repeat, 1 ch, turn.
9th Row: 1 dc into first tr, * 5 ch, 1 dc into centre tr of next shell, a shell into next dc, 1 dc into next loop, (5 ch, 1 dc into next loop) twice, 5 ch, 1 dc into next tr, 15 ch, 1 dc into next tr; repeat from * omitting 1 dc 15 ch and 1 dc at end of last repeat, 1 dc into 3rd of 5 ch, 5 ch, turn.
10th Row: 1 dc into first loop, * (5 ch, 1 dc into next loop) twice, a shell into next dc, 1 dc into centre tr of next shell, 5 ch, 1 dc into next loop, 2 ch, 1 tr into next dc, 13 ch, 1 tr into next dc, 2 ch, 1 dc into next loop; repeat from * omitting 13 ch, 1 tr 2 ch and 1 dc at end of last repeat, 1 ch, turn.
11th Row: 1 dc into first tr, * 5 ch, 1 dc into next loop, 5 ch, 1 dc into centre tr of next shell, a shell into next dc, 1 dc into next loop, 5 ch, 1 dc into next loop, 5 ch, 1 dc into next tr, 13 ch, 1 dc into next tr; repeat from * omitting 1 dc 13 ch and 1 dc at end of last repeat, 1 dc into 3rd of 5 ch, 5 ch, turn.
12th Row: 1 dc into first loop, * 5 ch, 1 dc into next loop, a shell into next dc, 1 dc into centre tr of next shell, (5 ch, 1 dc into next loop) twice, 2 ch, 1 tr into next dc, 7 ch, working over ch loops of previous 3 rows work 1 dc over next 3 loops, 7 ch, 1 tr into next dc, 2 ch, 1 dc into next loop; repeat from * omitting 7 ch 1 dc 7 ch 1 tr 2 ch and 1 dc at end of last repeat, 1 ch, turn.
13th Row: 1 dc into first tr, (5 ch, 1 dc into next loop) twice, 5 ch, 1 dc into centre tr of next shell, a shell into next dc, 1 dc into next loop, 5 ch, 1 dc into next tr, 15 ch, 1 dc into next tr; repeat from * omitting 1 dc 15 ch and 1 dc at end of last repeat, 1 dc into 3rd of 5 ch, 5 ch, turn.
14th Row: 1 dc into first loop, * a shell into next dc, 1 dc into centre tr of next shell, (5 ch, 1 dc into next loop) 3 times, 2 ch, 1 tr into next dc, 13 ch, 1 tr into next dc, 2 ch, 1 dc into next loop; repeat from * omitting 13 ch 1 tr 2 ch and 1 dc at end of last repeat, 1 ch, turn.
Repeat 3rd to 14th row 8 times more then 3rd to 8th row again.
Next Row: 1 dc into first tr, * 4 ch, 1 dc into centre tr of next shell, (4 ch, 1 dc into next loop) 3 times, 4 ch, 1 dc into next tr, 12 ch, 1 dc into next tr; repeat from * omitting 1 dc 12 ch and 1 dc at end of last repeat, 1 dc into 3rd of 5 ch. Fasten off.

Damp and pin out to measurements.

Joining

Place wrong sides of sections together, attach thread to one long side approximately 2.5 cm (1 in) from corner and working over both sections work a row of dc neatly round 3 sides ending approximately 2.5 cm (1 in) after last corner. Now working over front

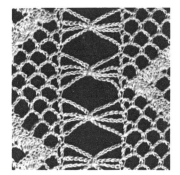

Close-up, Long Cushion

section only continue to work in dc ending with 1 ss into first dc. Fasten off.

Making Up

Cut 2 sections from fabric 51 × 33 cm (20 × 13 in). 1.5 cm (½ in) seam allowance has been given. Place sections right sides together, edges even. Baste and stitch leaving an opening sufficiently wide for pad insertion. Turn to right side, insert pad and slipstitch opening. Slip crochet over pad and sew opening.

Chairbacks and Television Runner

Materials Required

Clark's Anchor Stranded Cotton : 3 skeins each Cobalt Blue 0132, Muscat Green 0281 ; 2 skeins each Jade 0188, Almond Green 0263 ; 1 skein Cobalt Blue 0134. Use 3 strands throughout.
70 cm (¾ yd) lime green furnishing fabric, as in illustration, 120 cm (48 in) wide.
1 Milward 'Gold Seal' crewel needle No. 7.

The finished size of the runner is approximately 20 × 63 cm (8 × 25 in), the chairbacks approximately 41 × 61 cm (16 × 24 in).

Long Cushion

Cutting Out and Making Up

Cut two pieces from fabric 44 × 68 cm ($17\frac{1}{4}$ × 27 in) for chairbacks and one piece 24 × 67 cm ($9\frac{1}{2}$ × $26\frac{1}{2}$ in) for runner. Fold chairback pieces across the centre lengthwise, runner piece widthwise and crease lightly. The pattern gives one large and one small motif. With short side of chairback piece facing, trace motifs (see Tracing instructions, page 19) as given, with large motif placed centrally on to fold and 11.5 cm ($4\frac{1}{2}$ in) from lower edge. Repeat small motif to the left, spacing evenly. With long side of runner piece facing, trace small motif centrally on to right-hand side 3 cm ($1\frac{1}{4}$ in) from fold. Turn motif and repeat 5.5 cm ($2\frac{1}{4}$ in) to the right. Turn fabric and repeat on other side. Follow the Key on page 105 for the embroidery. All parts similar to numbered parts are worked in the same colour and stitch. Press the embroidery on the wrong side. Make up chairback, taking 4 cm ($1\frac{1}{2}$ in) hem at lower edge and 1.5 cm ($\frac{1}{2}$ in) hems on other three sides. Make up runner, taking 1.5 cm ($\frac{1}{2}$ in) hems.

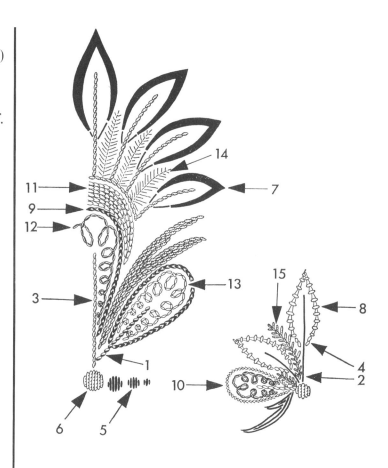

Close-up of Motif,
Chairbacks and Television Runner

Chairbacks and Television Runner

Key to Pattern

1 – 0134
2 – 0132
3 – 0263
4 – 0281 } Stem Stitch

5 – 0132
6 – 0263 } Satin Stitch

7 – 0132
8 – 0281 } Spanish Knotted Feather Stitch

9 – 0132
10 – 0188
11 – 0281 } Chain Stitch

12 – 0134
13 – 0281 } Back Stitch

14 – 0188
15 – 0263 } Fly Stitch

Pattern for Chairbacks and Television Runner

105

Chapter 6

LOOSE COVERS

The term 'loose cover' is slightly misleading as the covers do not fit loosely, but are made to fit snugly over a chair or settee, usually fully upholstered, and can easily be removed for washing or dry-cleaning.

They can also be used to change the appearance of a room, by making them up in a light coloured fabric for the summer months, and reverting to the original upholstery during the winter.

There is now a variety of ready-made stretch covers on the market but they tend to be limited to chairs in rather basic styles, and most people prefer something more individual.

Ideally loose covers should be made when the chair or suite is new. A loose cover may be made to give a new lease of life to an old or worn chair but first check that the framework is sound, and the chair thoroughly clean otherwise the dirt could quickly damage the new fabric.

If properly made, a loose cover should give the appearance of an upholstered chair with all seams and pipings in correct positions. Nothing looks worse than a cover which does not fit properly over the arms, at the top of the back and round cushion edges. Success depends on having plenty of time and a love of precision work. It is also advisable to choose, for a first attempt, a simple design of chair and a textured fabric without a too-definite pattern.

Careful exact measurements are taken of each section of the chair, paper patterns are made from these and then transferred on to a cheap calico or muslin, marking with pencil, seam and hem allowances and amounts to be tucked in round the seat of the chair (called 'tuck-in allowance'). This muslin cover should have each section labelled, the correct grain of fabric marked by arrows, and, in the case of identical pieces, marked left- or right-hand side. This pattern will then form a permanent basis for the first and any future covers required.

Choosing the Fabric

There are two main considerations to be borne in mind :
a) It must be of firm texture, closely woven and shrink-resistant. The fabric will only retain its shape after constant washing or dry-cleaning if it is of close weave and firm texture. Loosely woven or slub fabrics quickly lose their shape and the frequent movement of the fabric in a loose cover makes them wear out more quickly.

Linen, cotton damask, repp and chintz are all suitable hard-wearing fabrics, but check with the retailer that the one you choose can be washed or dry-cleaned and will not shrink or fade. If there is a risk of shrinkage this will have to be taken into account when buying, cutting out and making up and this makes for extra difficulties.

b) Decide whether it is to be self coloured or patterned. Unless starting from scratch, the present décor of the room will have to be taken into account.

Plain, self coloured fabrics tend to look dirty rather more quickly and require washing or cleaning more often than patterned. On the other hand a fabric with a large bold design, the motif of which has to be centralized in several places on the cover, may be wasteful, because so much extra fabric will have to be bought.

Textured fabrics, or those with a small pattern or an all-over design are most economical and easiest to handle.

Taking Measurements for Paper Pattern

1. Remove cushions from chair.
2. Note position of seams and piping.
3. Note sections with tuck-in allowances.
4. On the chair, mark central lines with tailor's chalk or pins on Outside Back, Inside Back, Seat and Front. (Test on fabric before marking with chalk, as some makes are not easily brushed off.)
5. Measure each section and make a paper pattern as in instructions listed below. (See diagram 1).

Measure and make patterns of following sections:

1. Back of chair A–B, A1–B1.
2. Front of chair C–D, C1–D1.
3. Seat over front to top of valance D–E, F–G.
4. Inner edge of arm, over arm to top of valance F–H, I–J.
5. Front arm panel K.
6. Back gusset L. Length by breadth.
7. Valance M – allow 1½ times the measurement for a frilled valance or twice the measurement of lower edge for box pleats with equal pleats and spaces, or allow approximately at each corner 30 cm (12 in) for an 8 cm (3 in) pleat.

Measuring and Cutting Out

See chart as guide to amount of fabric. Allow sufficient fabric for covering piping cord, approximately 1 m (1 yd) fabric. Allow fabric for each cushion; extra for matching patterns or where a motif is to be centralized.

Once the pattern sections have been made and clearly marked, cut out pieces in calico or muslin. Leave the following allowances when cutting:

Seams – 2.5 cm (1 in)
Hems – 5 cm (2 in)
Tuck-in on section 2, 23 cm (9 in) at D
Tuck-in on section 3, 23 cm (9 in) at D, F and G
Tuck-in on section 4, 23 cm (9 in) at F

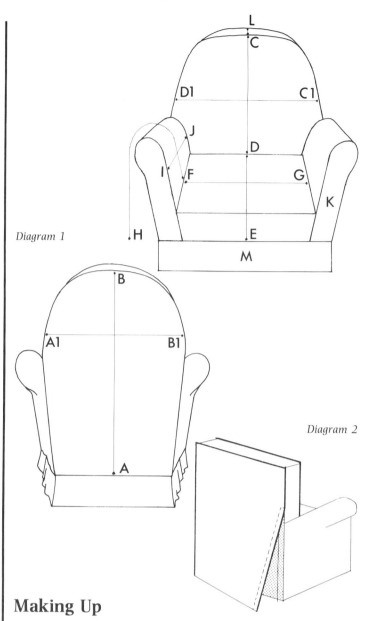

Diagram 1

Diagram 2

Making Up

Neaten the seams by hand or using zig-zag machine stitch. Pin the calico sections together and place over chair, wrong side uppermost; try on chair, taking in darts if necessary (on rounded corners). Make any necessary alterations noting that patterns match, centre lines are straight. Cut out sections in fabric, pin as before and try again on chair. Insert the piping (page 79), removing a few pins at a time; clip piping if necessary. Remove cover by opening a back seam. The cover can now be basted together. Stitch, leaving the lower edge of back section open. To complete the cover, a frill or valance is sewn to the lower edge M. Complete the back opening by using snap fastener tape, or a zip using the concealed method of insertion (diagram 2).

Settee Cover

When making a cover for a settee follow the same procedure, having an opening at right and left back sides. When fabric has to be joined, eg across back width of settee, space joins evenly. For cushions, make patterns to fit and make up.

AMOUNT OF FABRIC NEEDED FOR LOOSE COVERS

	Plain or Small Print	Larger Print		Plain or Small Print	Larger Print
Armchair (1 cushion)	6.40–6.90 m (7–7½ yd)	7.40–8.30 m (8–9 yd)	**Wing Chair** (1 cushion)	6.90–7.40 m (7½–8 yd)	7.80–8.30 m (8½–9 yd)
Plus frilled Valance	8.70–9.20 m (9½–10 yd)	9.20–9.70 m (10–10½ yd)	Plus frilled Valance	7.40–7.80 m (8–8½ yd)	8.30–8.70 m (9–9½ yd)
Plus box pleated Valance	9.20–9.70 m (10–10½ yd)	9.70–10.10 m (10½–11 yd)	Plus box pleats	7.80–8.30 m (8½–9 yd)	8.70–9.20 m (9½–10 yd)
Plus corner pleats	7.80–8.70 m (8½–9½ yd)	8.70–9.20 m (9½–10 yd)	Plus corner pleats	7.4·–7.80 m (8–8½ yd)	8.30–8.70 m (9–9½ yd)
Settee (3 cushions)	11.00–11.90 m (12–13 yd)	12.90–13.80 m (14–15 yd)	**Easy-Chair** (wooden arms)	2.80–3.20 m (3–3½ yd)	3.20–3.70 m (3½–4 yd)
Plus frilled Valance	17.90–18.30 m (19½–20 yd)	17.90–18.30 m (19½–20 yd)	Plus frilled Valance	3.70–4.20 m (4–4½ yd)	4.20–4.60 m (4½–5 yd)
Plus box pleats	16.50–18.30 m (18–20 yd)	17.00–18.80 m (18½–20½ yd)	Plus box pleats	4.20–4.60 m (4½–5 yd)	4.60–5.10 m (5–5½ yd)
Plus corner pleats	14.70–15.10 m (16–16½ yd)	15.60–16.50 m (17–18 yd)	Plus corner pleats	3.70–4.20 m (4–4½ yd)	4.20–4.60 m (4½–5 yd)

Loose Covers fitted on Three Piece Suite

Chapter 7

TABLE LINEN

Every home, whether it be a flat, a villa, a mansion or even a caravan, needs some form of table linen. The words table linen cover a wide range of articles and could include a checked gingham cloth for the kitchen; a set of mats for the tea trolley; a delicate traycloth and napkins when apéritifs are being served; a long refectory cloth for a family dinner and, last but not least, and possibly the most popular of all in our present life, lunch and dinner mats. These latter are a boon to the busy housewife, as they are so easy to care for and launder.

Depending upon the location and use, a wide range of fabrics may be used. Brightly checked gingham is excellent for informal occasions and, though attractive unadorned, it can be made more individual by the addition of a crochet lace edging or by a motif or border embroidered in bold Cross Stitch.

Lightweight furnishing fabrics of smooth texture, which are normally available in a wide range of both bright and subtle colours, are ideal for lunch and dinner mats and also for trolley sets. For elegant dining, a somewhat finer fabric is required. Fine linen is traditional, but unfortunately it is becoming more and more expensive and also difficult to find. An excellent alternative is fabric in cotton/polyester or cotton/Dacron which can be bought by the metre (yard) (see page 44/5). This is made in a good range of colours, but if a more striking colour scheme is needed, attention should be paid to the range of sheets in this fabric made by well-known manufacturers. A single bed size sheet would provide more than enough fabric for quite a large tablecloth and the remnants could be used for a matching trolley set or mats for occasional tables.

We all know the difficulty of searching for something of correct size and colour and how frustrating it can be. Now with the aid of this book it is possible to select your fabric and make it up to the correct measurements.

The materials required and the finished sizes are included for all the articles illustrated in this chapter, but obviously these sizes can be adjusted to suit specific requirements. Measure your table, tray or trolley carefully, adding extra for hems and not forgetting the 'drop' required for a tablecloth. The amount of fabric needed can be calculated with the aid of graph paper — one small square equalling 2.5 cm (1 in). Table mats can be made to any convenient size, rectangular, oval or circular. These two latter shapes may be finished with bias binding.

When it comes to decoration, the choice is wide — embroidered borders or motifs of various designs, or edging and insertions of delicate crochet lace. If you cannot crochet, a cotton lace makes a good substitute.

Lunch Mats

Materials Required

The amounts given are for three mats.
Clark's Anchor Stranded Cotton: 3 skeins Coffee 0381; 2 skeins Beige 0379; 1 skein each Nasturtium 0328 and Magenta 063. Use 6 strands for Laid Threads in Couching, 4 strands for Satin Stitch and 3 strands for rest of the embroidery.
Clark's Anchor Soft Embroidery: 1 skein Coffee 0381. 50 cm ($\frac{1}{2}$ yd) bronze furnishing fabric, as in illustration, 120 cm (approx. 48 in) wide.
1 Milward 'Gold Seal' chenille needle No. 19 for Soft Embroidery and 6 strands of Stranded Cotton; 1 crewel needle No. 7 for 4 and 3 strands.

The finished size of each mat is approximately 30 × 41 cm (12 × 16 in).

Cutting Out and Making Up

Cut three pieces from fabric 34 × 44 cm ($13\frac{1}{2}$ × $17\frac{1}{4}$ in). The pattern gives the complete motif. With long side facing, trace the motif (see Tracing instructions, page 19) centrally on to fabric 5 cm (2 in) from left-hand side. Follow the Key for the embroidery. All parts similar to numbered parts are worked in the same colour and stitch. Press the embroidery on the wrong side. Make up, taking 1.5 cm ($\frac{1}{2}$ in) hems.

Key to Pattern

S represents Soft Embroidery
   1 — 063 — French Knots
   2 — 063 — Buttonhole Stitch
   3 — 0328 ⎫
   4 — 0379 ⎭ Satin Stitch
S 5 — 0381 — Stem Stitch
   6 — 0381 — Couching
S 7 — 0381 — Laid Threads ⎫ Couching
   8 — 0381 — Tying Stitch ⎭

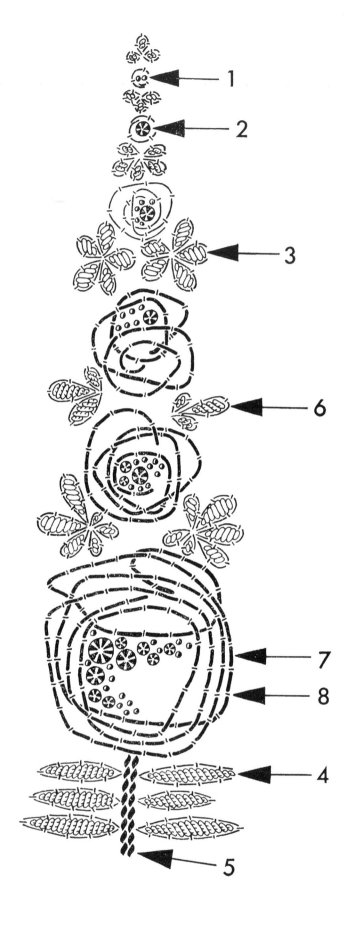

Close-up of Motif, Lunch Mats

Lunch Mats

Traycloth

Materials Required

Clark's Anchor Stranded Cotton: 1 skein each Cyclamen 086, 088, Violet 0102 and Moss Green 0267. Use 1 strand for Straight Stitch Stars, 3 strands for rest of the embroidery.

50 cm ($\frac{1}{2}$ yd) slate blue furnishing fabric, as in illustration, 120 cm (approx. 48 in) wide.

1 each Milward 'Gold Seal' crewel needles Nos. 7 and 8 for 3 strands and 1 strand respectively.

The finished size of the traycloth is approximately 35 × 51 cm (14 × 20 in).

Cutting Out and Making Up

Cut one piece from fabric 39 × 54 cm (15½ × 21½ in). The pattern gives the complete design. With long side facing, trace the motif (see Tracing instructions, page 19) centrally on to fabric 6.5 cm (2½ in) from left-hand side. Follow the Key below for the embroidery. All parts similar to numbered parts are worked in the same colour and stitch. Press the embroidery on the wrong side. Make up, taking 1.5 cm (½ in) hems.

Key to Pattern

1 – 086
2 – 088   } Straight Stitch Stars
3 – 0102
4 – 0267

5 – 086
6 – 088   } Back Stitch
7 – 0102

8 – 086   } Satin Stitch
9 – 088

10 – 086 – Double Knot Stitch

11 – 0102 – Outlined Herringbone Stitch

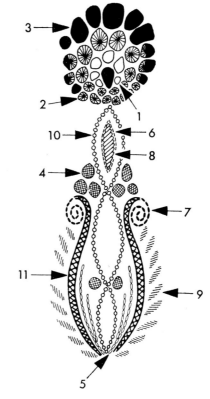

Pattern for Traycloth

Traycloth

115

Traycloth with Border Motifs

Materials Required

Clark's Anchor Pearl Cotton No. 5 (10 g) : 2 balls White 0402.

50 cm (½ yd) yellow evenweave fabric, as in illustration, 130 cm (approx. 52 in) wide, 29 threads to 2.5 cm (1 in) (sufficient fabric for two traycloths).
1 Milward 'Gold Seal' tapestry needle No. 20.

The finished size of the traycloth is 53 × 38 cm (21 × 15 in).

Cutting Out and Making Up

Cut 57 × 42 cm (22½ × 16½ in) from fabric for traycloth. The pattern gives a section of the design showing the corner turning. The background squares of the pattern represent the threads of fabric. Follow the Key on page 117 for the embroidery. Commence at right-hand corner (arrow on pattern) 9 cm (3½ in) from edges of fabric. On long sides work 5 of the long motifs A separated by the small motifs B between corners; and on short sides, 3 motifs A separated by motifs B between corners. Continue the borders as shown on all sides. On small motifs B, after the outlining Satin Stitch blocks are completed, cut and withdraw 4 fabric threads, miss 4 threads and cut 4 threads each way of fabric. The parts where threads are cut out are shown by blank spaces on pattern. The Woven Bars are then worked over the 4 loose threads, 5 rows of weaving in each bar. The Twisted Bars are worked obliquely across the open spaces. The Eyelet Holes and Four-Sided Stitch are worked over a square of 4 fabric threads. The Satin Stitch pyramids are 13 stitches over 4, 6, 8 and 10 threads; the blocks are 5 stitches over 4 threads; the mitred corner of inner border has 5 stitches into the same place at the inside and 2 threads between each stitch at the outside. The Straight Stitch is over 4 threads and also 2 threads obliquely. See pages 20–29 for method of working the stitches. Trim the margins even and finish with 1.5 cm (½ in) hem.

Traycloth with Border Motifs

Key to Pattern

1 — Satin Stitch
2 — Eyelet Holes
3 — Woven Bars
4 — Twisted Bars
5 — Straight Stitch
6 — Four-Sided Stitch

Pattern for Traycloth with Border Motifs

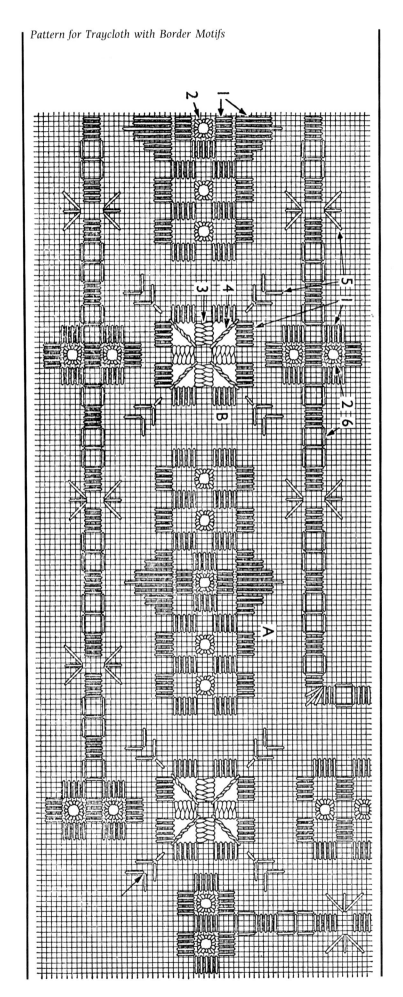

Trolley Set

Materials Required

Clark's Anchor Stranded Cotton: 3 skeins each Indigo 0127, Jade 0188, Moss Green 0269; 2 skeins each Cyclamen 088 and Muscat Green 0280. Use 6 strands for Laid Threads in Couching, 3 strands for rest of the embroidery.

70 cm ($\frac{3}{4}$ yd) royal blue furnishing fabric, as in illustration, 120 cm (approx. 48 in) wide – sufficient for two trolley cloths and two napkins.

1 Milward 'Gold Seal' crewel needle No. 7.

The finished size of the trolley cloths is 41×61 cm (16×24 in); the napkins 27 cm ($10\frac{1}{2}$ in) square.

Cutting Out and Making Up

Cut two pieces from fabric 44×64 cm ($17\frac{1}{4} \times 25\frac{1}{2}$ in) and two pieces 30 cm (12 in) square. Fold large pieces across the centre widthwise and crease lightly. The pattern gives the complete design. With long side facing, trace the design as given (see Tracing instructions, page 19) 2 cm ($\frac{3}{4}$ in) to the left of fold and 5 cm (2 in) from lower edge. Turn fabric and repeat on other long side. Follow the Key on page 120 for the embroidery. All parts similar to numbered parts are worked in the same colour and stitch. Press the embroidery on the wrong side. Make up, taking 1.5 cm ($\frac{1}{2}$ in) hems.

Trolley Set

Close-up of Motif, Trolley Set

Key to Pattern

1 — 0127 ⎫
2 — 0269 ⎭ Stem Stitch

3 — 088 ⎫
4 — 0127 ⎬ French Knots
5 — 0188 ⎭

6 — 0127 — Daisy Stitch

7 — 0127 ⎫
8 — 0188 ⎪
9 — 0269 ⎬ Double Daisy Stitch
10 — 0280 ⎭

11 — 088 ⎫
12 — 0188 ⎬ Double Knot Stitch
13 — 0280 ⎭

14 — 088 ⎫
15 — 0188 ⎪
16 — 0269 ⎬ Couching
17 — 0280 ⎭

18 — 0127 ⎫
19 — 0269 ⎭ Closed Herringbone Stitch

20 — 088 ⎫
21 — 0269 ⎭ Satin Stitch

22 — 0127 ⎫
23 — 0269 ⎭ Fly Stitch

24 — 0127 ⎫
25 — 0269 ⎬ Straight Stitch
26 — 0280 ⎭

27 — 0127 — Back Stitch

Key to Pattern for Trolley Set

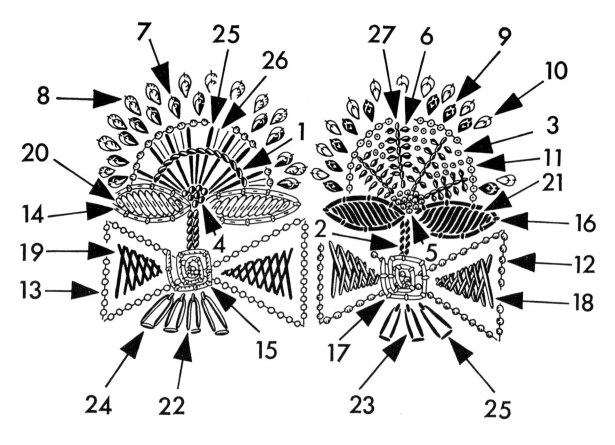

Coffee Tablecloth

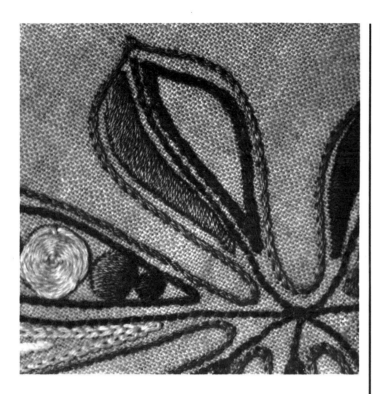

Coffee Tablecloth

Materials Required

Clark's Anchor Stranded Cotton: 4 skeins Tapestry shade 0903; 3 skeins Tapestry shade 0905; 2 skeins each Tapestry shade 0885, 0887; 1 skein White 0402. Use 3 strands throughout.
1 m (1 yd) fine turquoise embroidery fabric, as in illustration, 90 cm (approx. 36 in) wide.
3 m (3¼ yd) white bobble braid.
1 Milward 'Gold Seal' crewel needle No. 7.

The finished size of the illustrated tablecloth is approximately 87 cm (34½ in) in diameter, excluding braid.

Instructions

Fold the fabric in half both ways and crease lightly. These folds act as a guide when placing the first section of the design. The pattern gives one third of the design, consisting of two motifs joined at tips of leaves. Trace the design as given on to fabric (see Tracing instructions, page 19) with the joining of tips of leaves 16 cm (6½ in) from centre. To complete, trace the given section twice more on to remaining two thirds of fabric, spacing evenly. To ensure correct positioning insert a pin through the tracing and fabric at the centre point and turn tracing round pin. Follow pattern and Key for the embroidery. All parts similar to numbered parts are worked in the same colour and stitch. Press embroidery on the wrong side. To make up, mark a circle 89 cm (35 in) in diameter on the wrong side of fabric and cut round outline. Turn up raw edge 6 mm (¼ in) to the right side and machine stitch or zig-zag stitch. Place braid over the raw edge and machine stitch in position.

Close-up of Motif, Coffee Tablecloth

Key to Pattern

1 – 0402	
2 – 0885	
3 – 0887	Satin Stitch
4 – 0903	
5 – 0905	
6 – 0885	
7 – 0887	Spider's Web Filling
8 – 0903	
9 – 0905	
10 – 0402	
11 – 0903	Stem Stitch
12 – 0905	
13 – 0885	
14 – 0887	Chain Stitch
15 – 0905	
16 – 0885	
17 – 0887	Double Knot Stitch
18 – 0903	Stem Stitch Filling
19 – 0905	Back Stitch

Pattern for Coffee Tablecloth

Coffee Table Mat

Coffee Table Mat

Materials Required

Coats Chain Mercer-Crochet Cotton No. 20 (20 g).
1 ball Mid Buttercup 442; 2 balls Dk. Jade 524 and
3 balls Jade 521. This model is worked in these three
shades, but any other shades of Mercer-Crochet may
be used.
Milward steel crochet hook 1.25 (no. 3).

Tension

Size of motif — 12 cm ($4\frac{3}{4}$ in) from point to point.

Measurements

48 × 55 cm (19 × $21\frac{3}{4}$ in).

Motif (make 19)

Using Mid Buttercup commence with 4 ch.
1st Row: 11 tr into 4th ch from hook, 1 ss into 4th
of 4 ch.
2nd Row: 2 dc into same place as ss, 2 dc into each
st, 1 ss into first dc.
3rd Row: 1 dc into same place as ss, * 3 ch, miss
1 dc, 1 dc into next dc; repeat from * ending with
3 ch, 1 ss into first dc.
4th Row: 1 ss into next loop, 3 ch, 4 tr into same
loop, 5 tr into each loop, 1 ss into 3rd of 3 ch.
Fasten off.
5th Row: With right side facing and working behind
previous 2 rows attach Dk. Jade to any free dc on 2nd
row, 1 dc into same place as join, * 4 ch, 1 dc into
next free dc; repeat from * ending with 4 ch 1 ss
into first dc.
6th Row: 1 ss into next st and into loop, 1 dc into
same loop, * 5 ch, 1 dc into next loop; repeat from *
ending with 2 ch, 1 tr into first dc.
7th Row: 1 dc into loop just formed, * 16 ch, 1 ss
into 13th ch from hook, 3 ch, 1 dc into next loop;
repeat from * omitting 1 dc at end of last repeat, 1 ss
into first dc.
8th Row: 4 ch, * 17 tr into next 13 ch loop (a petal
made), 1 ch, 1 tr into next dc, 1 ch; repeat from *
omitting 1 tr and 1 ch at end of last repeat, 1 ss into
3rd of 4 ch. Fasten off.
9th Row: With right side facing miss 8 sts on any
petal, attach Jade to next st, 1 dc into same place as
join * 9 ch, miss 8 tr on next petal, into next st
work 1 hlf tr 3 ch and 1 hlf tr, 9 ch, miss 8 tr on
next petal, 1 dc into next st; repeat from * omitting
1 dc at end of last repeat, 1 ss into first dc.
10th Row: 3 ch, * 9 tr into next loop, 1 tr into next
hlf tr, 5 tr into next sp, 1 tr into next hlf tr, 9 tr into
next loop, 1 tr into next dc; repeat from * omitting
1 tr at end of last repeat, 1 ss into 3rd of 3 ch.
11th Row: 3 ch, 1 tr into each of next 12 tr, * 3 tr
into next tr, 1 tr into each of next 25 tr; repeat
from * omitting 13 tr at end of last repeat, 1 ss into
3rd of 3 ch.

12th Row: 3 ch, 1 tr into each of next 13 tr, * 3 tr
into next tr, 1 tr into each of next 27 tr; repeat from *
omitting 14 tr at end of last repeat, 1 ss into 3rd of
3 ch. Fasten off.

Damp and pin out to measurements.

Making Up

Sew motifs together (see pattern for placing of motifs).

Pattern for Coffee Table Mat

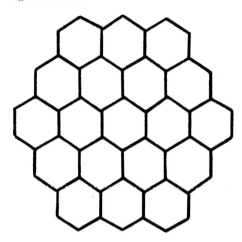

Close-up of motif, Coffee Table Mat

125

Trolley Cloth

Materials Required

Coats Chain Mercer-Crochet Cotton No. 20 (20 g).
4 balls. This model is worked in shade 521 (Jade), but
any other shade of Mercer-Crochet may be used.
Milward steel crochet hook 1.25 (no. 3).
70 cm ($\frac{3}{4}$ yd) dark purple furnishing fabric 120 cm
(approx. 48 in) wide.

Tension

Depth of Edging — 3 cm ($1\frac{1}{4}$ in).
Depth of Trimming — 2 cm ($\frac{3}{4}$ in).
5 scallops — 7 cm ($2\frac{3}{4}$ in).

Measurements

Finished size of Edging — 67 × 47 cm ($26\frac{1}{2}$ × $18\frac{1}{2}$ in).
Finished size of Trimming — 51 × 30 cm (20 × 12 in).

Abbreviations

ch — chain; dc — double crochet; tr — treble; dbl tr —
double treble; st(s) — stitch(es); ss — slip stitch.

Edging (make 2)

Commence with 10 ch, join with a ss to form a ring.
1st Row: 3 ch, 9 tr into ring, * 10 ch, 1 ss into last tr,
2 ch, 1 ss into same place as last tr made, turn, 9 tr
into ring (2 scallops made); repeat from * along side
until 40 scallops have been worked not including
corner, or number required having an even number of
scallops, 2 ch, 1 ss into same place as last tr made,
10 ch, remove loop from hook, insert hook into last ch
and draw dropped loop through, 1 ss into ring just
made, 3 ch, 9 tr into ring (corner turned); repeat from
first * along next side until 27 scallops have been
worked including corner, or number required having
an uneven number of scallops, work other two sides
and corners to correspond having 41 scallops on
second long side ending last repeat before last corner,
2 ch, 1 ss into same place as last tr made, 5 ch, 1 ss
into 3rd of 3 ch on first scallop, 5 ch, remove loop
from hook, insert hook into same place as second last
ss and draw dropped loop through, 1 ss into loop just
made, 3 ch, 9 tr into ring, 1 ss into first ring.
2nd Row: 4 ch, 6 dbl tr into same ring, * 4 ch, 1 dc
into centre tr of next scallop, 4 ch, 7 dbl tr into next
ring; repeat from * to within corner, 4 ch, 1 dc into
centre tr of next scallop, 4 ch, miss 4 tr, leaving the
last loop of each on hook work 1 dbl tr into 1st of
2 ch on same scallop and 3rd of 3 ch on next scallop,
thread over and draw through all loops on hook (a
joint dbl tr made at corner), 4 ch, miss 4 tr, 1 dc into
next tr, 4 ch, 7 dbl tr into next ring; repeat from
first * omitting 7 dbl tr at end of last repeat, 1 ss into
4th of 4 ch.
3rd Row: 4 ch, 1 dbl tr into same place as ss, 2 dbl tr
into next dbl tr, remove loop from hook, insert hook
into 4th of 4 ch and draw dropped loop through (a

starting popcorn st made), * 1 ch, 2 dbl tr into each of
next 3 dbl tr, remove loop from hook, insert hook into
first dbl tr of dbl tr group and draw dropped loop
through (a popcorn st made over 3 sts), 1 ch, 2 dbl tr
into each of next 2 dbl tr, remove loop from hook,
insert hook into first dbl tr of dbl tr group and draw
dropped loop through (a popcorn st made over 2 sts),
5 ch, 1 dc into 3rd ch from hook (a picot made), 1 ch,
3 dc into each of next 2 loops, 4 ch, a picot, 2 ch, a
popcorn st over 2 sts; repeat from * to within joint
dbl tr at corner, 4 dbl tr into joint dbl tr, remove loop
from hook, insert hook into first dbl tr of dbl tr group
and draw dropped loop through (a popcorn st made at
corner), 5 ch, a picot, 1 ch, 3 dc into each of next
2 loops, 4 ch, a picot, 2 ch, a popcorn st over 2 sts;
repeat from first * omitting a popcorn st at end of last
repeat, 1 ss into starting popcorn st. Fasten off.

Heading for Edging

Attach thread to first free loop to left of any corner,
3 ch, 2 tr into same ring, * 5 ch, 1 dc into centre tr of
next scallop, 5 ch, 3 tr into next ring; repeat from * to
within 2 rings at corner, 2 tr into next loop, leaving
the last loop of each on hook work 1 tr into same loop
and 1 tr into next loop, thread over and draw through
all loops on hook (a joint tr made), 2 tr into same loop
as last tr; repeat from first * ending with 5 ch, 1 dc
into centre tr of next scallop, 5 ch, 1 ss into 3rd of
3 ch. Fasten off.

Trimming (make 2)

1st Row: Work as 1st row of Edging having 30
scallops or number required having an even number
of scallops not including corner along first side and 17
scallops or number required having an uneven number
of scallops along second side including corner, work
other two sides to correspond.
2nd Row: 3 ch, 2 tr into same ring, * 5 ch, 1 dc into
centre tr of next scallop, 5 ch, 3 tr into next ring;
repeat from * to within corner, 5 ch, 1 dc into centre
tr of next scallop, 5 ch, miss 4 tr, a joint dbl tr over
1st of 2 ch on same scallop and 3rd of 3 ch on next
scallop, 5 ch, 1 dc into centre tr of same scallop, 5 ch,
3 tr into ring; repeat from first * omitting 3 tr at end
of last repeat, 1 ss into 3rd of 3 ch. Fasten off.

Heading

As Heading for Edging.

Damp and pin out to measurements.

Making Up

Cut two pieces of fabric 44 × 64 cm ($17\frac{1}{2}$ ×
$25\frac{1}{2}$ in). Turn in 1.5 cm ($\frac{1}{2}$ in) hems, mitre corners
and slipstitch in position. Sew edging to edge of trolley
cloth. Place trimming centrally on trolley cloth
approximately 5 cm (2 in) from edge and sew in
position.

Trolley Cloth

Chapter 8

Lampshades

Well-proportioned Lampshades

Every home requires some form of lighting, and the choice depends upon the situation, size and function of the room. Normally there will be a central ceiling fitting, and further light may be obtained from a standard lamp, wall lights or table lamps.

Most lamps need some form of shade, which will cut the glare of the bulb and also provide a decorative feature. If selected with care and thought a lampshade can be an attractive part of the décor, and in the evening when lit, emit a warm and welcoming light.

Lampshades can be of many different sizes and shapes and the choice will be determined by various factors. If the shade is for a central fitting the size of the room must be studied ; if for a standard or table lamp the base and the shade must be in proportion. The sketches on this page illustrate 'right' and 'wrong' – and the latter need no further explanation.

The choice of fabric is very important: not only must it allow the light to come through, but it must be sufficiently opaque to hide the glare of the bulb. A wide variety of fabrics is suitable, ranging from fine organdie to evenweave linen, and including parchment. Fine fabric should be used for draped or pleated shades; this usually needs to be lined.

Lining also gives a more professional finish to lampshades. For shaped shades the fabric and lining should be cut on the true bias of the fabric.

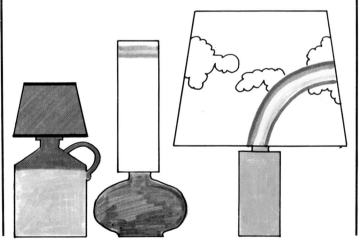

Badly-proportioned Lampshades

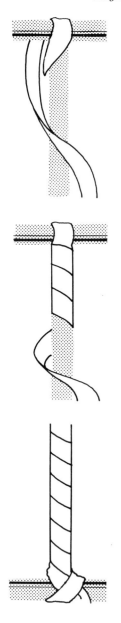

Diagram 1

About binding Frames

Before a lampshade is made, the frame must be tightly bound. A fine bias binding is best for this purpose and Coats Nainsook bias binding is ideal. To make the binding of the frame easier, first roll up the bias binding like a wheel and secure the end to the roll with a pin. When binding, release about 30 cm (12 in) at a time. This will prevent the bias binding becoming tangled round the rings and struts of the frame. If the lampshade is made of washable fabrics and the trimmings or braid sewn on, then the rings and struts should be painted before being bound. Use two coats of gloss or enamel paint. The complete lampshade may then be immersed in warm, soapy water for cleaning and the frame will not rust and mark the fabric.

All the wires on the lampshade frame must be bound except the gimble (this is the attachment which fits on to the lamp), and the wires supporting it. The binding should be very tight and overlap when being wound round the wires. If a shaped frame with vertical struts is being used, the vertical struts must be bound first. For each strut, start at the top and fold about 4 cm (1½ in) of the binding over the top ring and down the strut. Hold this in place and, working from top to lower end, wind binding evenly down to the base of the strut (diagram 1). Anchor at lower edge by winding in a figure-of-eight round lower ring and strut. Cut binding, turn in raw edge and secure with a few stitches. When all the vertical wires have been bound, bind the top and lower rings. Your frame is now ready for covering.

Pendant Lampshade, Lunch Mats and Glass Mats

Pendant Lampshade

Materials Required

Clark's Anchor Stranded Cotton: 7 skeins Peacock Blue 0170; 5 skeins White 0402. Use 6 strands for Satin Stitch, 3 strands for the rest of the embroidery.
40 cm (⅜ yd) pale blue evenweave embroidery fabric, as in illustration, 21 threads to 2.5 cm (1 in), 150 cm (approx. 60 in) wide.
1 piece of lampshade parchment 30 × 130 cm (12 × 51 in).
2 lampshade rings, one with fitting, 41 cm (16 in) in diameter.
Coats bias binding for rings.
Coats Drima (polyester) thread.
1 each Milward 'Gold Seal' tapestry needles No. 20 for 6 strands and No. 24 for 3 strands.

The finished lampshade is 30 cm (12 in) high, and has a diameter of 41 cm (16 in).

Instructions

Cut a piece from fabric 34 × 132 cm (13½ × 52 in)

Pendant Lampshade, Lunch Mats and Glass Mats

and mark the centre both ways with a line of basting stitches. With one long side of fabric facing commence the embroidery at the blank arrow on pattern, 31 threads up from crossed basting stitches and work the section as given following Key opposite for the design and stitches used. Repeat as given five times more on each side, then work half of section at each end. Turn fabric and repeat, commencing at the blank arrow on pattern, 85 threads up from crossed basting stitches. Work squared Edging Stitch on long sides 37 threads from the embroidery on one side and 91 threads from the embroidery on the other side. Press the embroidery on the wrong side.

Making Up

Bind rings (diagram 1). For ease of sewing, a row of holes can be made 3 mm ($\frac{1}{8}$ in) from top and lower edges of parchment by using an unthreaded sewing machine and a large stitch. Overlap short ends of parchment 1.5 cm ($\frac{1}{2}$ in) and glue together. Sew rings to top and lower edges of parchment. Fold fabric right sides together, short ends meeting. Baste and stitch 1.5 cm ($\frac{1}{2}$ in) from short ends, matching the embroidery. Trim seam. Turn to right side, pull fabric over parchment and sew to rings.

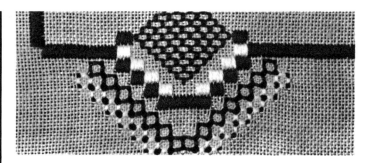

Close-up of Motif, Pendant Lampshade etc

Key to Pattern

1 – 0170
2 – 0402 } Satin Stitch
3 – 0170
4 – 0402 } Double Faggot Filling Stitch
5 – 0170 – Honeycomb Filling Stitch

Pattern for Pendant Lampshade, Lunch Mats and Glass Mats

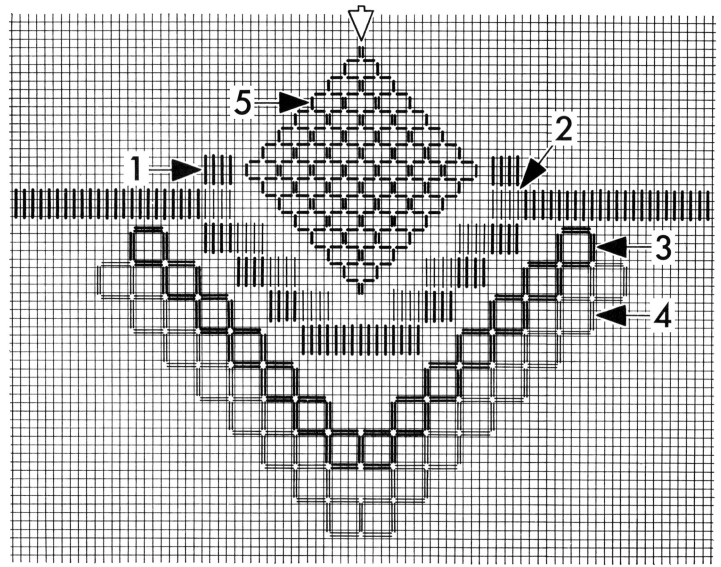

Lunch Mats and Glass Mats

Materials Required

The following amounts make 3 Lunch Mats and 3 Glass Mats.

Clark's Anchor Stranded Cotton: 8 skeins each Peacock Blue 0170; 8 skeins White 0402. Use 6 strands for Satin Stitch, 3 strands for the rest of the embroidery.

60 cm (⅝ yd) pale blue medium weight evenweave fabric, as in illustration, 21 threads to 2.5 cm (1 in), 150 cm (approx. 60 in) wide.

1 each Milward 'Gold Seal' tapestry needles No. 20 for 6 strands and No. 24 for 3 strands.

The finished size of each lunch mat is approximately 30 × 41 cm (12 × 16 in); each glass mat is approximately 11.5 cm (4½ in) square.

Instructions

Cut three pieces from fabric 35 × 46 cm (14 × 18 in) for lunch mats and three pieces 16.5 cm (6½ in) square for glass mats. Mark the centre both ways on each piece with a line of basting stitches. The pattern gives a section of the design, centre indicated by blank arrow which should coincide with the basting stitches. The pattern also shows the arrangement of the stitches on the threads of the fabric, represented by the background lines. With one long side of each large piece of fabric facing, commence the embroidery at the blank arrow on pattern, 40 threads down from crossed basting stitches and work section given, following pattern and Key for the design and stitches used. With the exception of the Satin Stitch, each stitch must be pulled firmly. Repeat given section once more on each side. Turn fabric and repeat on other long side. To complete the design, work Satin Stitches over four threads in Kingfisher along short sides to join Satin Stitch on long sides as shown in photograph. To finish off the edge, work a Buttonhole Stitch Hem (as instructed on page 22) on all sides of the embroidery to form a rectangle 30 × 41 cm (12 × 16 in). On small pieces of fabric, commence the embroidery at blank arrow on pattern, 15 threads above crossed basting stitches and work section given, omitting the Satin Stitches in 0170 on each side of central section as shown. Turn fabric and complete other half to correspond. Work Squared Edging Stitch on all sides of the embroidery to form an 11.5 cm (4½ in) square.

Diagram 2

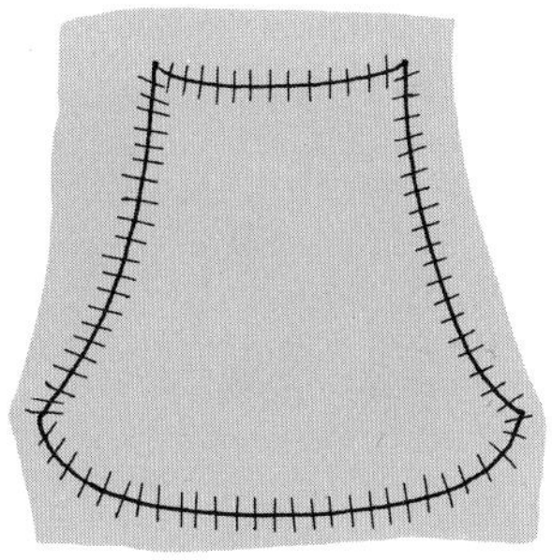

Diagram 3

Pleated Draped Lampshade

Materials Required

1 lampshade frame with six side struts.
The one illustrated measures 33 cm (13 in) across the base, 16.5 cm (6½ in) across the top and 23 cm (9 in) in height.
1 m (1 yd) fine fabric, 115 cm (approx. 45 in) wide.
70 cm (¾ yd) lining fabric, 115 cm (approx. 45 in) wide.

Diagram 4

Pleated Draped Lampshade

Plain Fitted Lampshade

Coats bias binding.
Trimming.
Coats Drima (polyester) thread.

Bind lampshade frame. See page 130.

Cutting Out

Measure your frame from the base of a side strut diagonally across one strut to the top of the next strut (diagram 2, page 133). To this figure add 9 cm ($3\frac{1}{2}$ in) and cut two strips across width of fabric to this measurement. Pin lining fabric on the 'bias' across one half of the frame (diagram 3), pin and re-pin until a smooth fit is achieved. Tack or mark with marking chalk the finished seam line on sides, top and lower edge of the pinned shape. Unpin from frame. Trim lining to within 1.5 cm ($\frac{1}{2}$ in) at side edges and to within 4 cm ($1\frac{1}{2}$ in) from top and lower edges. Use this piece as a pattern to cut out a second lining section – also on the bias.

Making Up

With wrong sides facing, baste side seams of lining sections. Stitch 6 mm ($\frac{1}{4}$ in) outside finished seam line, trim seam, turn wrong side out and complete a french seam by stitching on finished seam line. Pull the lining right side out over frame, matching seams to side struts. Oversew top and lower edges to binding on rings. Trim close to stitching.

To form the pleats take one strip of main fabric and turn under 1.5 cm ($\frac{1}{2}$ in) on one selvedge edge. Pin

one end of the folded edge to the ring at the base of a side strut, stretch diagonally across one strut and pin to the ring at the top of the next strut. Make a 6 mm ($\frac{1}{4}$ in) pleat 2.5 cm (1 in) from folded edge and pin to base ring. Following the straight grain of the fabric, take pleat to the top ring (pleat will be deeper at the top) and pin 1 cm ($\frac{3}{8}$ in) from folded edge. Fabric must be pulled taut at all times. Continue pleating in this way (diagram 4). To join a new length of fabric, turn one selvedge edge under 1.5 cm ($\frac{1}{2}$ in) and continue pleating using folded edge as next pleat, and overlapping end of previous strip 1.5 cm ($\frac{1}{2}$ in). When shade is evenly and completely covered, trim off excess fabric on the straight grain of fabric, leaving 1.5 cm ($\frac{1}{2}$ in) to tuck under first pleat. Oversew the pleats to the binding at the top and lower rings. Trim close to stitching. Sew trimming in place round the top and lower edges of shade.

Plain Fitted Lampshade

Materials Required

1 lampshade frame with side struts. (The one pictured measures 33 cm (13 in) across the base, 16.5 cm ($6\frac{1}{2}$ in) across the top and 23 cm (9 in) in height.)
50 cm ($\frac{1}{2}$ yd) fabric 115 cm (approx. 45 in) wide.
50 cm ($\frac{1}{2}$ yd) lining fabric 115 cm (approx. 45 in) wide.
Coats bias binding.
Trimming.
Coats Drima (polyester) thread.

Bind lampshade frame (page 130).

Cutting Out

Pin lining fabric on the bias across one half of the frame (diagram 3) pin and re-pin until smooth fit is achieved. Baste or mark with marking chalk the finished seam line on sides, top and lower edge of the pinned shape. Unpin from frame. Turn to within 1.5 cm ($\frac{1}{2}$ in) at sides and to within 4 cm ($1\frac{1}{2}$ in) at top and lower edges. Use this piece as a pattern to cut out a second lining section and two sections from main fabric also on the bias.

Making Up

With wrong sides facing baste side seams of lining section together. Stitch 6 mm ($\frac{1}{4}$ in) outside finished seam line. Trim seam, turn wrong side out and complete a french seam by stitching on finished seam line. Pull the lining right side out over frame, matching seams to side struts. Oversew top and lower edges to binding on rings. Trim close to stitching. The outer cover is made up and attached in the same way. Sew trimming in place at top and lower edges. If main fabric used is sufficiently dense to prevent struts from showing through it, the lining should go to the inside of the frame to hide the struts and should be attached after the outer cover is sewn in place.

135

Shadow-work Lampshade and Cheval Runner

Shadow-work Lampshade

Materials Required

Clark's Anchor Stranded Cotton: 3 skeins White 0402;
2 skeins each Parrot Green 0254, Muscat Green 0281,
Gorse Yellow 0303; 1 skein Buttercup 0295. Use
2 strands for Stem Stitch, 3 strands for the rest of the
embroidery.
30 cm ($\frac{1}{3}$ yd) white organdie 90 cm (approx. 36 in)
wide.
30 cm ($\frac{1}{3}$ yd) very fine white cotton for lining, 90 cm
(approx. 36 in) wide.
1 m (1 yd) elastic cord.
Tiffany lampshade frame 23 cm (9 in) in diameter ×
21.5 cm ($8\frac{1}{2}$ in) in height.
1 m (1 yd) white fringing, 10 cm (4 in) deep.
Coats bias binding for frame.
Coats Drima (polyester) thread.
1 each Milward 'Gold Seal' crewel needles No. 7 for
3 strands and No. 8 for 2 strands.

Instructions

Cut one piece from organdie and one piece from
lining 76 × 28 cm (30 × 11 in). Fold organdie
across the centre widthwise and crease lightly. The
pattern gives one complete motif. With one long side
of organdie facing, trace as given (see Tracing
instructions, page 19) centrally on to fold. Repeat
twice more on each side, spacing 1.5 cm ($\frac{1}{2}$ in) apart.
Follow Key for the embroidery. All parts similar
to numbered parts are worked in the same colour and
stitch. Press the embroidery on the wrong side.

Making Up

Bind frame (diagram 1).
1.5 cm ($\frac{1}{2}$ in) has been allowed for seams. Place
embroidered section to lining, right sides together,
edges even. Baste and stitch each long edge on seam
line, leaving an 8 cm (3 in) opening on one long side
near the beginning of the machine stitching.

Trim seams to 6 mm ($\frac{1}{4}$ in). Pull the short end of
fabric through to meet the other short end, keeping
right sides together, seams matching. Baste and stitch
the short raw ends to form a circle. Trim seams to
6 mm ($\frac{1}{4}$ in) and press. Pull to the right side through
the opening. Slipstitch open edges together. To form
the casings, make a line of machine stitching 6 mm
($\frac{1}{4}$ in) from upper and lower edge. Pull lampshade
over frame. To insert elastic, slit lining seam at the
casings. Insert elastic and pull firmly to fit frame. Tie
the ends tightly. Sew fringing round lower edge.

Cheval Runner

Materials Required

Clark's Anchor Stranded Cotton: 2 skeins each Muscat
Green 0281, White 0402; 1 skein each Parrot Green
0254, Buttercup 0295 and Gorse Yellow 0303. Use
2 strands for Stem Stitch, 3 strands for the rest of the
embroidery.

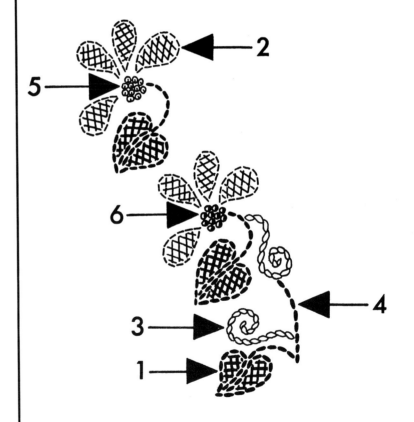

Key to Pattern

1 – 0281	Shadow-work
2 – 0402	
3 – 0254	Stem Stitch
4 – 0281	Back Stitch
5 – 0295	French Knots
6 – 0303	

30 cm (⅓ yd) white organdie, 90 cm (approx. 36 in) wide.
1 each Milward 'Gold Seal' crewel needles No. 7 for 3 strands and No. 8 for 2 strands.

The finished size of the runner is approximately 74 × 25 cm (29 × 10 in).

Instructions

Cut a piece from fabric 79 × 30 cm (31 × 12 in). Fold across the centre both ways and crease lightly. The pattern gives one complete motif. With one long side of fabric facing, trace as given (see Tracing instructions, page 19) centrally on to upper half of widthwise fold 2 mm ($\frac{1}{16}$ in) up from lengthwise fold. Repeat once more on each side, spacing 1.5 cm ($\frac{1}{2}$ in) apart. To complete one half of the design, trace half of the given motif on each side as shown in photograph, spacing evenly. Turn fabric and repeat on other half. Follow Key on page 137 for the embroidery. All parts similar to numbered parts are worked in the same colour and stitch. Press the embroidery on the wrong side.

Making Up

Turn back 1.5 cm ($\frac{1}{2}$ in) hems on all sides, mitre corners and slipstitch.

Standard Lampshade and Cushion

Lampshade

Materials Required

Clark's Anchor Stranded Cotton: 39 skeins Black 0403; 10 skeins Amber Gold 0308; 8 skeins Orange 0326. Use 6 strands for Satin Stitch, 3 strands for the rest of the embroidery.
1.60 m (1¾ yd) white evenweave embroidery linen, 29 threads to 2.5 cm (1 in), 56 cm (approx. 22 in) wide.
1 piece lampshade parchment 147 × 41 cm (58 × 16 in).
2 lampshade rings, one with fitting, 46 cm (18 in) in diameter.
Coats bias binding for rings.
Coats Drima (polyester) thread.
1 each Milward 'Gold Seal' tapestry needles No. 20 (for 6 strands) and No. 24 (for 3 strands).

Instructions

The pattern gives a section of the design showing the arrangement of the stitches on the threads of the fabric, represented by the background lines. With one long side of fabric facing, commence the embroidery

Close-up, Standard Lampshade and Cushion Design

Pattern for Shadow-work Lampshade and Cheval Runner

Standard Lampshade and Cushion

at blank arrow on pattern 1.5 cm ($\frac{1}{2}$ in) from right-hand side and 5 cm (2 in) from lower edge and work section given, following pattern and Key on this page. Continue the embroidery in pattern across the fabric to within 1.5 cm ($\frac{1}{2}$ in) from opposite end. Now work central section of diamond shaped Satin Stitches only — 58 threads above as shown in photograph, then once more 14 threads above previous one. To complete the design, work a row of the octagonal shapes from pattern, 4 cm ($1\frac{1}{2}$ in) from top edge. Press the embroidery on the wrong side.

Making Up

Bind rings (diagram 1). For ease of sewing a row of holes can be made 3 mm ($\frac{1}{8}$ in) from top and lower edges of parchment, using an unthreaded sewing machine and a large stitch. Overlap short ends of parchment 1.5 cm ($\frac{1}{2}$ in) and glue together. Sew rings to top and lower edges of parchment. Fold fabric right sides together with embroidery matching. Baste and stitch close to the embroidery. Trim seam. To mark finished edges of shade, fold fabric to the wrong side 1.5 cm ($\frac{1}{2}$ in) from top edge of embroidery and 2.5 cm (1 in) from lower edge of embroidery. Trim fabric to 1.5 cm ($\frac{1}{2}$ in) from fold on each edge. Turn up raw edges 6 mm ($\frac{1}{4}$ in) and baste. Pull fabric over parchment and sew to rings.

Cushion

Materials Required

Clark's Anchor Stranded Cotton: 9 skeins Black 0403; 4 skeins Orange 0326; 2 skeins White 0402. Use 6 strands throughout.
50 cm ($\frac{1}{2}$ yd) gold medium weight evenweave embroidery linen, 20 threads to 2.5 cm (1 in), 140 cm (approx. 54 in) wide.
Pad to fit.
1 Milward 'Gold Seal' tapestry needle No. 20.
The finished size of the cushion is approximately 58 × 35 cm (23 × 14 in).

Instructions

Cut two pieces from fabric 61 × 38 cm (24 × 15 in). The pattern gives a section of the design showing the arrangement of the stitches on the threads of the fabric, represented by the background lines. With short side of one piece facing, commence the embroidery at blank arrow on pattern 1.5 cm ($\frac{1}{2}$ in) from right-hand side and 5 cm (2 in) from lower edge and work section given, following pattern and Key. Continue the design across the fabric to within 1.5 cm ($\frac{1}{2}$ in) from opposite side. Now work central section of diamond shaped Satin Stitches only, 58 threads above as shown in photograph, then once more 14 threads above previous one. To complete the design, work a row of the octagonal shapes from pattern, 2.5 cm (1 in) from top edge. Press the embroidery on the wrong side.

Making Up

Make up cushion taking 1.5 cm ($\frac{1}{2}$ in) seams.

Key to Pattern

Lampshade	—	Cushion	
1 – 0308	–	0402	} Satin Stitch
2 – 0403	–	0403	
3 – 0326	–	0326	– Back Stitch
4 – 0326	–	0326	– Cross Stitch

Pattern for Standard Lampshade and Cushion

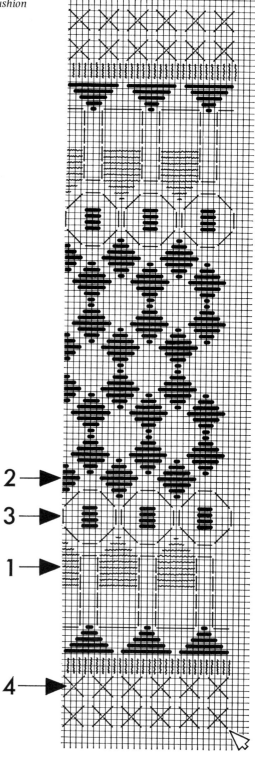

Lampshade Cover

Lampshade Cover

Materials Required

Coats Chain Mercer-Crochet Cotton No. 20 (20 g).
3 balls. This model is worked in shade 524 (Dk. Jade), but any other shade of Mercer-Crochet may be used.
Milward steel crochet hook 1.25 (no. 3).
50 cm ($\frac{1}{2}$ yd) lampshade parchment, 74 cm (approx. 29 in) wide.
50 cm ($\frac{1}{2}$ yd) fabric, 90 cm (approx. 36 in) wide in contrasting colour.
2 lampshade rings, one with fitting, 20 cm (8 in) in diameter.
Coats bias binding for rings.
Coats Drima (polyester) thread.

Tension

First 3 rows 1.5 cm ($\frac{1}{2}$ in).

Measurements

66 × 23 cm (26 × 9 in).

Abbreviations

ch – chain; dc – double crochet; tr – treble; dbl tr – double treble; quad tr – quadruple treble; sp – space; st(s) – stitch(es); ss – slip stitch.

Instructions

Commence with 5 ch.

1st Row: * 1 dbl tr into 5th ch from hook, 11 ch; repeat from * 30 times more omitting 5 ch at end of last repeat and being careful not to twist work 1 ss into same place as first dbl tr. (31 loops made).
2nd Row: 1 ss into first loop, 3 ch, 4 tr into same loop, * 7 ch, 5 tr into next loop; repeat from * ending with 7 ch, 1 ss into 3rd of 3 ch.
3rd Row: 1 ss into next tr, * 1 dc into next tr, into next sp work 5 tr 3 ch 1 ss into last tr (a picot made)

and 4 tr, miss 2 tr; repeat from * ending with 1 ss into first dc.
4th Row: 3 ch, 1 tr into each of next 2 tr, * 7 ch, miss 5 tr, 1 tr into each of next 5 sts; repeat from * omitting 3 tr at end of last repeat, 1 ss into 3rd of 3 ch.
5th Row: 1 dc into same place as ss, * into next sp work 5 tr a picot and 4 tr, miss 2 tr, 1 dc into next tr; repeat from * omitting 1 dc at end of last repeat, 1 ss into first dc.
Repeat last 2 rows once more.
8th Row: 1 ss into each of next 5 tr and into picot, 1 dc into same picot, * 11 ch, 1 dc into next picot; repeat from * ending with 5 ch, 1 quad tr into first dc.
9th Row: 8 ch, 1 tr into top of last quad tr, * 6 ch, into centre ch of next loop work 1 tr 5 ch and 1 tr (a V st made); repeat from * ending with 6 ch, 1 ss into 3rd of 8 ch.
10th Row: 1 ss into each of next 3 ch, 8 ch, 1 tr into same place as last ss, * 3 ch, 1 dc into next loop, 3 ch, a V st into centre ch of next V st; repeat from * omitting a V st at end of last repeat, 1 ss into 3rd of 8 ch.
11th Row: 1 ss into each of next 3 ch, 8 ch, 1 tr into same place as last ss, * 6 ch, a V st into centre ch of next V st; repeat from * ending with 6 ch, 1 ss into 3rd of 8 ch.
12th Row: 1 ss into next sp, 3 ch, 4 tr into same sp, * 7 ch, 5 tr into next V st; repeat from * ending with 7 ch, 1 ss into 3rd of 3 ch.
Repeat 3rd to 12th row twice more then 3rd to 7th row again. Fasten off.

Heading

1st Row: With right side facing attach thread to any loop on opposite side of first row, 5 dc into same loop, * 7 dc into next sp, 5 dc into next loop; repeat from * ending with 7 dc into next sp, 1 ss into first dc.
Fasten off.

Damp and pin out to measurements.

Making Up

Bind rings (see page 130). Cut bonding parchment 23 × 67 cm (9 × 26$\frac{1}{2}$ in).
Cut fabric 25 × 68 cm (10 × 27 in).
For ease of sewing a row of holes can be made 3 mm ($\frac{1}{8}$ in) from top and lower edges of parchment by using an unthreaded sewing machine and a large stitch.
Overlap short ends of parchment 1.5 cm ($\frac{1}{2}$ in) and glue together.
Sew rings to top and lower edges of parchment.
Fold fabric right sides together, baste and stitch 1.5 cm ($\frac{1}{2}$ in) from edge of short ends. Trim seam. Turn to right side.
Turn back 1.5 cm ($\frac{1}{2}$ in) to wrong side on long edges then turn raw edges up 6 mm ($\frac{1}{4}$ in) and baste. Pull fabric over parchment and sew to rings. Pull crochet over fabric and sew to lampshade.

Chapter 9

WALL PANELS

This chapter contains a selection of designs in embroidery and crochet for all kinds of wall panels and hangings. Use your skill and imagination to make the basic designs or your own individual variations, using different backing materials, colours and motifs.

Among the embroidered designs many interesting techniques can be seen, including corded stitchery, chunky French knots and decorative fringing. A wide variety of fabrics is available to make a basis for your embroidery — in fact, almost any fabric is suitable, so long as it is firmly woven.

Crochet's image has changed radically in recent years. No longer is it used only in the traditional manner for cheval sets, doilies and lunch mats. Here you see it used in unconventional ways to produce attractive wall panels.

Flower Panel (Free-Style)

Materials Required

Coats Anchor Tapisserie Wool: 3 skeins Terra Cotta 0340; 2 skeins each Terra Cotta 0337, Coffee 0381, Olive Green 0422, Sage Green 0843; 1 skein each Terra Cotta 0336, Olive Green 0424, Amber Gold 0565. Use 3 thicknesses of wool to work French Knots.
Clark's Anchor Stranded Cotton: 2 skeins Amber Gold 0305; 1 skein Coffee 0381. Use 4 strands for Straight Stitch, 6 for remainder of embroidery.
Piece 68 × 81 cm (27 × 32 in) pale gold medium weight furnishing fabric.
1.20 m (1¼ yd) No. 6 piping cord.
1.20 m (1¼ yd) No. 5 piping cord.
1 m (1 yd) No. 4 piping cord.
Picture frame and backing board to fit embroidery.
2 picture rings.
Milward 'Gold Seal' chenille needle No. 18 for Tapisserie Wool.
Milward chenille heavy embroidery needle for 3 thicknesses of Tapisserie Wool.
1 each Milward 'Gold Seal' crewel needles No. 6 for 4 strands, No. 5 for 6 strands Stranded Cotton.

The finished size of the picture is approximately 43 × 54 cm (17 × 21¼ in).

Mounting and Framing instructions are on page 146.

Instructions

The tracing gives the complete design. Trace as given

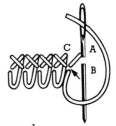

Diagram 1
Velvet Stitch

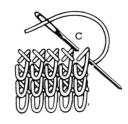

Flower Panel (Free-Style)

centrally on to fabric. Mount the fabric as given in instructions on page 146. Follow the pattern and Key for the embroidery. All parts similar to numbered parts are worked in the same colour and stitch. Press the embroidery on the wrong side, taking care not to flatten the Velvet Stitch (see below) or piping cord.

Velvet Stitch

This stitch resembles the pile of an Oriental carpet. It is worked from left to right in rows working from the bottom upwards (see diagram 1). Bring the thread through at arrow, insert the needle at A; bring out again at arrow; re-insert needle at A leaving a loop of thread at the bottom (to keep regularity in the length of loops it can be worked over a thick knitting needle, not shown in diagram). Bring the needle out at B, insert at C, bring out again at B in readiness for the next stitch. After all the rows have been worked, cut the loops and trim evenly, taking care not to trim the tufts too short.

Key to Pattern

1 – 0336 No. 4 piping cord ⎤ Overcast
2 – 0337 No. 5 piping cord ⎬ Stitch or
3 – 0340 No. 6 piping cord ⎦ Trailing
4 – 0337 ⎤
5 – 0340 ⎬ Straight Stitch
6 – 0381 (S) ⎦
7 – 0422 ⎤
8 – 0565 ⎬ French Knots
9 – 0843 ⎦
10 – 0381 – Velvet Stitch
11 – 0424 – Chain Stitch
12 – 0305 (S) Satin Stitch
13 – 0305 (S) Back Stitch
14 – 0381 (S) Buttonhole Stitch
(S) represents Stranded Cotton

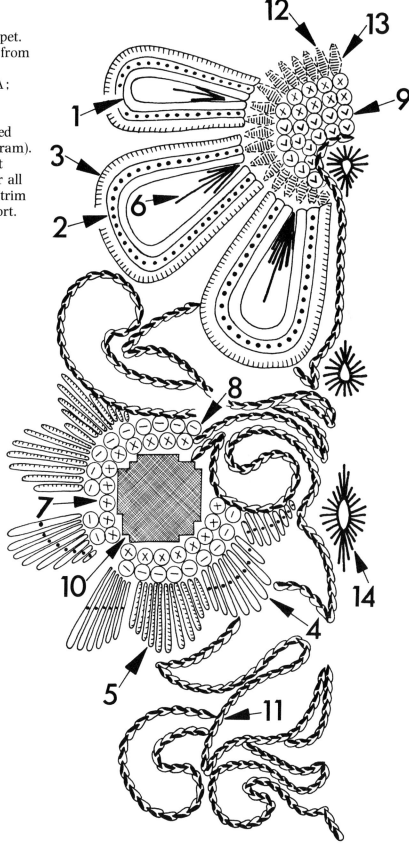

145

Mounting and Framing Panels

It is suggested that the panels and pictures be made up professionally. However, simple instructions are given for making up each article at home. If the latter is decided upon it is advisable to purchase the picture frame and backing board after the embroidery has been completed.

Pattern for Flower Panel

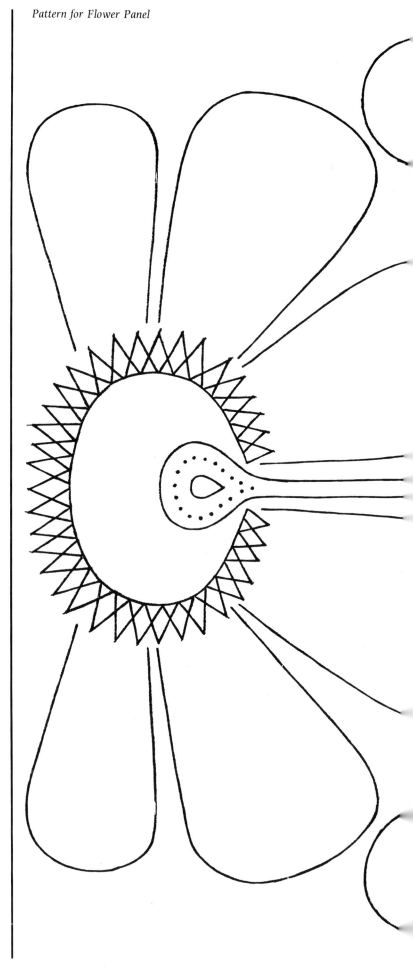

Diagram 2

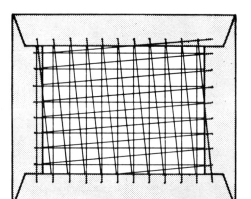

Mounting (see diagram 2)

Place the embroidery centrally over the backing board, fold the surplus fabric to the back and secure at top with pins into edge of board. Pull firmly over the lower edge and pin in position. Repeat on side edges pulling fabric until it lies taut on the board. Secure at the back by lacing from side to side both ways with a strong thread. Remove pins.

Framing (see diagram 3)

Place glass (if desired) and embroidery in frame with small panel pins. Paste a sheet of brown paper over the back edge of the frame to seal. Screw in two picture rings approximately one third of the height from the top. Attach a piece of cord to the rings.

Diagram 3

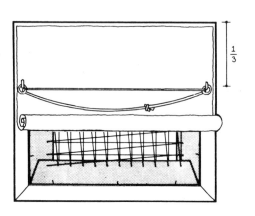

Snow Crystal Panel

Snow Crystal Panel

Materials Required

Coats Chain Mercer-Crochet Cotton No. 20 (20 g).
3 balls. This model is worked in White, but any
shade of Mercer-Crochet may be used.
Milward steel crochet hook 1.25 (no. 3).
70 cm ($\frac{3}{4}$ yd) purple velvet, 90 cm (approx. 36 in)
wide.
60 cm ($\frac{5}{8}$ yd) silver leather cloth.
7 large translucent sequins for motif centres.
36 oblong pearls for motif points.
1 packet small pink beads for centre motif.
1 packet small purple beads for outer braid.
Piece of plywood 51 cm (20 in) in diameter for
mounting.
Piece of felt 51 cm (20 in) in diameter for
backing.

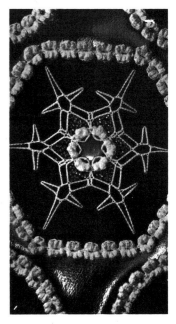

*Close-up of centre motif,
Snow Crystal Panel*

Tension

Centre Motif — 13 cm (5 in) in diameter.
Outer Motif — 9.5 cm ($3\frac{3}{4}$ in) in diameter measured
over 2nd and 5th points.
Braid — 1 repeat — 1.5 cm ($\frac{1}{2}$ in).

Measurements

51 cm (20 in) in diameter.

Abbreviations

ch — chain; dc — double crochet; tr — treble;
dbl tr — double treble; st — stitch; ss — slip stitch.

Centre Motif

Commence with 5 ch.
1st Row: 1 dbl tr into 5th ch from hook, * 6 ch,
1 dbl tr into 5th ch from hook; repeat from * 4 times
more, 1 ch, remove loop from hook, taking care not
to twist insert hook into first ch worked and draw
dropped loop through (a joining ss made). 6 rings.
2nd Row: * 1 dc into next ch, 2 ch, 5 tr into next
ring, remove loop from hook, insert hook into first of
tr group and draw dropped loop through (a popcorn
st made), 2 ch, 5 dbl tr into same ring, remove loop
from hook, insert hook into first of 5 dbl tr and draw
dropped loop through (a large popcorn st made), 2 ch,
a popcorn st into same ring, 2 ch; repeat from *
ending with 1 ss into first dc.
3rd Row: 3 ch, 1 tr into same place as ss, * 13 ch,
2 tr into next dc; repeat from * ending with 13 ch,
1 ss into 3rd of 3 ch.
4th Row: 3 ch, * 1 tr into next tr, 6 ch, miss 6 ch,
1 tr into next ch, 14 ch, 1 tr into 14th ch from
hook, 21 ch, 1 tr into 21st ch from hook, 14 ch,
1 tr into 14th ch from hook, 1 tr into same place
as 4th last tr made, 6 ch, 1 tr into next tr; repeat
from * omitting 1 tr at end of last repeat, 1 ss into
3rd of 3 ch. Fasten off.

Outer Motif (make 6)

Work as Centre Motif for 2 rows.

3rd Row: 1 dc into same place as ss, 21 ch, 1 dc into next dc, 25 ch, 1 dc into next dc, 21 ch, 1 dc into next dc, 29 ch, 1 dc into next dc, 33 ch, 1 dc into next dc, 29 ch, 1 ss into first dc. Fasten off.

Centre Braid

Commence with 4 ch.

1st Row: 1 dbl tr into 4th ch from hook, * 5 ch, 1 dbl tr into 4th ch from hook; repeat from * 34 times more, 1 ch, a joining ss into first ch worked. 36 rings.

2nd Row: * 1 dc into next ch, into next ring work 1 ss 2 ch (a popcorn st, 2 ch) 3 times and 1 ss; repeat from * 4 times more, 1 dc into next ch, into next ring work 1 ss 2 ch a popcorn st 2 ch a large popcorn st 2 ch a popcorn st 2 ch and 1 ss (a corner ring); repeat from first * 5 times more, 1 ss into first dc. Fasten off.

3rd Row: Working along opposite side, attach thread to same ch as first dc to left of any corner, 1 dc into same place as join, * into next ring work 1 ss 2 ch (a popcorn st, 2 ch) 3 times and 1 ss, 1 dc into same ch as next dc; repeat from * 4 times more, into next corner ring work 1 ss 2 ch (a popcorn st, 2 ch) twice and 1 ss, 1 dc into same ch as next dc; repeat from first * 5 times more omitting 1 dc at end of last repeat, 1 ss into first dc. Fasten off.

Outer Braid (make 6)

1st Row: Work as Centre Braid until 31 rings have been completed, do not turn.

2nd Row: * Into next ring work 1 ss 2 ch (a popcorn st, 2 ch) 3 times and 1 ss, 1 dc into next ch; repeat from * along side omitting 1 dc at end of repeat, 1 ss into first ch worked, do not turn, working along opposite side repeat from first * working last ss into top of last ring. Fasten off.

Joining Strip (make 12)

Commence with 29 ch.

1st Row: 1 dc into 2nd ch from hook, 1 dc into each ch. Fasten off.

Damp and pin out to shape.

Making Up

Pattern gives one sixth of the design. Leather cloth may be cut in one piece by making a paper copy from the pattern (broken line shows the joining).

Mark centre of fabric both ways with a line of basting stitches. Cut leather cloth and sew centrally to fabric. Sew centre braid and outer braids to edge of leather cloth as shown in illustration. Sew centre motif in position over sequin.

Place outer motifs to spaces between spokes with a joining strip on each side as shown in illustration,

having sequin in each centre as before and sew neatly. Decorate with beads as shown in illustration.

Mounting

Secure all round with pins into edge of board. Trim fabric on wrong side to within 8 cm (3 in) and lace in position.

Pattern for Snow Crystal Panel

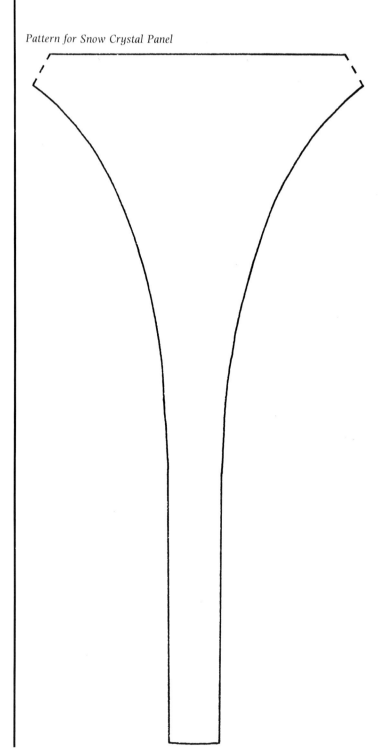

Panel

Panel

Materials Required

Coats Chain Mercer-Crochet Cotton No. 20 (20 g).
1 ball each Cerise 494, Indian Pink 2101,
Lt. Rose Pink 402, Blush Pink 624, Lt. Brown 476,
and Carnation Pink 693.
Coats Chain Mercer-Crochet Cotton No. 40 (20 g).
1 ball each Lt. Brown 476, Lt. Rose Pink 402 and
White. This model is worked in these shades, but any
other shades of Mercer-Crochet may be used.
Milward steel crochet hooks 1.25 (no. 3) for No. 20
Crochet Cotton and 1.00 (no. 4) for No. 40 Crochet
Cotton.
70 cm ($\frac{3}{4}$ yd) pale green fabric 90 cm (approx. 36 in)
wide.
70 cm ($\frac{3}{4}$ yd) fine cotton fabric 90 cm (approx. 36 in)
wide for backing.
Piece of cardboard 68 × 35 cm (27 × 14 in).
1 packet small white beads for flowers B, G, M and T.
1 packet small gold beads for leaves K.
1 packet bronze bugle beads for leaves H and T.
1 packet pink bugle beads for flower T.

Tension

Size of Flower A – 2.5 cm (1 in) in diameter.

Measurements

68 × 35 cm (27 × 14 in).

Flowers and leaves are worked in order from left to right.

Flower A

Using Blush Pink commence with 5 ch.
1st Row: Into 5th ch from hook work (1 tr, 1 ch)
8 times, 1 ss into 4th of 5 ch.
2nd Row: 1 ss into first sp, 4 ch, 2 dbl tr into same
sp, 3 dbl tr into each sp, 1 ss into 4th of 4 ch.
3rd Row: 1 dc into same place as ss, 1 dc into back
loop only of each st, 1 ss into first dc. Fasten off.

Stem

Using Lt. Brown No. 40 commence with 5 ch.
1st Row: 1 tr into 4th ch from hook, 1 tr into each
ch, 2 ch, turn.
2nd Row: Miss first tr, 1 tr into each tr, 1 tr into
next ch, 2 ch, turn.

Repeat last row until stem measures 5 cm (2 in)
omitting turning ch at end of last row. Fasten off.

Leaf (make 2)

Using Lt. Brown No. 20 commence with 13 ch.
1st Row: 1 dc into 2nd ch from hook, 1 hlf tr
into next ch, leaving the last loop of each on hook
work 1 tr into each of next 2 ch, thread over and
draw through all loops on hook (a 2 tr cluster made),

a 2 dbl tr cluster working 1 dbl tr into each of next
2 ch, 1 trip tr into each of next 5 ch, into next ch
work 1 dbl tr 3 ch and 1 ss, 4 ch, working into
opposite side of commencing ch, 1 dbl tr into same ch,
1 trip tr into each of next 5 ch, a 2 dbl tr cluster
over next 2 ch, a 2 tr cluster over next 2 ch, 1 hlf tr
into next ch, 1 dc into next ch, 1 ss into first dc.
Fasten off.

Flower B Seed (make 12)

Using White commence with 5 ch, join with a ss to
form a ring.
1st Row: Into ring work (1 dc, 2 tr) 4 times, 1 ss
into first dc. Fasten off.

Stem

Work as Stem A for 8.5 cm ($3\frac{1}{4}$ in), do not fasten off,
1 ch, turn.
Next Row: 1 dc into each tr, 1 dc into 2nd of 2 ch,
5 ch, turn.
Next Row: 2 dbl tr into first dc, 4 tr into next dc,
into next dc work 2 dbl tr and 1 trip tr, turn.
Next Row: 1 ss into first st, 28 ch, 1 ss into first of
28 ch, 1 ss into next st, (32 ch, 1 ss into first of 32 ch,
1 ss into next st, 26 ch, 1 ss into first of 26 ch, 1 ss
into next st) 3 times, 26 ch, 1 ss into first of 26 ch,
1 ss into next st, 32 ch, 1 ss into first of 32 ch, 1 ss
into next st, 26 ch, 1 ss into first of 26 ch, 1 ss into
same place as second last ss. Fasten off.

Flower C

Using Indian Pink commence with 4 ch.
1st Row: 11 tr into 4th ch from hook, 1 ss into
4th of 4 ch.
2nd Row: 2 dc into same place as ss, 2 dc into back
loop of each tr, 1 ss into first dc.
3rd Row: * 4 ch, 1 trip tr into same place as last ss,
a 2 trip tr cluster into next dc, into next dc work 1
trip tr 4 ch and 1 ss, 1 ss into next dc; repeat from *
to end. Fasten off.
4th Row (inner ring): Using Blush Pink commence
with 8 ch, 1 dc into 2nd ch from hook, 1 dc into
next ch, 1 hlf tr into each of next 2 ch, 1 tr into each
of next 3 ch, * 3 ch, turn, miss first tr, 1 tr into each
of next 2 tr, 1 hlf tr into each of next 2 hlf tr, 1 dc
into each of next 2 dc, 1 ch, turn, 1 dc into each of
next 2 dc, 1 hlf tr into each of next 2 hlf tr, 1 tr
into each of next 2 tr, 1 tr into 3rd of 3 ch; repeat
from * 12 times more.
5th Row (edging): * 4 ch, a 2 tr cluster into 4th
ch from hook, 1 ss into 3rd of next 3 ch on previous
row, 4 ch, a 2 tr cluster into 4th ch from hook,
1 ss into next tr; repeat from * ending with 4 ch, a
2 tr cluster into 4th ch from hook, 1 ss into next ch,
cut thread leaving an end, join at 4th row to
correspond. Fasten off.
6th Row (outer ring): Using Cerise commence with
84 ch, join with a ss to form a ring, 3 ch, 1 tr into

each ch, 1 ss into 3rd of 3 ch.

7th Row: 1 dc into same place as ss, * 3 ch, 3 tr into same place as last dc, miss 2 tr, 1 dc into next tr; repeat from * omitting 1 dc at end of last repeat, 1 ss into first dc. Fasten off.

8th Row: Working from the back of previous row attach Carnation Pink to back loop of 2nd tr missed, 1 dc into same place as join, * 9 ch, miss 3 free tr on 6th row, 1 dc into back loop of next tr; repeat from * omitting 1 dc at end of last repeat, 1 ss into first dc.

9th Row: Into each loop work 1 dc 1 hlf tr 9 tr 1 hlf tr and 1 dc, 1 ss into first dc. Fasten off.

Stem

Work as Stem A commencing with 6 ch instead of 5 for 18 cm (7 in).

Leaf (make 2)

Using Lt. Brown No. 20 commence with 18 ch.

1st Row: 1 hlf tr into 2nd ch from hook, 1 hlf tr into each ch, do not turn.

2nd Row: 1 dc over bar of last hlf tr, 25 ch, 1 dc over ch at opposite end, 25 ch, 1 ss into first dc.

3rd Row: Into same place as ss work 2 hlf tr 1 tr and 2 half tr, 1 hlf tr into each st, 1 ss into back loop of first half tr.

4th Row: 1 hlf tr into same place as ss, working into back loop only of each st work 1 hlf tr into next st, into next st work 2 hlf tr 1 tr and 2 hlf tr, 1 hlf tr into each of next 23 sts, 2 hlf tr into next st, 1 hlf tr into each of next 7 sts, 2 hlf tr into next st, 1 hlf tr into each of next 21 sts, 1 ss into first hlf tr. Fasten off.

Flower D

Using White commence with 5 ch, join with a ss to form a ring.

1st Row: 4 ch, 20 dbl tr into ring, 1 ss into 4th of 4 ch.

2nd Row: 1 dc into same place as ss, 1 dc into back loop of each dbl tr, 1 ss into first dc. Fasten off.

Stem

Work as Stem A for 4 cm (1½ in).

Leaf (make 2)

Using Lt. Brown No. 20 commence with 8 ch.

1st Row: 1 dc into 2nd ch from hook, 1 hlf tr into next ch, a 2 tr cluster over next 2 ch, a 2 dbl tr cluster over next 2 ch, into next ch work 1 dbl tr 3 ch and 1 ss, 4 ch, working into opposite side of commencing ch, 1 dbl tr into same ch, a 2 dbl tr cluster over next 2 ch, a 2 tr cluster over next 2 ch, 1 hlf tr into next ch, 1 dc into next ch, 1 ss into first dc. Fasten off.

Flower E

Work as Flower C for 2 rows. Fasten off.

3rd Row: Attach Blush Pink to same place as last ss and work as 3rd row of Flower C.

4th Row: Using Indian Pink commence with 48 ch, join with a ss to form a ring, 3 ch, 1 tr into each ch, 1 ss into 3rd of 3 ch.

5th Row: As 7th row of Flower C.

Stem

Work as Stem A for 13 cm (5 in).

Leaf (make 4)

As Leaf A.

Flower F

Using White commence with 5 ch, join with a ss to form a ring.

1st Row: 4 ch, 20 dbl tr into ring, 1 ss into 4th of 4 ch. Fasten off.

2nd Row: Attach Lt. Rose Pink No. 40 to same place as ss, 1 dc into same place as join, 1 dc into back loop only of each st, 1 ss into first dc. Fasten off.

3rd Row: Using Lt. Rose Pink No. 40 work as 4th row of Flower C working repeat 10 times instead of 12.

4th Row: As 5th row of Flower C.

Stem

As Stem D.

Leaf (make 2)

As Leaf D.

Flower G

Work as Flower B making Stem 16.5 cm (6½ in).

Flower H

Using Lt. Rose Pink No. 20 commence with 32 ch, join with a ss to form a ring.

1st Row: 1 dc into same place as ss, 1 dc into each ch, 1 ss into first dc.

2nd Row: 1 dc into same place as ss, * miss 1 dc, 7 tr into next dc, miss 1 dc, 1 dc into next dc; repeat from * omitting 1 dc at end of last repeat, 1 ss into first dc. Fasten off.

3rd Row: Using Blush Pink commence with 65 ch, join with a ss to form a ring, 1 hlf tr into same place as ss, 1 hlf tr into each ch, 1 ss into first hlf tr. Fasten off.

Using sewing needle and Cerise darn a filling in centre of ring as shown in illustration on page 151.

Stem

Work as Stem A for 10 cm (4 in).

Leaf (make 4)

Using Lt. Brown No. 20 commence with 50 ch, remove loop from hook, insert hook into 3rd ch made and draw dropped loop through (a joining st made).
1st Row: * 1 hlf tr into next ch, (insert hook into next ch and draw thread through) twice, thread over and draw through all loops on hook; repeat from * 4 times more, 1 hlf tr into each ch to within joining st, 1 hlf tr into each of next 2 sts, 1 ss into next ch. Fasten off.

Flower I

Work as Flower D making Stem 2.5 cm (1 in).

Flower J

Work as Flower D.
Next Row: Using Lt. Rose Pink No. 20 work as 4th row of Flower C working repeat 11 times instead of 12.
Next Row: As 5th row of Flower C.

Stem

Work as Stem A for 7.5 cm (2¾ in).

Leaf (make 2)
As Leaf H.

Flower K

Using Indian Pink commence with 7 ch, join with a ss to form a ring.
1st Row: 3 ch, 21 tr into ring, 1 ss into 3rd of 3 ch.
2nd Row: 4 ch, 1 dbl tr into same place as ss, 2 dbl tr into back loop only of each tr, 1 ss into 4th of 4 ch.
3rd Row: 1 dc into same place as ss, * 21 ch, 1 dc into back loop only of next dbl tr; repeat from * ending with 21 ch, 1 ss into first dc. Fasten off.
4th Row: Attach Blush Pink to any 21 ch loop, 2 dc into same place as join, * 2 ch, 2 dc into next loop; repeat from * ending with 2 ch, 1 ss into first dc.
5th Row: 3 ch, 1 tr into each st, 1 ss into 3rd of 3 ch. Fasten off.
6th Row: Attach White to 4th of 4 ch on 2nd row, 1 dc into same place as join, 1 dc into front loop of each dbl tr, 1 ss into first dc.
7th Row: As 2nd row of Flower H.

Outer Row

Small Ring (make 30)
Using White commence with 5 ch, join with a ss to form a ring.
1st Row: 10 dc into ring, 1 ss into first dc. Fasten off.

Stem

Commence with 8 ch and work as Stem A for 20 cm (8 in).

Leaf (make 2)

Using Lt. Brown No. 20 commence with 58 ch, join with a ss to form a ring.
1st Row: Into same place as ss work 2 hlf tr 1 tr and 2 hlf tr, 1 hlf tr into each of next 28 ch, into next ch work 2 hlf tr 1 tr and 2 hlf tr, 1 hlf tr into each ch, 1 ss into first hlf tr. Fasten off.

Flower L

Using Blush Pink work as Flower C for 1 row. Fasten off.
Attach Indian Pink to same place as ss and work as 2nd and 3rd rows of Flower C.
4th Row: Using Blush Pink commence with 44 ch, join with a ss to form a ring, 4 ch, 1 dbl tr into same place as ss, 2 dbl tr into each ch, 1 ss into 4th of 4 ch.
5th Row: 3 ch, 1 tr into each st, 1 ss into 3rd of 3 ch. Fasten off.

Stem

Work as Stem A for 6 cm (2¼ in).

Leaf (make 2)

Commence with 40 ch and work as Leaf H.

Flower M

Work as Flower B making Stem 10.5 cm (4¼ in).

Flower N

As Flower D.

Flower O

As Flower F.

Stem

Work as Stem A for 8 cm (3 in).

Leaf (make 2)

As Leaf A.

Flower P

Using Indian Pink commence with 36 ch and work as Flower H for 1 row.
2nd Row: As 3rd row of Flower C.
Using sewing needle and Blush Pink darn a filling in centre of ring as before.

Stem

Work as Stem A for 4.5 cm (1¾ in).

Leaf (make 2)

Using Lt. Brown No. 20 commence with 30 ch, join with a ss to form a ring.

1st Row: Into same place as ss work 2 hlf tr 1 tr and 2 hlf tr, 1 hlf tr into each of next 14 ch, into next ch work 2 hlf tr 1 tr and 2 hlf tr, 1 hlf tr into each ch, 1 ss into first hlf tr. Fasten off.

Flower Q

Using Cerise commence with 36 ch, join with a ss to form a ring.

1st Row: 1 dc into same place as ss, 1 dc into each ch, 1 ss into first dc.

2nd Row: 1 dc into same place as ss, * into next dc work 1 dc 21 ch and 1 dc, 1 dc into next dc, 17 ch, miss 3 dc, 1 dc into next dc; repeat from * omitting 1 dc at end of last repeat, 1 ss into first dc. Fasten off.

3rd Row: Attach Lt. Rose Pink No. 20 to first ch on any 17 ch loop, 4 ch, * 1 dbl tr into each of next 5 ch, 2 dbl tr into each of next 5 ch, 1 dbl tr into each of next 6 ch (a petal made), miss 1 dc, working behind next 21 ch loop work 1 dc between next 2 dc, 1 dbl tr into first ch on next 17 ch loop; repeat from * omitting 1 dbl tr at end of last repeat, 1 ss into 4th of 4 ch. Fasten off.

4th Row: Attach Carnation Pink to any 21 ch loop, 1 dc into same place as join, * 9 ch, 1 dc into each of centre 2 dbl tr on next petal, 9 ch, 1 dc into next 21 ch loop; repeat from * omitting 1 dc at end of last repeat, 1 ss into first dc.

5th Row: 3 ch, 1 tr into each st, 1 ss into 3rd of 3 ch.

6th Row: As 7th row of Flower C.

Centre

Using Cerise make 7 small rings as on Flower K.

Stem

Work as Stem C for 11.5 cm (4½ in).

Leaf (make 2)

As Leaf C.

Flower R

Using Carnation Pink work as Flower A.

Stem

Work as Stem A for 3 cm (1¼ in).

Leaf (make 2)

As Leaf A.

Flower S

As Flower F.

Stem

As Stem L.

Leaf (make 2)

As Leaf D.

Flower T

Using Cerise work as Flower P for 2 rows.
Using sewing needle and Blush Pink darn a filling in centre as before.

Stem

Work as Stem C for 21 cm (8¼ in).

Leaf (make 6)

As Leaf H.

Flower U

As Flower D.

Outer Row: Make 8 small rings as on Flower K.

Stem

As stem O.

Leaf (make 2).

As Leaf P.

Damp and pin out to shape.

Making Up

We recommend that the panel be made up on a large embroidery frame as this will make it easier to position the crochet to the fabric. Place cotton backing to wrong side of fabric and tack together, marking out centrally the finished size of panel. Mount the fabric centrally on to frame and place the crochet to the fabric as shown in illustration, leaving a space of 2.5 cm (1 in) at each short end. Sew neatly in place. Decorate with beads as shown in illustration or as desired.

Mounting

Place the fabric centrally over the backing board, fold the surplus fabric to the back and secure at top with pins into the edge of board. Pull firmly over the lower edge and pin in position. Repeat on side edges, pulling fabric until it lies taut on the board. Secure at the back by lacing from side to side, vertically and horizontally with a strong thread. Remove pins. Frame as desired.

Rya Stitch Hanging (Counted)

Materials Required

Coats Anchor Tapisserie Wool: 4 skeins each Sea Green 0506, Violet 097; 3 skeins Plum 0869; 2 skeins each Oyster 0983, 0981, Plum 0871, Sea Green 0507, Violet 096; 1 skein each Smoke 0987, Cyclamen 0577, 087. Use 2 thicknesses of wool to

Key to Pattern

⊡	087	
☑	096	
▣	097	
◬	0506	
▲	0507	
◉	0577	Cross Stitch
☑	0869	
◪	0871	
⊡	0981	
⊠	0983	
▣	0987	

⬮	096	
⬮	097	
⬮	0507	
⬮	0869	Rya Stitch
⬮	0871	
⬮	0983	
⬮	0987	

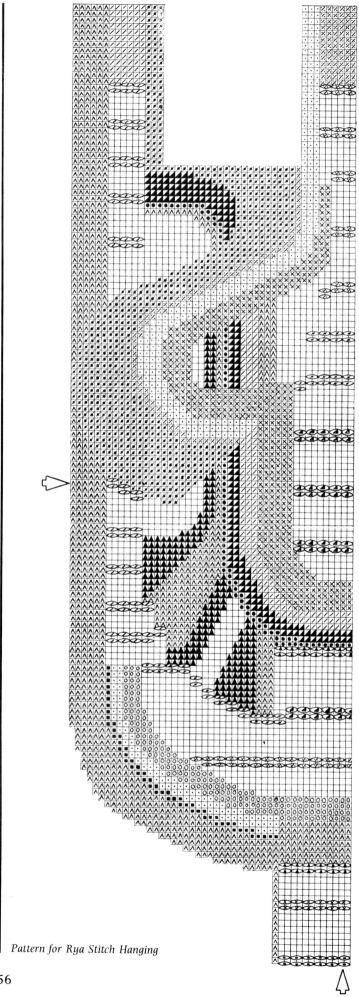

Pattern for Rya Stitch Hanging

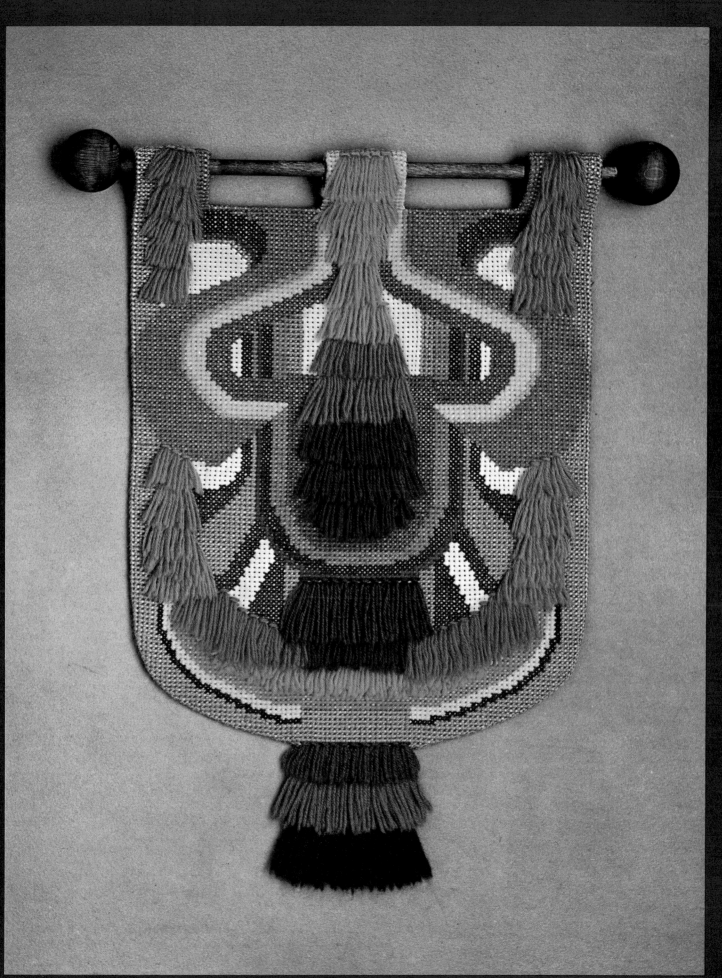

Rya Stitch Hanging

Diagram 4 Rya Stitch

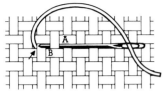

4A

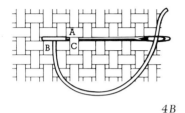

4B

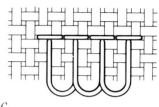

4C

work Rya Stitch (see below), 1 thickness for remainder of embroidery.
60 cm ($\frac{5}{8}$ yd) cream square weave fabric, 6 squares to 2.5 cm (1 in).
50 cm ($\frac{1}{2}$ yd) matching medium weight furnishing fabric, 120 cm (approx. 48 in) wide for backing
Rod to fit.
1 Milward 'Gold Seal' tapestry needle No. 18.

The finished size of the hanging is approximately 56 × 38 cm (22 × 15 in).

Suitable fabric brand is Penelope Binca Canvas K023 – cream (100% cotton).

Instructions

Mark the centre of the fabric both ways with a line of basting stitches. Mount the fabric as given in the instructions on page 146. The pattern gives half the design, centre indicated by blank arrows, which should coincide with the basting stitches. The Cross Stitch is worked over 1 square of fabric, 6 crosses to 2.5 cm (1 in), the Rya Stitch over 2 squares of fabric. It is important when working Cross Stitch that the upper half of all crosses lie in the same direction. Commence the design centrally and follow the Key for the embroidery. Work other half to correspond. Press the embroidery on the wrong side.

Making Up

Cut a piece from backing fabric 46 × 63 cm (18 × 25 in). Trim hanging to 1.5 cm ($\frac{1}{2}$ in) from embroidery. Place backing fabric to embroidery, right sides together. Baste close to embroidery and stitch, leaving an opening for turning to right side. Trim, clip corners and turn to the right side. Slipstitch open edges together. Fold over top tabs to wrong side to form loops and sew in position.

Rya Stitch

This stitch is worked from left to right using double thickness of thread working from the bottom row upwards; for simplicity the stitch diagram shows one thickness only.
(4A) – bring the thread through at arrow, insert the needle 2 holes to the right at A, bring thread through 1 hole to the left at B keeping the thread above the needle. (4B) – insert the needle 1 hole to the right of A at C and bring through again at A, 1 hole to the left, keeping the thread below the needle. Hold down the loop of thread the required length with the left thumb and continue in this way to the end of the row. (4C) – when complete cut the loops of thread to form a fringe.

158

Train Panel (Free-Style)

Materials Required

Clark's Anchor Stranded Cotton: 2 skeins each Lilac 0107, Parma Violet 0108, Moss Green 0268, Amber Gold 0308, Tangerine 0313, Cinnamon 0371, White 0402; 1 skein each Carnation 027, Magenta 063, Parrot Green 0255, Orange 0324. Use 6 strands for French Knots and Buttonhole Stitch, 4 for remainder of embroidery.
Piece 84 × 58 cm (33 × 23 in) yellow medium weight furnishing fabric.
Picture frame and backing board to fit embroidery.
2 Picture rings.
1 each Milward 'Gold Seal' crewel needles No. 5 for 6 strands, No. 6 for 4 strands.

The finished size of the picture is approximately 59.5 × 37 cm ($23\frac{1}{2}$ × $14\frac{1}{2}$ in).

Mounting and Framing instructions page 146.

Instructions

The tracing gives the complete design. Trace as given centrally on to fabric. Mount the fabric as given in instructions on page 146. Follow the pattern and Key for the embroidery. All parts similar to numbered parts are worked in the same colour and stitch. Press the embroidery on the wrong side.

Close-up of motif, Train Panel

Train Panel

159

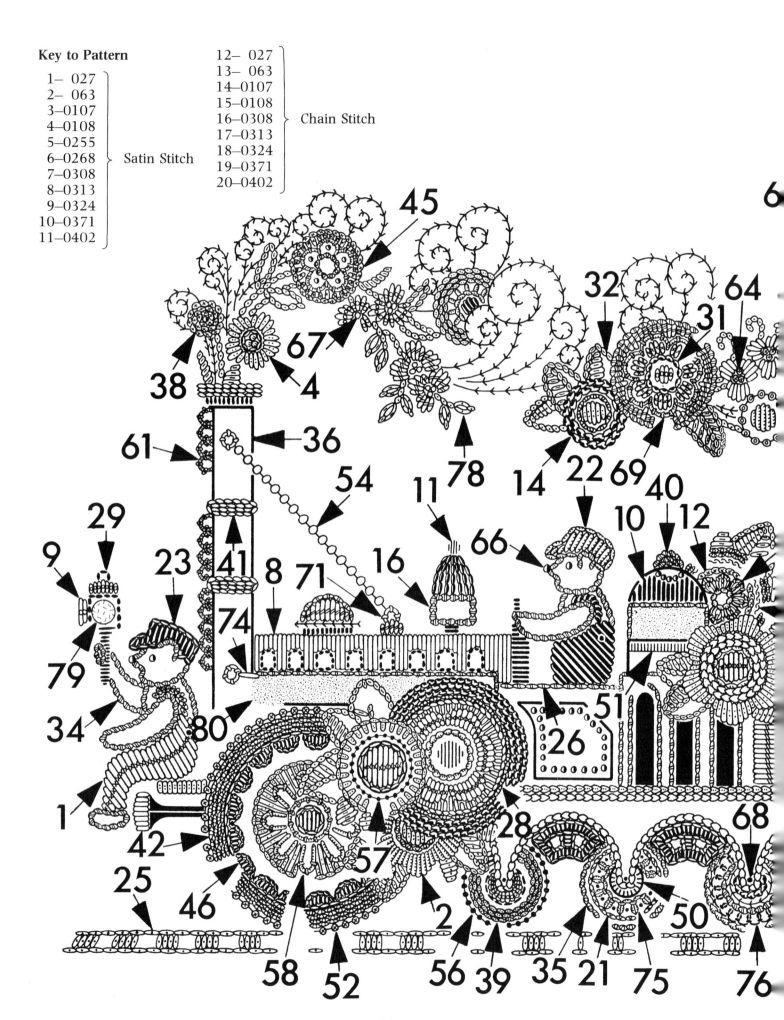

Key to Pattern

Satin Stitch:
1– 027
2– 063
3–0107
4–0108
5–0255
6–0268
7–0308
8–0313
9–0324
10–0371
11–0402

Chain Stitch:
12– 027
13– 063
14–0107
15–0108
16–0308
17–0313
18–0324
19–0371
20–0402

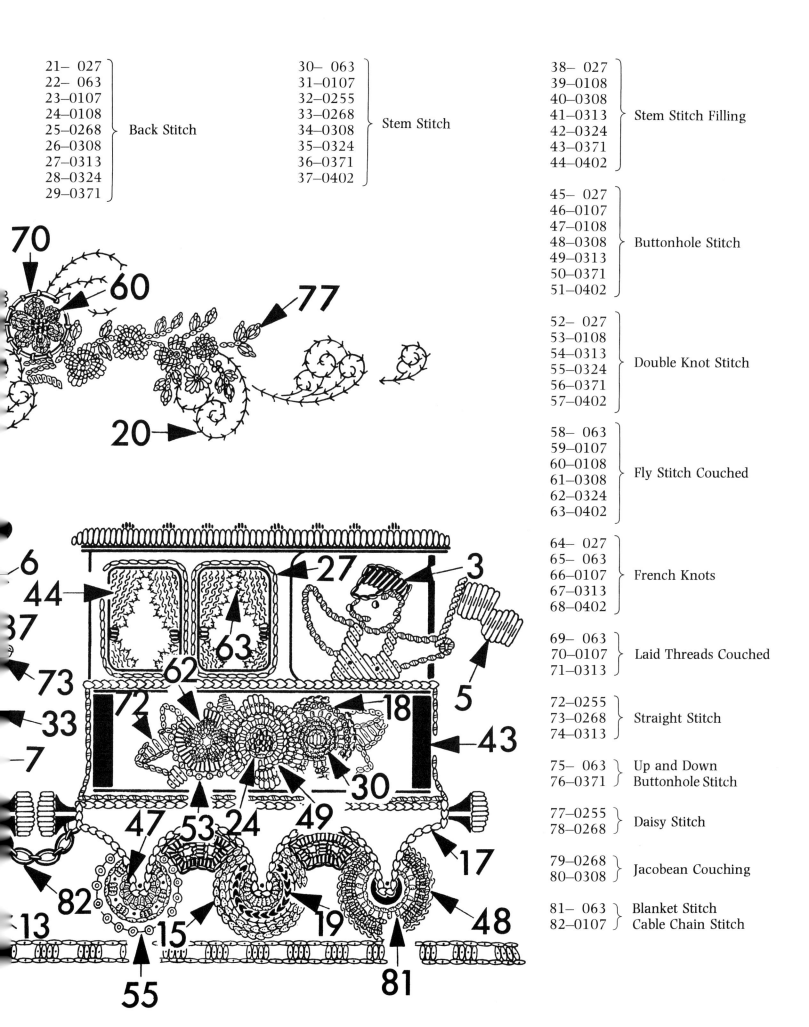

21– 027
22– 063
23–0107
24–0108
25–0268 } Back Stitch
26–0308
27–0313
28–0324
29–0371

30– 063
31–0107
32–0255
33–0268
34–0308 } Stem Stitch
35–0324
36–0371
37–0402

38– 027
39–0108
40–0308
41–0313 } Stem Stitch Filling
42–0324
43–0371
44–0402

45– 027
46–0107
47–0108
48–0308 } Buttonhole Stitch
49–0313
50–0371
51–0402

52– 027
53–0108
54–0313
55–0324 } Double Knot Stitch
56–0371
57–0402

58– 063
59–0107
60–0108
61–0308 } Fly Stitch Couched
62–0324
63–0402

64– 027
65– 063
66–0107 } French Knots
67–0313
68–0402

69– 063
70–0107 } Laid Threads Couched
71–0313

72–0255
73–0268 } Straight Stitch
74–0313

75– 063 } Up and Down
76–0371 } Buttonhole Stitch

77–0255 } Daisy Stitch
78–0268

79–0268 } Jacobean Couching
80–0308

81– 063 } Blanket Stitch
82–0107 } Cable Chain Stitch

161

Chapter 10

Rugs

Rugmaking is a very satisfying and rewarding handicraft, and there is nothing quite like a hand-made rug to add beauty and luxury to the home. To make rugs in embroidery stitches, count out the stitches on the canvas threads in exactly the same way as for embroidery and tapestry. The only difference is that you are working on a rug canvas instead of a finer tapestry canvas or embroidery linen.

Attractive rugs can also be made in both knitting and crochet, as can be seen on page 170. One is developed using brightly coloured knitted patchwork shapes on a dramatic black background, and the other a Mexicana-style striped design in crochet.

Patons Brown Check Canvas is made in widths from 30 to 150 cm (12 to 60 in).

Starting and Finishing

The following instructions apply to all rugs (except in some special cases such as circular rugs). On your length of canvas, the first and last few centimetres are folded back and pressed flat, and the first and last few rows of stitches are worked through the double canvas as follows: turn under 5 cm (2 in) of canvas at start, then as you work down the length, count off threads required to finish the rug design, then turn back the surplus canvas for last few rows.

To Start the Stitching

Thread needle with length of colour stated and run it in and out of canvas before bringing it out at left selvedge in first hole from folded edge, or point stated. In the majority of designs, all rows are worked from left to right.

Turkey Rug Wool is made in cut packs or skeins. Rugs worked in embroidery stitches use skeins. Work with a rug needle, which is short and thick and has a large eye and blunt end.

Finishing off Selvedges

Short ends are oversewn or fringed and selvedges are covered with Binding Stitch (see page 168).

Pressing Stitched Rugs

Lay finished rug face down on a suitably padded surface and pull to shape, although there should be little or no distortion with a stitched rug. Using a hot iron and damp cloth, press well and carefully all over including the side edges.

Cleaning the Turkey Rugs

Clean regularly by shaking off all loose dirt and dust, and use suction cleaner on back of rug to remove grit.

Florentine Rug

Otherwise use damp (not wet) cloth wrung out in a solution of detergent. Do not use soap preparations as they may contain excessive alkali. Rugs should not be allowed to become wet through, and on no account should you try to wash the rug in a tub or washing machine. Shampooing machines are not recommended.

After cleaning, hang rug as quickly as possible on a line outside, away from bright sunlight, so that plenty of air can get into the fabric.

Turkey rugs can also be dry-cleaned, and no damage will arise from the use of any of the recognized home dry-cleaning liquids.

Florentine Rug

The striking zig-zag patterning is worked in Florentine Stitch, which covers the canvas solidly with small blocks of stitches over 4 threads of the canvas, to give an attractive and hardwearing texture.

Materials Required

1.60 m (1¾ yd) of 68 cm (27 in) wide Turkey Brown Check Canvas.
30 (50 g) skeins Patons Turkey Rug Wool: 9 skeins Lt Tan 863; 7 skeins each Scarlet 850, Marigold 838 and Orange 837.
Rug needle.

The finished size of the rug is 68 × 142 cm (27 × 56 in).

Instructions

Turn under about 8 cm (3 in) across one cut end of canvas and, omitting spare thread on folded edge (fringe is worked over this later), work first few rows through double thickness. The pattern gives half the design and one repeat of stripe in depth. Each upright block of 4 small squares on pattern represents a Florentine Stitch (see chapter 1) worked over 4 threads of canvas.

To complete each row, work to centre stitch (arrowed), then work back from centre stitch to end, noting that 1 hole of canvas will be left unworked at end of every row (this is taken in with Binding stitch later).

Start work at lower left corner of canvas with first row of Lt Tan points, (see arrow on pattern), first stitch over first 4 double threads up from folded edge of canvas. Follow in rows with the colours indicated on pattern and repeat downwards below first row of Lt Tan stitches to fill in lower triangles of each point, as shown on pattern.

The 4 full rows are repeated up canvas until the 11th row of Lt Tan points has been worked, but before reaching the end of design, count off numbers of threads required to complete rug and, allowing spare thread on folded edge for fringe, turn under spare canvas and work last few rows through double thickness as at beginning. Repeat rows of colours to fill in each triangle across top of rug.
Using Lt Tan, work Binding Stitch over each selvedge

(diagram 1), taking in spare hole of canvas up right side by folding selvedge over on top of this and binding over doubled canvas, pulling the wool as tightly as possible.

Cut remaining wool into 20 cm (8 in) lengths and fringe ends over spare thread (diagram 2). Press finished rug on wrong side under a damp cloth.

Bokhara Rug

Bokhara, capital and forbidden city of the old province of Turkestan, gives its name to a particular type of rich, colourful carpet. The growing popularity of these designs is due to their beauty of colour and simplicity of design, indicative in some ways of the wild and colourful life of this nomadic people.

The original Bokhara designs were beautifully hand-woven by nomads, and brought warmth, colour and comfort into their primitive homes. Their carpets and camel rugs used the limited materials available from their flocks, and the colouring dyes were obtained from the scant vegetation of the impoverished land. Designs show a wonderful consistency of pure traditional design, tribal custom and colour over the centuries.

One of the easiest to recognize among oriental carpets, Bokharas are made up principally of octagonal and diamond forms, and the colouring is usually a rich crimson interspersed with black, gold or cream. Although generally termed Bokharas, these rugs were often made hundreds of miles from the city itself and sold there by returning nomads.

Materials Required

2 m (2¼ yd) of 90 cm (36 in) wide Patons Brown Check Canvas.
50 skeins Patons Turkey Rug Wool as follows:
22 skeins Dk Rose 990; 11 skeins Lt Biscuit 973; 10 skeins Black 52; 4 skeins Brick Dust 910 and 3 skeins Cardinal 924.
Rug needle.

The finished size of the rug is 91 × 182 cm (36 × 72 in).
Starting and Finishing notes are given on page 165. Read these before beginning. Design is worked in Single Cross Stitch throughout. See diagram on page 22. The pattern gives just over a quarter of the design, and each square equals a stitch on the canvas.

Instructions

To complete each row, work back from centre stitch arrowed. Note that colour of stitches in centre medallions is reversed on right-hand side of centre Black line: work Brick Dust stitches in Cardinal and Cardinal stitches in Brick Dust. See extensions on pattern.

To complete other half of rug, work back as follows: for Border, work the 27 Border stitches marked by centre dotted row at top left on pattern. For Centre Panel, work from centre line marked at

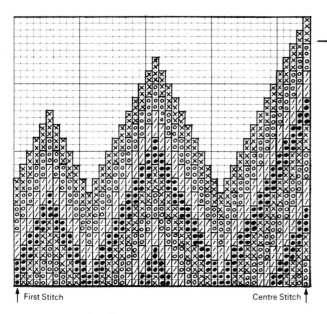

Pattern for Florentine Rug

Key to Pattern

 863   838

 850 837

Diagram 1 Binding Stitch

Diagram 2 Fringing

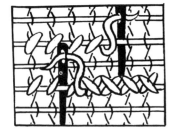

Diagram 3

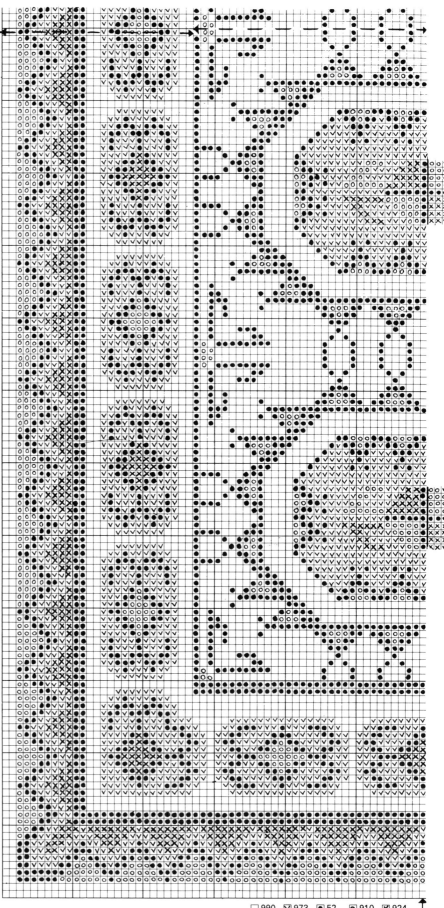

Pattern for Bokhara Rug

☐ 990 ☑ 973 ● 52 ◉ 910 ☒ 924

Bokhara Rug

Patchwork Rug and Crochet Rug

top right.

The 3 rows given above these lines are to clarify the continuation of the design. It is advisable to work the design first, then fill in Dk Rose background later. Finish as described on page 165, working Binding Stitch and oversewing in Dk Rose.

Knitted Patchwork Design Rug

Materials Required

35 (50 g) skeins Patons Turkey Rug Wool: 11 skeins Black 52; 6 skeins each Lt Biscuit 973, Peacock 895, Flame 836 and Marigold 838.
Pair of size 00 needles.
Note: Octagonal patches can be made from oddments of double knitting wool by using 6 strands together.

Measurements

Approximately 68 × 130 cm (27 × 51 in).

Abbreviations

k – knit; st(s) – stitch(es); sl – slip; psso – pass slipped stitch over; tog – together.

Octagonal Patches

Make 8 from each of the 4 colours, ie 32 patches.
1st Row: Cast on 7 sts and k 1 row.
Working in Garter Stitch throughout, ie every row k, work as follows: Increase 1 st at each end of next and every alternate row until there are 15 sts.
K 10 rows. Decrease 1 st at each end of next and every alternate row until 7 sts remain. Cast off.

Black Diamond Shapes (Make 21)

1st Row: Cast on 2 sts and k 1 row.
2nd Row: Increase in first stitch, k 1.
3rd Row: Knit.
Continue in Garter Stitch, increasing 1 st at each end of next and every alternate row until there are 9 sts. K 2 rows.
Decrease 1 st at each end of next and every alternate row until 3 sts remain. K 1 row.
Next Row: sl 1, k 2 tog, psso. Fasten off.
End Borders: Make 2. Cast on 73 sts and k 3 rows.
Next Row: k 9, turn. *Continue on these 9 sts, decreasing 1 st at each end of next and every alternate row until 3 sts remain. K 1 row.
Next Row: sl 1, k 2 tog, psso. Fasten off. Rejoin wool to remaining sts and cast off 7 sts (1 st on needle after cast off). K 8, turn*. Repeat from * to * 3 times more.
Decrease 1 st at each end of next and every alternate row until 3 sts remain. K 1 row.
Next Row: sl 1, k 2 tog, psso. Fasten off.

Side Borders: Make 2. Cast on 2 sts and k 2 rows.
Next Row: Increase in first st, k 1. K 1 row. Increase 1 st at beg of next row: 4 sts. K 11 rows.
Increase 1 st at beg of next and every alternate row until there are 8 sts. K 1 row. Decrease 1 st at beg of next and every alternate row until 4 sts remain. K 11 rows. Repeat from * to * 6 times more.
Decrease 1 st at beg of next and every alternate row until 1 st remains.
Fasten off.

Making Up

Using a Flat Seam (see page 11) and Black wool, join the straight edges of each octagonal patch together, arranging colours as shown in illustration. Now stitch a Black diamond between each patch. Stitch end and side borders in position.

Using a warm iron and damp cloth, press rug carefully on wrong side. Using Black wool, work a line of Back Stitch (see page 20) over straight seams only, between the octagonal patches. The stitching is not worked where patches join the Black diamonds.

Striped Crochet Rug

Materials Required

30 (50 g) skeins Patons Turkey Rug Wool: 8 skeins Wedgwood 966; 7 skeins each Old Gold 964 and White 501; 4 skeins each Cardinal 924 and Scarlet 850.
No. 6.00 mm (4) Milward Disc hook.

Measurements

61 × 127 cm (24 × 50 in), including fringes.

Abbreviations

ch – chain; dc – double crochet; B – Wedgwood; R – Cardinal; W – White; G – Old Gold; S – Scarlet.

Instructions

Using B, make 70 ch.
Foundation Row: 1 dc in 2nd ch from hook, * 1 ch, miss 1 ch, 1 dc in next ch; repeat from * to end.
1st Row: * 1 ch, 1 dc in next 1 ch space of previous row; repeat from * to end. Repeat 1st row twice more. Break B.
Repeating 1st row throughout work in stripes as follows: 4 rows R; 4 rows W; 4 rows G; 4 rows B; 4 rows S; 4 rows W; 4 rows G; 4 rows B.
Repeat last 32 rows 3 times more. Fasten off.
Cut remaining wool into 15 cm (6 in) lengths and fringe ends by folding each length in half and knotting through every stitch. Press finished rug on wrong side under a damp cloth.

Chapter 11

Here are some colourful crochet designs which would brighten up any nursery or bedroom. Once you have mastered the basic crochet stitches given in Chapter 1, you will find it quite easy to make them. Children will love the 'Parachute' Lampshade Cover, from which their favourite toy can be hung, while the detail on the House Panel will charm any little boy or girl. Add a special touch with the Owl Picture or the Filet Curtain, or make the useful and decorative Pyjama Case.

House Panel

Materials Required

Coats Chain Mercer-Crochet Cotton No. 20 (20 g). 3 balls Carnation Pink 693, 1 ball each of Dk. Jade 524, Pale Lavender 690, Tan 477, Brown 579, Cream 602, Lt. Navy Blue Spec. 8749, Turkey Red 700, Parrot Green 463, Straw Yellow 582, and Marigold 538. This model is worked in these eleven shades, but any other shades of Mercer-Crochet may be used.
Milward steel crochet hook 1.25 (no. 3).
Piece of navy blue felt 51 × 49.5 (20 × $19\frac{1}{2}$ in).
Coats Drima (polyester) thread.

Tension

1 brick — 1.6 × 2.5 cm ($\frac{5}{8}$ × 1 in).

Measurements

51 × 24 cm (20 × $9\frac{1}{2}$ in).

Lower Section (Bricks)

Using Carnation Pink commence with 9 ch.
1st Row: 1 dc into 2nd ch from hook, 1 dc into each ch, (1 ch, turn, 1 dc into each of next 8 dc) 6 times, 1 ch, turn (a half brick made at beginning of row), * 1 dc into first dc, 6 ch, miss 6 dc, 1 dc into next dc, 1 ch, turn, 1 dc into first dc, 1 dc into each of next 6 ch, 1 dc into next dc, (1 ch, turn, 1 dc into each of next 8 dc) 10 times, 1 ch, turn (a brick made); repeat from * 8 times more, 1 dc into each of next 8 dc, 9 ch, turn.
2nd Row: 1 dc into 2nd ch from hook, 1 dc into each ch, (1 ch, turn, 1 dc into each of next 8 dc) 6 times, miss 6 rows of last brick made on previous row, 1 ss into next row end, 1 ch, turn (a half brick joined at beginning of row), * 1 dc into first dc, 6 ch, miss 6 dc, 1 dc into next dc, 1 ch, turn, 1 dc into first dc, 1 dc into each of next 6 ch, 1 dc into next dc, (1 ch, turn, 1 dc into each of next 8 dc) 10 times, miss 5 rows of next brick on previous row, 1 ss into next row end, 1 ch, turn (a brick joined); repeat

from * 8 times more, joining last brick to end half brick to correspond, 1 dc into each of next 8 dc, 9 ch, turn.

Make 3 more rows of bricks as 2nd row.

6th Row (Divide for Windows): 1 dc into 2nd ch from hook, 1 dc into each ch, (1 ch, turn, 1 dc into each of next 8 dc) 6 times, miss 6 rows of last brick made on previous row, 1 ss into next row end, 1 ch, turn, 1 dc into first dc, 6 ch, miss 6 dc, 1 dc into next dc, 1 ch, turn, 1 dc into first dc, 1 dc into each of next 6 ch, 1 dc into next dc, (1 ch, turn, 1 dc into each of next 8 dc) twice, miss 4 rows of brick on previous row, 1 ss into next row end, 1 ch, turn, 1 dc into each of next 8 dc, 9 ch, turn.

7th Row: 1 dc into 2nd ch from hook, 1 dc into each ch, (1 ch, turn, 1 dc into each of next 8 dc) 10 times, miss 6 rows of half brick on previous row, 1 ss into next row end, 1 ch, turn, 1 dc into each of next 8 dc, 9 ch, turn.

8th Row: As 6th row of bricks omitting turning ch. Fasten off.

6th Row (continued): Miss 1 brick and 10 rows of next brick on 5th row, attach thread to next row end, 9 ch, turn, ** 1 dc into 2nd ch from hook, 1 dc into each ch, (1 ch, turn, 1 dc into each of next 8 dc) 6 times, miss 5 rows of next brick on 5th row, 1 ss into next row end, 1 ch, turn, * 1 dc into first dc, 6 ch, miss 6 dc, 1 dc into next dc, 1 ch, turn, 1 dc into first dc, 1 into each of next 6 ch, 1 dc into next dc, (1 ch, turn, 1 dc into each of next 8 dc) 10 times, miss 5 rows of next brick on 5th row, 1 ss into next row end, 1 ch, turn; repeat from * twice more, 1 dc into each of next 8 dc, 9 ch, turn; repeat from ** twice more omitting turning ch at end of row. Fasten off.

6th Row (continued): Miss next brick and 5 rows of following brick on 5th row, attach thread to next row end, 9 ch, turn and work as 7th row of bricks.

7th Row (continued): As 8th row of bricks (first section) turning with 9 ch at end of last row.

8th Row: As 7th row of bricks (first section).

9th Row: As 1st row of bricks joining where necessary, turning with 1 ch at end of row.

10th Row: Working across row ends, 1 dc into each row end. Fasten off. Using Pale Lavender make 2 ch and leave aside.

11th Row: Attach Pale Lavender to last dc, 4 ch, turn, 1 tr into 4th ch from hook, 1 tr into each dc, attach length of ch already worked to last dc, 1 tr into each of next 2 ch. Fasten off.

Middle Section

1st and 2nd Rows: As 1st and 2nd rows of Lower Section.

3rd Row (Divide for Window): 1 dc into 2nd ch from hook, 1 dc into each ch, (1 ch, turn, 1 dc into each of next 8 dc) 6 times, miss 6 rows of last brick made, 1 ss into next row end, 1 ch, turn, * 1 dc into first dc, 6 ch, miss 6 dc, 1 dc into next dc, 1 ch,

turn, 1 dc into first dc, 1 dc into each of next 6 ch, 1 dc into next dc, (1 ch, turn, 1 dc into each of next 8 dc) 10 times, miss 5 rows of next brick on previous row, 1 ss into next row end, 1 ch, turn; repeat from * once more, 1 dc into first dc, 6 ch, miss 6 dc, 1 dc into next dc, 1 ch, turn, 1 dc into first dc, 1 dc into each of next 6 ch, 1 dc into next dc, (1 ch, turn, 1 dc into each of next 8 dc) twice, miss 5 rows of same brick on previous row, 1 ss into next row end, 1 ch, turn, 1 dc into each of next 8 dc, 9 ch, turn.

4th Row: 1 dc into 2nd ch from hook, 1 dc into each ch, (1 ch, turn, 1 dc into each of next 8 dc) 10 times, * miss 5 rows of next brick on previous row, 1 ss into next row end, 1 ch, turn, 1 dc into first dc, 6 ch, miss 6 dc, 1 dc into next dc, 1 ch, turn, 1 dc into first dc, 1 dc into each of next 6 ch, 1 dc into next dc, (1 ch, turn, 1 dc into each of next 8 dc) 10 times; repeat from * once more, miss 6 rows on half brick, 1 ss into next row end, 1 ch, turn, 1 dc into each of next 8 dc, 9 ch, turn.

5th Row: As 3rd row of bricks omitting turning ch at end of last row. Fasten off.

3rd Row (continued): Miss 3 bricks and 5 rows of next brick on 2nd row, attach thread to next row end, 9 ch, turn and work as 4th row of bricks.

4th Row (continued): As 3rd row of bricks (first side).

5th Row (continued): As 3rd row of bricks (second side).

6th Row: As 1st row of bricks joining where necessary, turning with 1 ch at end of row.

7th Row: As 10th row of Lower Section.

8th Row: As 11th row of Lower Section.

Top Section

Work as Middle Section for 6 rows.

7th Row: As 2nd row of bricks.

8th Row: As 10th row of Lower Section.

Shutter (make 4)

Using Dk. Jade commence with 9 ch.

1st Row: 3 dc into 2nd ch from hook, 1 dc into each of next 6 ch, 6 dc into next ch, work along opposite side of foundation ch, 1 dc into each of next 6 ch, 3 dc into next ch, working into back loop only 1 ss into first dc. Work into back loop only of each dc.

2nd Row: 1 dc into same place as ss, * 3 dc into next dc, 1 dc into each of next 8 dc, 3 dc into next dc, 1 dc into each of next 2 dc; repeat from * once more omitting 1 dc at end of repeat, 1 ss into first dc.

3rd Row: 1 dc into same place as ss, 1 dc into next dc, * 3 dc into next dc (centre dc at corner), 1 dc into each of next 10 dc, 3 dc into next dc (centre dc at corner), 1 dc into each of next 4 dc; repeat from * once more omitting 1 dc at end of repeat, 1 ss into first dc. Continue in this manner for 8 rows more having 2 dc more between corners on each row. Fasten off.

House Panel

Window Sill (make 2)

Using Pale Lavender commence with 31 ch.
1st Row: 1 dc into 2nd ch from hook, 1 dc into each ch, 1 ch, turn.
2nd and 3rd Rows: 1 dc into each dc, 1 ch, turn.
4th Row: 1 dc into each dc. Fasten off.

Window Box (make 2)

Using Tan commence with 36 ch.
1st Row: 1 dc into 2nd ch from hook, 1 dc into each ch, 1 ch, turn.
2nd Row: 2 dc into first dc, 1 dc into each dc to within last dc, 2 dc into last dc, 1 ch, turn.
Repeat last row 6 times more omitting turning ch at end of last row. Fasten off.

Leaf (make 8)

Using Parrot Green commence with 15 ch.
1st Row: 1 dc into 2nd ch from hook, 1 dc into each ch to within last ch, 3 dc into last ch (tip of leaf), 1 dc into each ch along opposite side of foundation ch, 1 dc into same place as last dc. Hereafter work into back loop only of each dc, 1 dc into each of next 11 dc, 1 ch, turn.
2nd Row: 1 dc into each dc to within centre dc of 3 dc group, into next dc work 1 dc 1 ch and 1 dc, 1 dc into each dc on other side to within last 4 dc from centre dc at tip of leaf, 1 ch, turn.
3rd Row: 1 dc into each dc to within 1 ch sp, into sp work 1 dc 1 ch and 1 dc, 1 dc into each dc on other side to within last 3 dc, 1 ch, turn.
4th Row: As 3rd row omitting turning ch. Fasten off.

Small Flower (make 2)

Using Straw Yellow commence with 7 ch, join with a ss to form a ring.
1st Row: 18 dc into ring, 1 ss into first dc.
2nd Row: 1 dc into same place as ss, * 3 ch, miss 2 dc, 1 dc into next dc; repeat from * omitting 1 dc at end of last repeat, 1 ss into first dc.
3rd Row: Into each loop work 1 dc 1 hlf tr 3 tr 1 hlf tr and 1 dc, 1 ss into first dc of previous row inserting hook from behind.
4th Row: 1 dc into same place as ss, * 4 ch, 1 dc into next dc on 2nd row inserting hook from behind; repeat from * 4 times more, 4 ch.
5th Row: Into each loop work 1 dc 1 hlf tr 5 tr 1 hlf tr and 1 dc, 1 ss into first dc. Fasten off.
6th Row: Attach Marigold to first hlf tr worked on previous row, 1 dc into same place as join, * (2 ch, 1 dc into next st) 6 times, 2 ch, (insert hook into next dc and draw thread through) twice, thread over and draw through all loops on hook, 2 ch, 1 dc into next hlf tr; repeat from * omitting 1 dc at end of last repeat, 1 ss into first dc. Fasten off.

Large Flower (make 2)

Work as small flower for 1 row. Fasten off.

2nd Row: Attach Marigold to same place as ss, 1 dc into same place as join, * 3 ch, miss 2 dc, 1 dc into next dc; repeat from * omitting 1 dc at end of last repeat, 1 ss into first dc.
3rd and 4th Rows: As 3rd and 4th rows of small flower.
5th Row: Into each loop work 1 dc 1 hlf tr 5 tr 1 hlf tr and 1 dc, 1 ss into first dc worked on 4th row.
6th Row: * 5 ch, 1 dc into next dc on 4th row; repeat from * 4 times more, 5 ch.
7th Row: As 5th row of small flower.
8th Row: Attach Straw Yellow to first hlf tr worked on previous row and work as 6th row of small flower.

Stems

Using Parrot Green make 4 lengths of braid 2.5 cm (1 in) long.

Braid

Commence with 2 ch, then holding this between the finger and thumb of the left hand work 1 dc into the first ch made (Diagram 1), turn, 1 dc into foundation loop of 2nd ch made inserting hook into back loop (Diagram 2), * turn, insert hook into 2 loops at side (Diagram 3), thread over and draw loop through, thread over and draw through remaining 2 loops; repeat from * for length required. Fasten off.

Door

Using Brown commence with 57 ch.
1st Row: 1 hlf tr into 3rd ch from hook, 1 hlf tr into each ch, 2 ch, turn.
2nd Row: Working into back loop only, miss first hlf tr, 1 hlf tr into each hlf tr, 1 hlf tr into next ch, 2 ch, turn.

Repeat 2nd row 14 times more omitting turning ch at end of last row. Fasten off.

Door Frame

1st Row: With right side facing attach Tan to last hlf tr worked, 1 dc into same place as join, 1 dc into each hlf tr, 3 dc into next ch, 1 dc over each row end to within next corner, 3 dc into next ch, 1 dc into each ch, 1 ch, turn.
2nd Row: 1 dc into each dc working 3 dc into centre dc at each corner. Fasten off.

Small Window Frame (make 2)

1st Row: With right side facing and using Tan attach thread to lower left hand corner of window and work 24 dc across bricks, insert hook into next dc and draw thread through, insert hook into next row end and draw loop through, thread over and draw through all loops on hook (a corner made), work 23 dc across top of window, make a corner as before then 24 dc across

176

bricks, 1 ch, turn.
2nd Row: 1 dc into each of first 23 dc, a corner over next 2 dc, 1 dc into each of next 21 dc, a corner over next 2 dc, 1 dc into each of next 23 dc. Fasten off.

Large Window Frame (make 2)

Work as small window frame having 39 dc between corners at top of window on 1st row and 37 dc on 2nd row.

Curtains (make 8)

Using Cream commence with 13 ch.
1st Row: 1 dc into 2nd ch from hook, 1 dc into each ch, 1 ch, turn.
2nd Row: 1 dc into each dc, 1 ch, turn.
3rd Row: Miss first dc, 1 dc into each dc, 1 ch, turn.
4th Row: 1 dc into each dc, 1 ch, turn.
Repeat last 2 rows 10 times more omitting turning ch at end of last row. Fasten off.

Grass (make 2)

Using Parrot Green commence with 32 ch.
1st Row: 1 tr into 4th ch from hook, 1 tr into each ch, 3 ch, turn.
2nd Row: Miss first tr, 1 tr into each tr, 1 tr into next ch. Fasten off.

Steps

Using Lt. Navy Blue commence with 75 ch.
1st Row: 1 tr into 4th ch from hook, 1 tr into each ch. Fasten off.
2nd Row: Attach Pale Lavender to last tr worked, 3 ch, turn, 1 tr into each tr, 1 tr into next ch, turn. Fasten off.
3rd Row: Miss 8 tr on previous row, attach Lt. Navy Blue to next tr, 3 ch, 1 tr into each tr to within last 8 sts. Fasten off.
4th Row: Attach Pale Lavender to last tr worked, 3 ch, turn, 1 tr into each tr, 1 tr into next ch. Fasten off.

Repeat last 2 rows once more turning with 3 ch at end of last row.

7th Row: Miss first tr, 1 tr into each tr, 1 tr into next ch. Fasten off.

Roof — First Row of Tiles

Using Turkey Red commence with 121 ch.
1st Row (wrong side): 1 dc into 2nd ch from hook, 1 dc into each ch, 1 ch, turn.
2nd to 5th Row: 1 dc into each dc, 1 ch, turn.
6th to 9th Row: 1 dc into each of first 12 dc, 1 ch, turn.
10th to 14th Row: Miss first dc, 1 dc into each dc, 1 ch, turn.
15th Row: Miss first dc, 1 dc into each of next 6 dc. Fasten off. (one tile made)

With right side facing attach thread to next dc on 5th row, 1 dc into same place as join, 1 dc into each of next 11 dc, 1 ch, turn and complete tile as before.

Make 8 more tiles as second tile.

Second Row of Tiles

Using Turkey Red commence with 109 ch and work as first row having 9 tiles.

Third Row of Tiles

Using Turkey Red commence with 97 ch and work as first row having 8 tiles.

Fourth Row of Tiles

Using Turkey Red commence with 85 ch and work as first row having 7 tiles.

Fifth Row of Tiles

Using Turkey Red commence with 73 ch and work as first row having 6 tiles.

Flower Pot (make 2)

Using Turkey Red commence with 15 ch and work as tiles for 4 rows.
5th to 11th Row: As 10th row of tiles.
12th Row: As 15th row of tiles.

Door Handle

Using Marigold commence with 2 ch.
1st Row: 6 dc into 2nd ch from hook.
2nd Row: (2 dc into next dc, 1 dc into next dc) 3 times. Cut thread leaving sufficient to lace through last row, draw up and fasten off.

Chimney

1st Row: With right side of last row of tiles facing miss 6 ch, attach Turkey Red to next ch, 1 dc into same place as join, 1 dc into each of next 11 ch, 1 ch, turn.
2nd to 29th Row: 1 dc into each dc, 1 ch, turn.
30th Row: 1 dc into each dc. Fasten off.
Attach Turkey Red to 18th ch from opposite end of row and complete chimney as before.

Making Up

Sew in place the following pieces: — curtains, window boxes, shutters, window sills, door handle, door, steps, grass border, flowers in pots and roof. Sew together.

Fold felt in half with short ends meeting; taking 1.5 cm ($\frac{1}{2}$ in) seam, sew short ends together. Press seam flat and turn to right side. Place crochet house over felt and cut felt to shape of crochet at each corner. Baste and stitch all round felt 3 mm ($\frac{1}{8}$ in) from edge. Sew crochet house to felt.

Sew flowers into upper window spaces.

Filet Curtain

Filet Curtain

Materials Required

Coats Chain Mercer-Crochet Cotton No. 20 (20 g).
6 balls. This model is worked in shade 795 (Amber Gold), but any other shade of Mercer-Crochet may be used.
Milward steel crochet hook 1.25 (no. 3).
8 curtain rings.

Tension

5 blks and 5 sps – 2.5 cm (1 in).

Measurements

53 × 72.5 cm (21 × 28½ in).

First Point

Commence with 6 ch.
1st Row: 1 tr into 4th ch from hook, 1 tr into each of next 2 ch, 5 ch, turn.
2nd Row: 1 tr into 4th ch from hook, 1 tr into next ch, 1 tr into next tr (1 blk increased at beginning of row), 2 ch, miss 2 tr, make a foundation tr into next st – to make a foundation tr, thread over hook, insert hook into next st and draw loop through, thread over and draw through 1 loop, thus making a ch st, thread over and complete as tr, make 3 more foundation tr by inserting hook into ch of previous

foundation tr (1 extension blk made at end of row), 5 ch, turn.
3rd Row: 1 increase blk, 2 ch, miss 2 tr, 1 tr into next tr (sp made over blk), 2 ch, miss 2 ch, 1 tr into next tr (sp made over sp), 1 sp, 1 extension blk, 5 ch, turn.
4th Row: 1 increase blk, 5 sps, 1 extension blk, 5 ch, turn.
5th Row: 1 increase blk, 3 sps, 2 tr into next sp, 1 tr into next tr (blk made over sp), 3 sps, 1 extension blk, 5 ch. Fasten off.

Second Point

Work as first point for 4 rows.
5th Row: Remove loop from hook, insert hook into 5th of 5 ch on last row of previous point and draw dropped loop through (joining made), 1 increase blk and complete as first point.

Make 11 more points in this manner turning with 8 ch at end of last point.

6th Row: 2 increase blks, (3 sps, 1 blk, 1 sp, 1 blk, 3 sps, 1 tr into each of next 5 ch, 1 tr into next tr) 12 times, 3 sps, 1 blk, 1 sp, 1 blk, 3 sps, 2 extension blks, 5 ch, turn.
7th Row: Follow pattern, turn.

179

Owl Picture

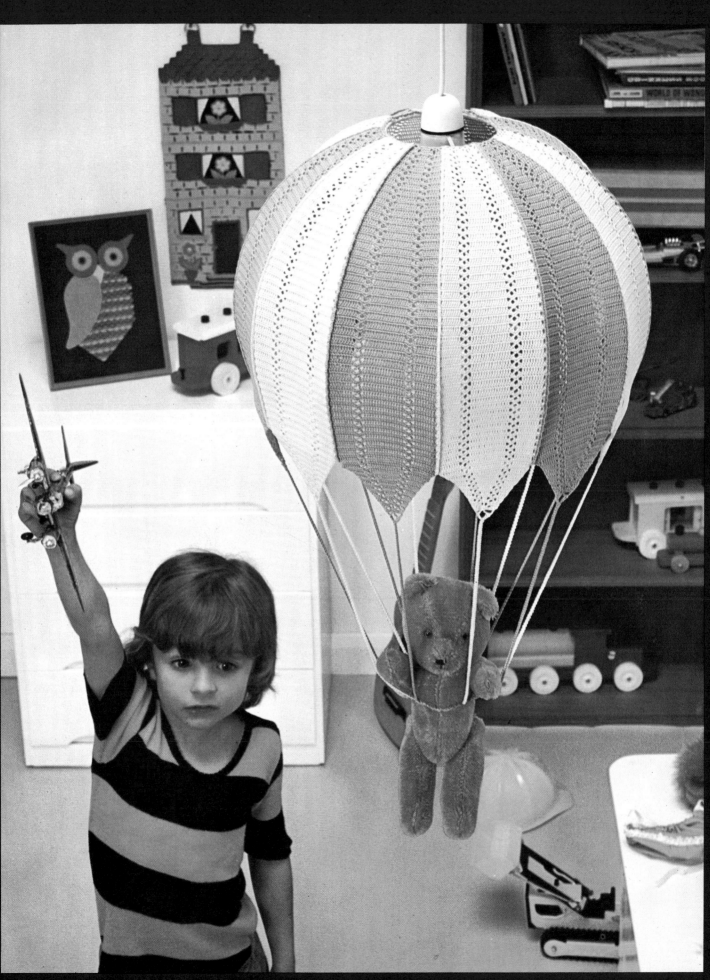

Lampshade Cover

Key to Pattern

⬒	Shell	
◨	Half Shell	Yellow
◖	DC	

⬒	Shell	
◪	Half Shell	Green
◪	DC	

⬒	Shell	
◩	Half Shell	Orange
◪	DC	

Close-up, Owl Picture

Pattern for Owl Picture

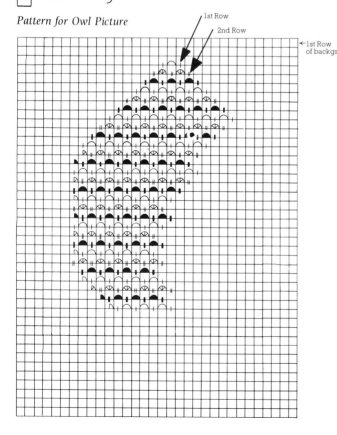

8th Row: 1 ss into each of first 4 tr (1 blk decreased at beginning of row), 3 ch, 2 tr into next sp, 1 tr into next tr (blk made over sp at beginning of row), 2 sps, 1 tr into each of next 3 tr (blk made over blk), 2 sps and continue to follow pattern to end of row, turn.

Follow pattern from 9th to 104th row turning with 5 ch at end of last row.

105th Row: Miss first 3 sts, 1 tr into next st, * 1 blk, 4 ch, 1 dc into 2nd ch from hook, 1 dc into each of next 2 ch, (1 ch, turn, 1 dc into each dc) twice, 1 blk, 1 sp; repeat from * to end of row. Fasten off.

Damp and pin out to measurements.

Space rings evenly and sew to last row.

Owl Picture

Materials Required

Coats Chain Mercer-Crochet Cotton No. 20 (20 g).
1 ball each Tangerine 687, Dk. Buttercup 962, Parrot Green 463, and 2 balls Brown 579. This model is worked in these four shades, but any other shades of Mercer-Crochet may be used.
Milward steel crochet hook 1.50 (no. 2½).
Piece of cardboard 30 × 23 cm (12 × 9 in).
40 cm (⅜ yd) fabric 90 cm (approx. 36 in) wide for covering cardboard.
Coats Drima polyester thread.

Tension

4 sps and 4 rows — 2.5 cm (1 in).

Measurements

Finished size of crochet background — 20 × 25 cm (8 × 10 in).
Thread is used double throughout.

Background

Using Brown commence with 101 ch.
1st Row: (right side): 1 tr into 8th ch from hook, * 2 ch, miss 2 ch, 1 tr into next ch; repeat from * ending with 5 ch, turn. (32 sps made)
2nd Row: Miss first tr, 1 tr into next tr, * 2 ch, miss 2 sts, 1 tr into next st; repeat from * ending with 5 ch, turn.

Repeat last row 40 times more. Fasten off.

Body

1st Row: Using Dk. Buttercup attach thread to sp marked by arrow on pattern, 1 dc into same sp as join, into next sp work 1 tr 3 dbl tr and 1 tr (a shell made), 1 dc into next sp. Fasten off Dk. Buttercup.
2nd Row: Using Parrot Green attach thread to sp

marked by arrow on pattern, 1 dc into same sp as join, (a shell into next sp, 1 dc into next sp) twice. Fasten off Parrot Green.

Continue to follow pattern for 8 rows more.

11th Row: Using Parrot Green attach thread to sp as shown on pattern, 1 dc into same sp, (a shell into next sp, 1 dc into next sp) 6 times, into next sp work 1 tr and 2 dbl tr (a half shell made). Fasten off Parrot Green.

Continue to follow pattern from 12th to 28th row. Fasten off.

Wing

Using Parrot Green commence with 13 ch.

1st Row: (right side): 2 tr into 4th ch from hook, 1 tr into each of next 8 ch, 3 tr into next ch, 1 ch, turn.

2nd Row: 1 dc into each tr, 1 dc into next st, 3 ch, turn.

3rd Row: Working into back loop only 2 tr into first dc, 1 tr into each dc to within last dc, 3 tr into next dc, 1 ch, turn.

Repeat last 2 rows twice more then 2nd row again.

9th Row: Working into back loop only miss first dc, 1 tr into each dc, 1 ch, turn.

10th Row: As 2nd row.

Repeat last 2 rows once more turning with 2 ch at end of last row.

13th Row: Working into back loop only 1 tr into first dc, 1 tr into each dc to within last 2 dc, leaving the last loop of each on hook work 1 tr into each of next 2 dc, thread over and draw through all loops on hook (a joint tr made over 2 sts), 1 ch, turn.

14th Row: 1 dc into first st, 1 dc into each tr, 2 ch, turn.

Repeat last 2 rows twice more turning with 3 ch at end of last row.

19th Row: Working into back loop only miss first dc, 1 tr into each dc to within last 3 dc, leaving the last loop of each on hook work 1 tr into each of next 3 dc, thread over and draw through all loops on hook (a joint tr made over 3 sts), 1 ch, turn.

20th Row: 1 dc into first st, 1 dc into each tr, 1 dc into next st, 3 ch, turn.

Repeat last 2 rows once more turning with 1 ch at end of last row.

23rd Row: Working into back loop only 1 dc into each of first 6 dc, 1 hlf tr into each of next 3 dc, 1 tr into each of next 4 dc, a joint tr over next 3 dc, 1 ch, turn.

24th Row: 1 dc into each st, 1 ch, turn.

25th Row: Working into back loop only 1 dc into each of first 6 sts, 1 hlf tr into each of next 3 sts, 1 tr into each of next 2 sts, a joint tr over next 3 sts, 1 ch, turn.

26th Row: As 24th row.

27th Row: Working into back loop only 1 dc into each of first 4 sts, 1 hlf tr into each of next 2 sts, 1 tr into each of next 3 sts, a joint tr over next 3 sts, 1 ch, turn.

28th Row: As 24th row.

29th Row: Working into back loop only 1 dc into each of first 4 sts, 1 hlf tr into each of next 2 sts, 1 tr into next st, a joint tr over next 3 sts, 1 ch, turn.

30th Row: As 24th row.

31st Row: Working into back loop only 1 dc into each of first 2 sts, 1 hlf tr into each of next 2 sts, 1 tr into next st, a joint tr over next 3 sts, 1 ch, turn.

32nd Row: As 24th row.

33rd Row: Working into back loop only 1 dc into each of first 2 sts, 1 hlf tr into next st, a joint tr over next 3 sts, 1 ch, turn.

34th Row: 1 dc into each st, 2 ch, turn.

35th Row: Working into back loop only miss first st and leaving the last loop of each on hook work 1 tr into each of next 3 sts, thread over and draw through all loops on hook and continuing to work over row ends work a row of dc neatly round wing ending with 1 ss into first dc. Fasten off.

Left Eye

Using Brown commence with 2 ch.

1st Row: 6 dc into second ch from hook, 1 ss into first dc.

2nd Row: 2 dc into same place as ss, 2 dc into each dc, 1 ss into first dc. Fasten off Brown.

3rd Row: Attach Parrot Green to same place as last ss, 2 dc into same place as join, * 1 dc into next dc, 2 dc into next dc; repeat from * ending with 1 dc into next dc, 1 ss into first dc. Fasten off Parrot Green.

4th Row: Attach Dk. Buttercup to same place as last ss, 2 dc into same place as join, * 1 dc into each of next 2 dc, 2 dc into next dc; repeat from * ending with 1 dc into each of next 2 dc, 1 ss into first dc.

5th Row: 2 dc into same place as ss, * 1 dc into each of next 3 dc, 2 dc into next dc; repeat from * ending with 1 dc into each of next 3 dc, 1 ss into first dc. Continue in this manner for 2 rows more increasing 6 sts on each row and having 1 dc more between each increase on each row. Fasten off Dk. Buttercup.

8th Row: Attach Tangerine to same place as last ss, 2 dc into same place as join, * 1 dc into each of next 6 dc, 2 dc into next dc; repeat from * ending with 1 dc into each of next 6 dc, 1 ss into first dc.

Continue increasing as before for 3 rows more.

Ear

1st Row: 1 dc into same place as ss, 1 dc into each of next 6 dc, 1 ch. turn.

2nd Row: 1 dc into each of first 4 dc, (insert hook into next st and draw thread through) 3 times, thread over and draw through all loops on hook, 1 ch, turn.
3rd Row: 1 dc into each st, 1 ch, turn.
4th Row: 1 dc into each of first 3 dc, (insert hook into next st and draw thread through) twice, thread over and draw through all loops on hook (a joint dc made over 2 sts), 1 ch, turn.
5th Row: As 3rd row.
6th Row: 1 dc into each of first 2 sts, a joint dc over next 2 sts, 1 ch, turn.
7th Row: As 3rd row.
8th Row: 1 dc into first dc, a joint dc over next 2 sts, 1 ch, turn.
9th Row: As 3rd row.
10th Row: A joint dc over first 2 sts. Fasten off.

Right Eye

Work as left eye for 11 rows.

Ear

1st Row: 1 dc into same place as ss, 1 dc into each of next 6 dc, 1 ch, turn.
2nd Row: Insert hook into first dc and draw thread through (insert hook into next dc and draw thread through) twice, thread over and draw through all loops on hook, 1 dc into each dc, 1 ch, turn.
3rd Row: 1 dc into each dc, 1 ch, turn.
4th Row: A joint dc over first 2 sts, 1 dc into each dc, 1 ch, turn.

Repeat 3rd and 4th rows twice more then 3rd row again.

10th Row: A joint dc over first 2 sts. Fasten off.

Beak

Using Dk. Buttercup commence with 11 ch.
1st Row (right side): 1 dc into 2nd ch from hook, 1 dc into each ch, 1 ch, turn.
2nd and 3rd Rows: 1 dc into each st, 1 ch, turn.
4th Row: A joint dc over first 2 sts, 1 dc into each dc to within last 2 dc, a joint dc over next 2 sts, 1 ch, turn.
5th Row: As 2nd row.

Repeat 4th and 5th rows twice more.

10th Row: A joint dc over first 2 sts, a joint dc over next 2 sts, 1 ch, turn.
11th Row: As 2nd row.
12th Row: A joint dc over first 2 sts. Fasten off.

Damp and pin out to measurements.

Making Up

Cut one piece from fabric 41 × 33 cm (16 × 13 in). Place background centrally to fabric and sew in

position. Place wing, eyes and beak to background and sew in position. Place the fabric centrally over the cardboard, fold the surplus fabric to the back and secure at top with pins into the edge of the board. Pull firmly over the lower edge and pin in position. Repeat on side edges pulling fabric until it lies taut on the board. Secure at the back by lacing from side to side, vertically and horizontally with strong thread. Remove pins.
Frame if desired.

Lampshade Cover

Materials Required

Coats Chain Mercer-Crochet Cotton No. 20 (20 g).
4 balls each Parrot Green 463 and Straw Yellow 582. This model is worked in these two shades, but any other shades of Mercer-Crochet may be used.
Milward steel crochet hook 1.25 (no. 3) and 1.50 (no. 2½).
Tiffany lampshade frame 28.5 cm (11¼ in) deep.
Bias binding for binding frame.
Soft toy.

Tension

First 8 rows – 2.5 cm (1 in).

Measurements

To fit lampshade 28.5 cm (11¼ in) deep and 99 cm (39 in) in circumference.

First Strip

Using Straw Yellow and 1.25 (no. 3) hook commence with 4 ch.
1st Row: 1 tr into 4th ch from hook, (3 ch, 1 tr into top of last tr) 4 times, turn.
2nd Row (wrong side): 1 ss into first loop, 3 ch, 2 tr into same loop, * into next loop work 1 tr 3 ch and 1 tr (a V st made), 3 tr into next loop; repeat from * ending with 1 ch, turn.
3rd Row: 1 dc into each of first 4 tr, 3 dc into next sp, 1 dc into each of next 5 tr, 3 dc into next sp, 1 dc into each of next 4 sts, 3 ch, turn.
4th Row: Miss first dc, 1 tr into each of next 2 dc, miss 2 dc, a V st into next dc, miss 2 dc, 1 tr into each of next 3 dc, miss 2 dc, a V st into next dc, miss 2 dc, 1 tr into each of next 3 dc, 1 ch, turn.

Repeat 3rd and 4th rows once more then 3rd row again.

8th Row: 1 tr into first dc, 1 tr into each of next 2 dc, miss 2 dc, a V st into next dc, miss 2 dc, 2 tr into next dc, 1 tr into next dc, 2 tr into next dc, miss 2 dc, a V st into next dc, miss 2 dc, 1 tr into each of next 2 dc, 2 tr into next dc, 1 ch, turn.
9th Row: 1 dc into each of first 5 tr, 3 dc into next

sp, 1 dc into each of next 7 tr, 3 dc into next sp, 1 dc into each of next 5 sts, 3 ch, turn.

10th Row: Miss first dc, 1 tr into each of next 3 dc, miss 2 dc, a V st into next dc, miss 2 dc, 1 tr into each of next 5 dc, miss 2 dc, a V st into next dc, miss 2 dc, 1 tr into each of next 4 dc, 1 ch, turn.

Repeat 9th and 10th rows once more then 9th row again.

14th Row: 1 tr into first dc, 1 tr into each of next 3 dc, miss 2 dc, a V st into next dc, miss 2 dc, 2 tr into next dc, 1 tr into each of next 3 dc, 2 tr into next dc, miss 2 dc, a V st into next dc, miss 2 dc, 1 tr into each of next 3 dc, 2 tr into next dc, 1 ch, turn.

15th Row: 1 dc into each of first 6 tr, 3 dc into next sp, 1 dc into each of next 9 tr, 3 dc into next sp, 1 dc into each of next 6 sts, 3 ch, turn.

16th Row: Miss first dc, 1 tr into each of next 4 dc, miss 2 dc, a V st into next dc, miss 2 dc, 1 tr into each of next 7 dc, miss 2 dc, a V st into next dc, miss 2 dc, 1 tr into each of next 5 dc, 1 ch, turn.

Repeat 15th and 16th rows once more then 15th row again.

Continue in this manner for 19 rows more increasing 4 sts as before on each increase row.

39th Row: 1 dc into each of first 10 tr, 3 dc into next sp, 1 dc into each of next 17 tr, 3 dc into next sp, 1 tr into each of next 10 sts, 3 ch, turn.

40th Row: Miss first dc, 1 tr into each of next 8 dc, miss 2 dc, a V st into next dc, miss 2 dc, 1 tr into each of next 15 dc, miss 2 dc, a V st into next dc, miss 2 dc, 1 tr into each of next 9 dc, 1 ch, turn.

Repeat last 2 rows 4 times more.

Change to 1.50 (no. 2½) hook.
Repeat 39th and 40th rows 8 times more.

Change to 1.25 (no. 3) hook.
Repeat 39th and 40th rows 10 times more then 39th row again turning with 2 ch instead of 3 ch at end of last row.

86th Row: Miss first dc, 1 tr into each of next 8 dc, miss 2 dc, a V st into next dc, miss 2 dc, leaving the last loop of each on hook work 1 tr into each of next 2 dc, thread over and draw through all loops on hook (a joint tr made over 2 dc), 1 tr into each of next 11 dc a joint tr over next 2 dc, miss 2 dc, a V st into next dc, miss 2 dc, 1 tr into each of next 7 dc, a joint tr over next 2 dc, 1 ch, turn.

87th Row: 1 dc into each of first 9 sts, 3 dc into next sp, 1 dc into each of next 15 sts, 3 dc into next sp, 1 dc into each of next 9 sts, 2 ch, turn.

88th Row: Miss first dc, 1 tr into each of next 7 dc, miss 2 dc, a V st into next dc, miss 2 dc, a joint tr

over next 2 dc, 1 tr into each of next 9 dc, a joint tr over next 2 dc, miss 2 dc, a V st into next dc, miss 2 dc, 1 tr into each of next 6 dc, a joint tr over next 2 dc, 1 ch, turn.

Continue in this manner for 9 rows more decreasing as before on each decrease row.

98th Row: Miss first dc, 1 tr into each of next 2 dc, miss 2 dc, a V st into next dc, miss 2 dc, leaving the last loop of each on hook work 1 tr into each of next 3 dc, thread over and draw through all loops on hook (a joint tr made over 3 dc), miss 2 dc, a V st into next dc, miss 2 dc, 1 tr into next dc, a joint tr over next 2 dc, 1 ch, turn.

99th Row: 1 dc into each of first 3 sts, (3 dc into next sp, 1 dc into each of next 3 sts) twice, 2 ch, turn.

100th Row: Miss first dc, a joint tr over next 2 dc, miss 1 dc, a V st into next dc, miss 2 dc, 1 tr into next dc, miss 2 dc, a V st into next dc, miss 1 dc, a joint tr over next 3 dc, 1 ch, turn.

101st Row: 1 dc into each of first 2 sts, 3 dc into next sp, 1 dc into each of next 3 tr, 3 dc into next sp, 1 dc into each of next 2 sts, 3 ch, turn.

102nd Row: Miss first 6 dc, 1 dbl tr into next dc, 5 ch, leaving the last loop of each on hook work 1 dbl tr into same place as last dbl tr miss 5 dc and 1 tr into next dc, thread over and draw through all loops on hook, 1 ch, turn.

103rd Row: 1 dc into first st, 5 dc into next sp, 1 dc into next dbl tr. Fasten off.

Second Strip

Using Parrot Green work as first strip.

Joining

1st Row: Place wrong sides together and working through both sections attach Parrot Green to row end of 2nd row, 3 dc over same row end, * 1 dc over next row end, 3 dc over next row end; repeat from * 40 times more, 1 dc over next row end. Fasten off.

Make 10 more strips alternating colours and joining as before joining last strip to first strip to correspond.

Top Edging

Using Parrot Green attach thread to opposite side of first loop on first strip, 3 dc into same loop, 3 dc into next loop, * 2 dc into next loop, 3 dc into each of next 4 loops; repeat from * omitting 6 dc at end of last repeat, 1 ss into first dc. Fasten off.

Cords

Using Parrot Green make 6 lengths of braid 23 cm (9 in) long.

To Make Braid

Commence with 2 ch, then holding this between the

finger and thumb of the left hand work 1 dc into the first ch made (Diagram 1, page 205), turn, 1 dc into foundation loop of 2nd ch made inserting hook into back loop (Diagram 2, page 205), *turn, insert hook into 2 loops at side (Diagram 3, page 205), thread over and draw loop through, thread over and draw through 2 loops on hook; repeat from* for length required.

Using Straw Yellow make 6 lengths of braid as before.

Using Parrot Green make one more length of braid to fit round soft toy.

Damp and pin out to measurements.

Making Up

Bind frame with bias binding. Slip crochet over frame and secure at top and between points at lower edge. Sew one length of braid for cord to each point, matching colours. Sew braid round soft toy then secure ends of cords to braid.

Pyjama Case

Materials Required

Coats Chain Mercer-Crochet Cotton No. 10 (20 g). 2 balls Black and 9 balls White. This model is worked in these two shades, but any other shades of Mercer-Crochet may be used.
Milward steel crochet hook 1.50 (no. 2½).
40 cm (⅜ yd) white fabric 90 cm (approx. 36 in) wide for lining.
Kapok for stuffing feet.
25 cm (10 in) white zip fastener.
Coats Drima (polyester) thread.

Tension

First 4 rows of body – 2.5 cm (1 in).

Measurements

37 × 28 cm (14½ × 11 in).

Head

Using Black commence with 16 ch.
1st Row: 2 dc into 2nd ch from hook, 1 dc into each ch to within last ch, 2 dc into next ch, 1 ch, turn.
2nd Row: Working into front loop only work 1 dc into each dc, 1 ch, turn.
3rd Row: 2 dc into first dc, 1 dc into each dc to within last dc, 2 dc into next dc, 1 ch, turn.

Repeat last 2 rows 7 times more.

18th Row: As 2nd row.
19th Row: 1 dc into each dc, 1 ch, turn.
20th Row: As 2nd row.
21st Row: As 3rd row.

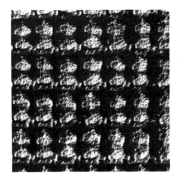

Close-up, Pyjama Case

Repeat last 4 rows 5 times more.

Repeat 18th and 19th rows 3 times more then 18th row again.

49th Row: Insert hook into first dc and draw loop through, insert hook into next dc and draw loop through, thread over and draw through all loops on hook (a joint dc made), 1 dc into each dc to within last 2 dc, a joint dc over next 2 dc, 1 ch, turn.
50th Row: Working into front loop only work 1 dc into each st, 1 ch, turn.

Repeat last 2 rows 9 times more then 49th row again.

70th Row: Working into front loop only work 1 dc into each of first 2 sts, 1 hlf tr into each of next 2 sts, 1 tr into each st to within last 4 sts, 1 hlf tr into each of next 2 sts, 1 dc into each of next 2 sts, 1 ch, turn.
71st Row: A joint dc over first 2 sts, 1 dc into next st, 1 hlf tr into next st, 1 tr into each st to within last 4 sts, 1 hlf tr into next st, 1 dc into next st, a joint dc over next 2 sts. Fasten off.

Ear (make 2)

Using Black commence with 2 ch.
1st Row: 1 dc into 2nd ch from hook, 1 ch, turn.
2nd Row: 3 dc into next dc, 1 ch, turn.
3rd Row: 1 dc into each dc, 1 ch, turn.
4th Row: As 3rd row of head.
5th Row: As 3rd row of ear.
6th Row: As 3rd row of head.
7th and 8th Rows: As 3rd row of ear.
9th Row: 2 dc into first dc, 1 dc into each dc, 1 ch, turn.
10th Row: As 3rd row.

Repeat last 2 rows 8 times more.

27th Row: 2 dc into first dc, 1 dc into each dc to within last 2 dc, a joint dc over next 2 dc, 1 ch, turn.
28th Row: 1 dc into each st, 1 ch, turn.
29th Row: 1 dc into each dc to within last 2 dc, a joint dc over next 2 dc, 1 ch, turn.
30th Row: As 28th row.

Repeat 27th to 30th row twice more.

39th Row: A joint dc over first 2 dc, 1 dc into each dc to within last 2 dc, a joint dc over next 2 dc, 1 ch, turn.
40th Row: As 28th row.

Repeat last 2 rows 4 times more.

49th Row: (Insert hook into next dc and draw thread through) 3 times, thread over and draw through all loops on hook. Fasten off.

Eye (make 2)

Using White commence with 16 ch.
1st Row: 1 dc into 2nd ch from hook, 1 dc into next ch, 1 hlf tr into next ch, 1 tr into next ch, 2 dbl tr into each of next 7 ch, 1 tr into next ch, 1 hlf tr into next ch, 1 dc into each of next 2 ch. Fasten off.

Mouth

First Section
Using White commence with 16 ch.
1st Row: 1 dc into 2nd ch from hook, 1 hlf tr into next ch, 2 tr into each of next 5 ch, 1 tr into next ch, 2 tr into each of next 5 ch, 1 hlf tr into next ch, 1 dc into next ch. Fasten off.

Second Section
1st Row: Using White commence with 15 ch, with wrong side of first section facing work 2 tr into centre tr of first section, 16 ch, turn.
2nd Row: 1 dc into 2nd ch from hook, 1 hlf tr into next ch, 2 tr into each of next 11 ch, 1 hlf tr into next ch, 1 dc into each of next 4 sts, 1 hlf tr into next ch, 2 tr into each of next 11 ch, 1 hlf tr into next ch, 1 dc into next ch. Fasten off.

Body

Using White commence with 118 ch.
1st Row: 1 dc into 2nd ch from hook, * 4 ch, miss 3 ch, 1 dc into next ch, 3 ch, miss 2 ch, 1 dc into next ch; repeat from * ending with 4 ch, miss 3 ch, 1 dc into next ch, 7 ch, turn.
2nd Row: 1 dbl tr into first dc, 2 ch, 6 dbl tr into next loop, remove loop from hook, insert hook into first dbl tr of dbl tr group and draw dropped loop through (a popcorn st made), 3 ch, a popcorn st into same loop, * 2 ch, 1 dbl tr into next loop, 2 ch, into next loop work a popcorn st 3 ch and a popcorn st; repeat from * ending with 2 ch, into next dc work 1 dbl tr 2 ch and 1 trip tr, 1 ch, turn.
3rd Row: 1 dc into first st, 2 ch, 1 dc into first sp * 3 ch, 1 dc into next sp, 4 ch, miss 2 popcorn sts, 1 dc into next sp; repeat from * ending with 3 ch, 1 dc into next sp, 2 ch, 1 dc into 5th of 7 ch, 7 ch, turn.
4th Row: 1 dbl tr into first dc, 2 ch, a popcorn st into next loop, * 2 ch, 1 dbl tr into next loop, 2 ch, into next loop work a popcorn st 3 ch and a popcorn st; repeat from * ending with 2 ch, 1 dbl tr into next loop, 2 ch, a popcorn st into next loop, 2 ch, into next dc work 1 dbl tr 2 ch and 1 trip tr, 1 ch, turn.
5th Row: 1 dc into first st, 4 ch, miss 2 sps and a popcorn st, 1 dc into next sp, * 3 ch, 1 dc into next sp, 4 ch, miss 2 popcorn sts, 1 dc into next sp; repeat from * ending with 3 ch, 1 dc into next sp, 4 ch, 1 dc into 5th of 7 ch, 7 ch, turn.
6th to 8th Row: As 2nd to 4th row.
9th Row: As 5th row turning with 4 ch instead of 7 ch.

10th Row: Into first loop work a popcorn st 3 ch and a popcorn st, * 2 ch, 1 dbl tr into next loop, 2 ch, into next loop work a popcorn st 3 ch and a popcorn st; repeat from * ending with 2 ch, 1 dbl tr into next dc, 1 ch, turn.

11th Row: 1 dc into first st, * 4 ch, miss 2 popcorn sts, 1 dc into next sp, 3 ch, 1 dc into next sp; repeat from * ending with 4 ch, 1 dc into 4th of turning ch, 6 ch, turn.

Repeat last 2 rows 14 times more turning with 4 ch instead of 6 ch at end of last row.

40th Row: A popcorn st into first loop, * 2 ch, 1 dbl tr into next loop, 2 ch, into next loop work a popcorn st 3 ch and a popcorn st; repeat from * omitting 3 ch and a popcorn st at end of last repeat, 1 dbl tr into next dc, 1 ch, turn.

41st Row: 1 dc into first st, 3 ch, miss 1 sp, 1 dc into next sp, * 4 ch, miss 2 popcorn sts, 1 dc into next sp, 3 ch, 1 dc into next sp; repeat from * working last dc into 4th of 4 ch, 4 ch, turn.

42nd Row: 1 dbl tr into first loop, * into next loop work a popcorn st 3 ch and a popcorn st, 2 ch, 1 dbl tr into next loop, 2 ch; repeat from * omitting 2 ch 1 dbl tr and 2 ch at end of last repeat, leaving the last loop of each on hook work 1 dbl tr into next loop and 1 trip tr into next loop, thread over and draw through all loops on hook, 1 ch, turn.

43rd Row: 1 dc into first st, 4 ch, * miss 2 popcorn sts, 1 dc into next sp, 3 ch, 1 dc into next sp, 4 ch; repeat from * ending with 1 dc into last dbl tr, 4 ch, turn.

Repeat 40th to 43rd row once more, omitting turning ch at end of last row. Fasten off.

Make another section to correspond. Do not fasten off. Place 2 sections wrong sides together.

Edging

1st Row: Working through both sections work a row of dc evenly across row ends having a multiple of 6 dc, working through front section only work a row of dc evenly along foundation ch having a multiple of 6 dc (opening made) and continuing to work through both sections complete other 2 sides to correspond ending with 1 ss into first dc.

2nd Row: 1 dc into same place as ss, * miss 2 dc, 7 tr into next dc, miss 2 dc, 1 dc into next dc; repeat from * omitting 1 dc at end of last repeat, 1 ss into first dc. Fasten off.

With right side facing attach thread to other section on other side of opening and work a row of dc along side. Fasten off.

Foot (make 4)

Using Black commence with 10 ch.

1st Row: 1 dc into 2nd ch from hook, 1 dc into each ch to within last ch, 3 dc into next ch, 1 ch, turn.

2nd Row: 2 dc into first dc, 1 dc into each dc, 1 ch, turn

3rd Row 1 dc into each dc, 1 ch, turn.

Repeat last 2 rows 5 times more.

14th to 17th Row: As 3rd row.

18th Row: Insert hook into first st and draw thread through, insert hook into next st and draw thread through, thread over and draw through all loops on hook (a joint dc made), 1 dc into each st, 1 ch, turn.

19th Row: 1 dc into each st, 1 ch, turn.

20th and 21st Rows: As 18th and 19th rows.

22nd Row: As 18th row.

23rd Row: 1 dc into each st to within last 2 sts, a joint dc over next 2 sts, 1 ch, turn.

Repeat last 2 rows 5 times more.

34th Row: A joint dc over first 2 sts, 1 dc into next st, 1 ch, turn.

35th Row: A joint dc over first 2 sts. Fasten off.

Damp and pin out to measurements.

Making Up

Sew ears and features to face of sheep. Sew face in position to one side of body (see illustration). Sew two foot sections together leaving an opening for stuffing. Stuff. Close opening and sew in position. Repeat with other foot.

Cutting Out

From fabric cut two pieces 37 × 28 cm (14½ × 11 in) and round off corners to fit outer edges of crochet case section.

Sewing

1.5 cm (½ in) seams have been allowed.
Insert zip between one long side of each lining section. Open zip. Baste and stitch remaining open edges right sides together. Turn to right side. Insert lining in case, slipstitch to top edges leaving shell edge at front free.

Chapter 12
NOVELTIES

When you have completed all your essential furnishings, you will find it is fun to make a few novelty items for your home, or as gifts.

In this chapter, there is a gay apron with matching oven gloves and lunch mats to brighten up everyday mealtimes, while for special occasions the pretty hostess apron and glass jackets provide protection from spills.

Gaily coloured fabric and attractive crochet trimmings make pomanders which are both decorative and sweet-smelling. Other pretty and practical items, such as a quilted tea cosy and a set of crochet coasters, are also included.

Apron, Oven Gloves and Lunch Mats

Apron

Materials Required

Clark's Anchor Stranded Cotton: 2 skeins each Peacock Blue 0170, Jade 0187; 1 skein each Peacock Blue 0167, Moss Green 0269, Muscat Green 0281, Buttercup 0298 and White 0402. Use 3 strands throughout.
1 m (1 yd) yellow medium weight furnishing fabric, as in illustration, 120 cm (approx 48 in) wide.
1 Milward 'Gold Seal' crewel needle No. 7.

Instructions

Cut the following pieces from fabric:
1 piece 122 × 61 cm (48 × 24 in) for skirt.
1 piece 63 × 9 cm (25 × 3½ in) for waistband.
2 pieces 84 × 9 cm (33 × 3½ in) for ties.
Fold skirt piece across the centre widthwise and crease lightly. Use upper section from the pattern as shown in photograph. With one long side of skirt piece facing, trace centrally on to fold 11.5 cm (4½ in) from lower edge (see Tracing instructions, page 19). Trace once more on each side spacing 2.5 cm (1 in) apart. Follow pattern and Key on page 193/4 for the embroidery. All parts similar to numbered parts are worked in the same colour and stitch. Press the embroidery on the wrong side.

Making Up

Apron skirt – turn back 1.5 cm (½ in) hem on each short side and stitch. Turn back 4 cm (1½ in) hem at lower edge and slipstitch in position. Run two rows of gathering stitches 6 mm (¼ in) apart and 6 mm (¼ in) from top edge. Turn back 1.5 cm (½ in) on short ends of waistband and baste. Pull up gathers on skirt to fit waistband and with right sides together stitch waistband to skirt 1.5 cm (½ in) from edge. Fold

Apron, Oven Gloves and Lunch Mats

in half lengthwise and slipstitch in position on wrong side to line of stitching. Turn in 6 mm (¼ in) hem on each long side and one short end of each tie and stitch. Pleat raw ends to fit open ends of waistband, insert ties and sew in position. Remove basting stitches.

Key to Pattern

1 – 0167
2 – 0170
3 – 0187 } Stem Stitch
4 – 0269
5 – 0281

6 – 0269 – Stem Stitch Filling

7 – 0167
8 – 0170
9 – 0187 } Satin Stitch
10 – 0281
11 – 0298

12 – 0298 } Back Stitch
13 – 0402

14 – 0170 } Double Knot Stitch
15 – 0187

16 – 0402 – French Knots

Oven Gloves

Materials Required

Clark's Anchor Stranded Cotton : 1 skein each Peacock Blue 0167, 0170, Jade 0187, Moss Green 0269, Muscat Green 0281, Buttercup 0298 and White 0402. Use 3 strands throughout.
50 cm (½ yd) yellow medium weight furnishing fabric, as in illustration, 120 cm (approx. 48 in) wide.
1 piece of wadding 38 × 20.cm (15 × 8 in).
1 Milward 'Gold Seal' crewel needle No. 7.

Instructions

Main section – cut 2 strips from fabric 75 × 19 cm (29½ × 7½ in).
Hand sections – cut 6 pieces 20 × 19 cm (8 × 7½ in) (4 from fabric, 2 from wadding).
Use one bird section from the pattern as shown in photograph. With short end of one hand section facing, trace centrally on to fabric (see Tracing instructions, page 19). Repeat on to one more hand section. Follow the pattern and Key above for the embroidery. All parts similar to numbered parts are worked in the same colour and stitch. Press the embroidery on the wrong side.

Making Up

Baste a piece of wadding to the wrong side of each end of one main section. Place one embroidered piece to each end of this section, right sides together, edges even. Baste and stitch 1.5 cm (½ in) from edges, curving the corners. Trim wadding close to the stitching, clip curves and turn to the right side. Make up remaining main section and hand sections in the same way, taking 1.5 cm (½ in) seams. Do not turn to

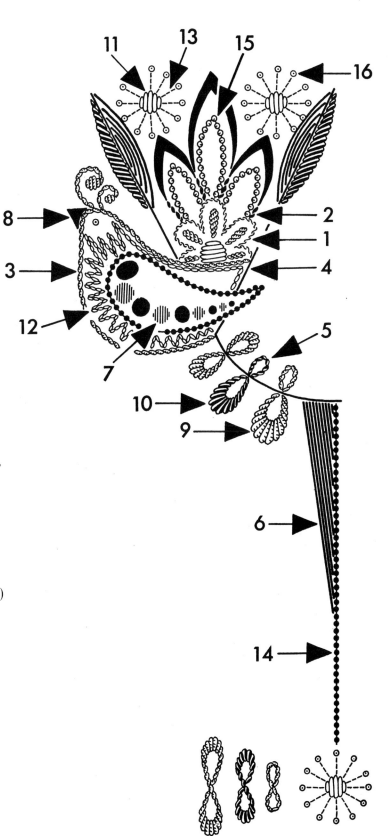

193

Pattern for Apron,
Oven Gloves and Lunch Mats

194

the right side. Insert inside the other section. Turn in the short ends and long sides and slipstitch together. Make a line of machine stitching along the short ends 6 mm ($\frac{1}{4}$ in) from slipstitching.

Lunch Mats

Materials Required

The following amounts make 3 mats.
Clark's Anchor Stranded Cotton: 2 skeins each Peacock Blue 0170, Jade 0187, Moss Green 0269 and Muscat Green 0281; 1 skein each Peacock Blue 0167, Buttercup 0298 and White 0402. Use 3 strands throughout.
50 cm ($\frac{1}{2}$ yd) yellow medium weight furnishing fabric, as in illustration, 120 cm (approx. 48 in) wide.
1 Milward 'Gold Seal' crewel needle No. 7.

The finished size of each mat is approximately 42 × 33 cm ($16\frac{1}{2}$ × 13 in).

Instructions

Cut three pieces from fabric 46 × 37 cm (18 × $14\frac{1}{2}$ in). The pattern gives the complete design. With long side of each piece facing, trace the main part of the design (see Tracing instructions, page 19) centrally on to fabric. Then trace one of the motifs within the dotted lines on to each corner, 5 cm (2 in) from long sides and 6.5 cm ($2\frac{1}{2}$ in) from short sides. Follow pattern and Key for the embroidery. All parts similar to numbered parts are worked in the same colour and stitch. Press the embroidery on the wrong side.

Making Up

Baste 1.5 cm ($\frac{1}{2}$ in) hems on all edges, mitre corners and slipstitch.

Quilted Tea Cosy

Materials Required

30 cm ($\frac{1}{3}$ yd) fabric, 90 cm (approx. 36 in) wide.
60 cm ($\frac{2}{3}$ yd) wadding, 90 cm (approx. 36 in) wide.
1 piece muslin, 30 × 25 cm (12 × 10 in).
80 cm ($\frac{7}{8}$ yd) cord.
1 skein Clarks Anchor Stranded Cotton to match fabric.
Coats Drima (polyester) thread.

Measurements

Length 28 cm (11 in); height 23 cm (9 in).

Cutting Out

Make a paper pattern to shape required.
Allowing 1.5 cm ($\frac{1}{2}$ in) for seams, using pattern;
From fabric   – cut 4 pieces (2 for lining)
From wadding – cut 8 pieces
From muslin   – cut 1 piece

Making Up

Trace pattern centrally onto right side of one fabric section. Place 4 pieces wadding, then muslin to wrong side of this section. Baste securely all over to hold in position. Using Back Stitch and three strands of stranded cotton embroider over traced lines. Baste remaining pieces of wadding to one other fabric section. Place quilted section to this fabric section, right sides together. Baste and stitch curved edge. Trim seams and turn to the right side. Place lining sections right sides together, baste and sew curved edges. Place lining inside cosy, turn in open edges, and sew together. Sew cord round edge of cosy as illustrated.

Pattern for Quilted Tea Cosy

195

Pomanders

Materials Required

Coats Chain Mercer-Crochet Cotton No. 20 (20 g).
1 ball. These models are worked in White, but any
shade of Mercer-Crochet may be used.
Milward steel crochet hook 1.25 (no. 3).
30 cm ($\frac{1}{4}$ yd) fabric, 90 cm (approx. 36 in) wide.
Lavender or Pot-Pourri.
1 spool Drima (polyester) multi-purpose thread to
match fabric.

Measurements

Length of Motif Strip – 11.5 cm ($4\frac{1}{2}$ in).

Abbreviations

ch – chain; dc – double crochet; tr – treble; dbl tr –
double treble; sp – space; st – stitch; ss – slip stitch.

Round Pomander

Motif Strip (make 6)
Small Motif (make 2)
Commence with 10 ch, join with a ss to form a ring.
1st Row: 3 ch, 4 tr into ring, remove loop from hook,
insert hook into 3rd of 3 ch and draw dropped loop
through (a starting popcorn st made), * 5 ch, 5 tr into
ring, remove loop from hook, insert hook into first tr
of tr group and draw dropped loop through (a
popcorn st made); repeat from * 4 times more, 5 ch,
1 ss into first popcorn st. Fasten off.

Centre Motif

Commence with 10 ch, join with a ss to form a ring.
1st Row: 3 ch, a starting popcorn st into ring, 2 ch,
1 dc into any loop on first motif, 2 ch, (a popcorn st
into ring of centre motif, 7 ch) twice, a popcorn st into
ring, 2 ch, 1 dc into any loop on second motif, 2 ch,
(a popcorn st into ring of centre motif, 7 ch) twice, 1 ss
into first popcorn st. Fasten off.

Edging

With right side facing attach thread to first free loop
to right of join on first motif, 4 ch, into same loop
work (1 tr, 1 ch) 3 times, ** into next free loop on
centre motif work (1 dbl tr, 1 ch) 4 times and 1 dbl tr,
5 ch, into next loop work (1 dbl tr, 1 ch) 5 times, into
first free loop on next motif work (1 tr, 1 ch) 4 times,
into next loop work (1 tr, 1 ch) 4 times, into next loop
work 1 dbl tr 1 ch 1 dbl tr 11 ch 1 dbl tr 1 ch and
1 dbl tr, 1 ch, * into next loop work (1 tr, 1 ch) 4
times; repeat from * once more; repeat from ** once
more omitting (1 tr, 1 ch) 4 times at end of repeat,
1 ss into 3rd of 3ch.
2nd Row: (1 dc into next sp, 3 ch) 8 times, * into
next loop work (1 dc, 3 ch) 4 times, (1 dc into next
sp, 3 ch) 14 times, into next loop work (1 dc, 3 ch)
8 times, (1 dc into next sp, 3 ch) 14 times; repeat from
* once more omitting (1 dc, 3 ch) 8 times at end of
last repeat, 1 ss into first dc. Fasten off.

Top

Work as small motif of motif strip for 1 row. *Do not
fasten off.*
2nd Row: 1 ss into first loop, 5 ch, into same loop
work (1 dbl tr, 1 ch) 4 times, * into next loop work
(1 dbl tr, 1 ch) 5 times; repeat from * ending with 1 ss
into 4th of 5 ch.
3rd Row: 1 dc into first sp, 3 ch, 1 dc into next sp,
* 1 ch, 1 dc into centre 3 ch loop of 11 ch loop on
any motif strip, 1 ch, (1 dc into next sp on top, 3 ch)
4 times, 1 dc into next sp; repeat from * joining each
motif strip to top in this manner omitting 1 dc, 3 ch,
1 dc at end of last repeat, 1 ss into first dc. Fasten off.

Tab

Make a chain desired length. Fasten off.

Damp and pin out to measurements.

Making Up

Make paper pattern from A. 1 square = 6 mm ($\frac{1}{4}$ in).
Arrow marks straight grain of fabric.
Cut 6 pieces from pattern.
6 mm ($\frac{1}{4}$ in) has been allowed for seams.
Place two sections, right sides together, edges even.
Baste and stitch one curved side. Repeat with
remaining sections to form shape, leaving an opening
on one side for stuffing. Turn to right side. Stuff
pomander and slipstitch open edges together. Sew
crochet in position as shown in illustration, securing
tab at top.

Diamond Pomander

Motif Strip (make 5)
As motif strip of Round Pomander.

Top

Commence with 8 ch, join with a ss to form a ring.
1st Row: 3 ch, a starting popcorn st into ring, (11 ch,
a popcorn st into ring) 4 times, 11 ch, 1 ss into first
popcorn st.
2nd Row: * Into next loop work (1 dc, 3 ch) 3 times
and 1 dc, 1 ch, 1 dc into centre 3 ch loop of 11 ch
loop on any motif strip, 1 ch, into same loop on top
work (1 dc, 3 ch) 3 times and 1 dc; repeat from *
joining remaining motif strips to top in this manner
ending with 1 ss into first dc. Fasten off.

Tab

Make a chain desired length. Fasten off.

Damp and pin out to measurements.

Making Up

Make paper pattern from B. 1 square = 6 mm ($\frac{1}{4}$ in).
Arrow marks straight grain of fabric.
Cut 5 pieces from pattern.
6 mm ($\frac{1}{4}$ in) has been allowed for seams.
Place two sections, right sides together, edges even.

Baste and stitch one side. Repeat with remaining sections to form shape, leaving an opening on one side for stuffing. Turn to right side. Stuff pomander and slipstitch open edges together. Sew crochet in position as shown in illustration, securing tab at top.

Edging for Apron and Glass Jackets

Edging for Apron

Materials Required

Coats Chain Mercer-Crochet Cotton No. 20 (20 g). 2 balls. This model is worked in shade 402 (Lt. Rose Pink), but any other shade of Mercer-Crochet may be used.

Pattern for Pomanders

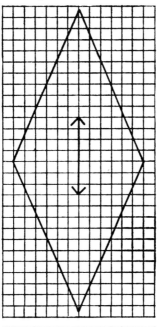

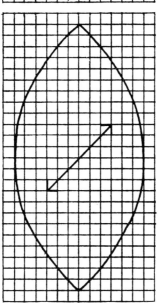

Pomanders

Close-up of motif, Pomanders

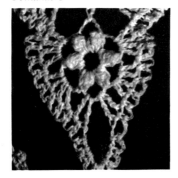

Hairpin Lace Staple 2 cm ($\frac{3}{4}$ in) wide.
Milward steel crochet hook 1.25 (no. 3).
70 cm ($\frac{3}{4}$ yd) organdie or any fine fabric 90 cm (approx. 36 in) wide.

Tension

15 loops — 2.5 cm (1 in) approximately.

Measurements

Depth of Edging — 5 cm (2 in) approximately.

Abbreviations

ch — chain; dc — double crochet; sp — space; ss — slip stitch.

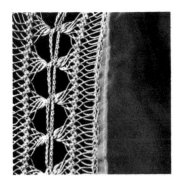

Close-up, Edging for Apron

How to Work the Lace

Use a crochet hook and Hairpin Lace Staple. Holding the crochet hook in the right hand, make a loop at end of ball thread and slip on to crochet hook. Take the Hairpin in the left hand and hold it flat between the thumb and first finger, with prong end uppermost and the round part downwards in the palm of the hand (see 1–7 below).

1. Make a loop at end of ball thread (diagram 1A).
2. Insert hook in loop and wind ball thread around right prong of Hairpin (diagram 1A).
3. Thread over hook and draw through loop, keeping loop at centre (diagram 1A).
4. Raise hook to a vertical position and turn Hairpin to the left (diagram 1B).

Edging for Apron and Glass Jackets

Close-up, Glass Jackets

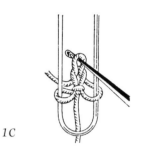

1C

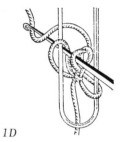

1D

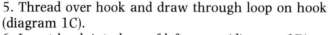

Diagram 1A

1B

5. Thread over hook and draw through loop on hook (diagram 1C).
6. Insert hook into loop of left prong (diagram 1D).
7. Thread over hook and draw loop through (2 loops on hook), thread over and draw through remaining 2 loops.

Repeat steps 4 to 7 until Hairpin is filled. Remove all loops, re-insert Hairpin into last 4 loops and continue as before for length required.

First Strip

Work a strip of Hairpin Lace 140 cm (55 in) long or length required, having a multiple of 5 loops on each side. Keep loops twisted throughout.

Heading

Attach thread to first loop on one side of Hairpin Lace Strip, 1 dc into same loop, 1 dc into each loop. Fasten off.

Edging

With right side facing attach thread to first 5 loops on opposite side of Hairpin Lace, 1 dc into same 5 loops, * 6 ch, 1 dc into next 5 loops; repeat from * to end. Fasten off.

Second Strip

Work another strip of Hairpin Lace 140 cm (55 in) long or length required having a multiple of 5 loops on each side.

1st Row: Attach thread to first 5 loops on one side of Hairpin Lace Strip, 1 dc into same 5 loops, 1 ss into corresponding dc of edging on first strip, * 6 ch, 1 dc into next 5 loops, 1 ss into next dc on first strip; repeat from * to end. Fasten off.

1st Row: With wrong side facing attach thread to first loop on opposite side of Hairpin Lace Strip, 1 dc into same loop, * 2 ch, 1 dc into next loop; repeat from * to end, turn.

2nd Row: 1 ss into first dc, * 1 dc into next sp, 4 ch, 1 ss into 3rd ch from hook, 1 ch; repeat from * ending with 1 dc into next sp. Fasten off.

Damp and pin out to measurements.

Making Up

Cut 1 piece 67 × 37 cm (26½ × 14½ in) for apron skirt. Cut 1 piece 42 × 10 cm (16½ × 4 in) for waistband. Cut 2 pieces 64 × 14 cm (25½ × 5½ in) for ties. Turn back 6 mm (¼ in) hem at sides and lower edge of apron skirt and sew neatly. Gather top to 39 cm (15½ in). With right sides together place one long edge of waistband centrally to skirt top and stitch together 1.5 cm (½ in) from the edge. Turn in 1.5 cm (½ in) on the other long edge and slipstitch to row of stitching at back of skirt. Fold in the surplus at the open ends of waistband. Turn back 6 mm (¼ in) hem on long side and short ends of ties. Baste and stitch. Pleat the raw edge of both ties to fit open end of waistband. Insert one at each end and slipstitch. Sew edging neatly to edge of apron.

Glass Jackets

Materials Required

Coats Chain Mercer-Crochet Cotton No. 20 (20 g).
2 balls. This model is worked in shade 524 (Dk. Jade), but any other shade of Mercer-Crochet may be used.
Milward steel crochet hook 1.25 (no. 3).
3 glass jackets may be worked from 1 ball.
Tubular elastic if desired.

Tension

First 5 rows – 5 cm (2 in) in diameter.

Measurements

Depth of jacket – 7 cm (2¾ in).

Abbreviations

ch – chain; dc – double crochet; ss – slip stitch; tr – treble.

Base

1st Row: Commence with 4 ch, 12 tr into 4th ch from hook, 1 ss into 4th of 4 ch.

2nd Row: 3 ch, 1 tr into same place as ss, 2 tr into each tr, 1 ss into 3rd of 3 ch.

3rd Row: 3 ch, * 2 tr into next tr (an increase made), 1 tr into next tr; repeat from * omitting 1 tr at end of last repeat, 1 ss into 3rd of 3 ch.

4th Row: 3 ch, 1 tr into next tr, * 2 tr into next tr, 1 tr into each of next 2 tr; repeat from * omitting 2 tr at end of last repeat, 1 ss into 3rd of 3 ch.

Continue in this manner for 2 rows more having 1 tr more between each increase on each row.

Side

1st Row: 3 ch, working into back loop only, 1 tr into each tr, 1 ss into 3rd of 3 ch.

2nd Row: 3 ch, 1 tr into each tr, 1 ss into 3rd of 3 ch.

3rd Row: 1 dc into same place as ss, * draw loop on hook out 6 mm (¼ in), thread over hook and draw through loop on hook, insert hook between loop and single thread of this ch and complete as for dc (knot stitch made), work another knot in same manner (a Solomon's knot made), miss 5 tr, 1 dc into next tr; repeat from * omitting 1 dc at end of last repeat, 1 ss into first dc.

4th Row: 3 ch, into same place as ss work 1 tr 3 ch 1 dc into 3rd ch from hook – a picot made – and 2 tr, * 1 Solomon's knot, miss 1 Solomon's knot, into next dc work 2 tr a picot and 2 tr (a shell made); repeat from * omitting a shell at end of last repeat, 1 ss into 3rd of 3 ch.

5th Row: 1 ss into each of next 5 sts and over knot st, 1 dc into next dc, * 1 Solomon's knot, miss a shell and 1 knot st, 1 dc into next dc; repeat from * omitting 1 dc at end of last repeat, 1 ss into first dc.

6th and 7th Rows: As 4th and 5th rows.

8th Row: 3 ch, * 2 tr over next knot st, 1 tr into next dc; repeat from * omitting 1 tr at end of last repeat, 1 ss into 3rd of 3 ch.

Repeat 3rd to 8th row once more.

Next Row: 3 ch, 1 tr into each tr, 1 ss into 3rd of 3 ch. Fasten off.

If desired, last row may be worked over tubular elastic.

Coasters

Abbreviations

ch – chain; dc – double crochet; tr – treble; dbl tr – double treble; trip tr – triple treble; sp – space; st(s) – stitch(es); ss – slip stitch.

Materials Required

Coats Chain Mercer-Crochet Cotton No. 20 (20 g).
2 balls. This model is worked in shade 687 (Tangerine),
but any other shade of Mercer-Crochet may be used.
Milward steel crochet hook 1.25 (no. 3).
1 piece of glass 18 cm (7 in) in diameter.
4 pieces of glass 10 cm (4 in) in diameter.

Tension

First 2 rows – 6.5 cm ($2\frac{1}{2}$ in) in diameter.

Measurements

Large Mat – 18 cm (7 in) in diameter.
Small Mat – 10 cm (4 in) in diameter.

Large Mat

Commence with 10 ch, join with a ss to form a ring.
1st Row: 3 ch, leaving the last loop of each on hook
work 2 dbl tr into ring, thread over and draw through
all loops on hook (a 2 dbl tr cluster made), (3 ch, a
3 dbl tr cluster into ring) 11 times, 3 ch, 1 ss into
first cluster.
2nd Row: 1 ss into next sp, 14 ch, 1 ss into 6th ch
from hook (a picot made), 4 ch, 1 dbl tr into same sp,
* 4 ch, 1 dc into next sp, 4 ch, into next sp work
1 dbl tr 10 ch 1 ss into 6th ch from hook 4 ch (a
picot loop made) and 1 dbl tr; repeat from * ending
with 4 ch, 1 dc into next sp, 4 ch, 1 ss into 4th of
14 ch.
3rd Row: 1 ss into each of next 4 ch and into picot,
4 ch, into same picot work 2 dbl tr 3 ch 3 dbl tr 5 ch
3 dbl tr 3 ch and 3 dbl tr, * 6 ch, into next picot work
3 dbl tr 3 ch 3 dbl tr 5 ch 3 dbl tr 3 ch and 3 dbl tr;
repeat from * ending with 6 ch, 1 ss into 4th of 4 ch.
4th Row: * 1 dc into next dbl tr, 3 ch, into next sp
work 1 tr 3 ch and 1 tr (a V st made), 3 ch, miss
1 dbl tr, 1 dc into next dbl tr, 3 ch, miss 3 sts, a V st
into next st, 3 ch, miss 1 dbl tr, 1 dc into next dbl tr,
3 ch, a V st into next sp, 3 ch, miss 1 dbl tr, 1 dc into
next dbl tr, into next sp work 3 dc 3 ch and 3 dc,
miss 1 dbl tr; repeat from * ending with 1 ss into first
dc.
5th Row: 1 ss into each of next 6 sts, 12 ch, * into
next V st work 1 tr a picot loop and 1 tr, 7 ch, 1 trip
tr into next V st, 13 ch, 1 ss into 6th ch from hook,
7 ch, 1 trip tr into next V st, 7 ch; repeat from *
omitting 1 trip tr and 7 ch at end of last repeat, 1 ss
into 5th of 12 ch.
6th Row: 1 ss into each of next 12 sts and into picot,
4 ch, into same picot work 2 dbl tr 3 ch 3 dbl tr 5 ch
3 dbl tr 3 ch and 3 dbl tr, * 6 ch, into next picot work
3 dbl tr 3 ch 3 dbl tr 5 ch 3 dbl tr 3 ch and 3 dbl tr;
repeat from * ending with 6 ch, 1 ss into 4th of 4 ch.
7th Row: As 4th row.
8th Row: 1 ss into each of next 6 sts, 12 ch, * 1 dc
into next V st, 9 ch, 1 tr into next V st, 7 ch, 1 tr into
next V st, 9 ch; repeat from * omitting 1 tr and 9 ch
at end of last repeat, 1 ss into 3rd of 12 ch.
9th Row: 1 ss into each of next 4 sts, 1 dc into same

loop, * 9 ch, 1 dc into next loop; repeat from *
ending with 9 ch, 1 ss into first dc.
10th Row: 3 ch, * 9 tr into next loop, 1 tr into next
dc; repeat from * ending with 9 tr into next loop, 1 ss
into 3rd of 3 ch.
11th Row: 3 ch, * leaving the last loop of each on
hook work 1 tr into each of next 2 sts, thread over
and draw through all loops on hook (a joint tr made),
1 tr into next st; repeat from * omitting 1 tr at end of
last repeat, 1 ss into 3rd of 3 ch.
12th Row: 1 dc into same place as ss, 1 dc into each
st, 1 ss into first dc.
13th Row: 1 dc into same place as ss, 1 dc into next
dc, * a joint dc over next 2 sts, 1 dc into each of next
2 dc; repeat from * omitting 2 dc at end of last repeat,
1 ss into first dc.
14th Row: As 12th row. Fasten off.

Small Mat (make 4)

Work as Large Mat for 4 rows.
5th to 9th Row: as 8th to 12th row of Large Mat.

Damp and pin out to measurements.
Slip over glass.

Bag

Materials Required

Coats Chain Mercer-Crochet Cotton No. 20 (20 g).
8 balls Raspberry 207 for bag and 1 ball each of
White and Mid Moss Green 789 for trimming. This
model is worked in these three shades, but any other
shades of Mercer-Crochet may be used.
Milward steel crochet hook 1.25 (no. 3).
1 m (1 yd) lining fabric, 90 cm (approx. 36 in) wide.
50 cm ($\frac{1}{2}$ yd) heavy Vilene or other bonded fibre
interlining, 80 cm (approx. 32 in) wide.
Coats Drima (polyester) thread.

Tension

First 7 rows – 2.8 cm ($1\frac{1}{8}$ in).

Measurements

Bag – 30 × 35 cm (12 × 14 in).

Bag Front and Back (both alike)

Using Raspberry commence with 148 ch.
1st Row: Into 4th ch from hook work 3 tr and
1 hlf tr, * miss 2 ch, into next ch work 1 dc 3 ch 3 tr
and 1 hlf tr; repeat from * ending with miss 2 ch,
1 dc into next ch, 5 ch, turn.
2nd Row: * Miss 3 tr, 1 dc into 3rd of 3 ch, 2 ch;
repeat from * omitting 2 ch at end of last repeat,
3 ch, turn.
3rd Row: Into first dc work 3 tr and 1 hlf tr, * into
next dc work 1 dc 3 ch 3 tr and 1 hlf tr; repeat
from * ending with 1 dc into 3rd of 5 ch, 5 ch, turn.

Bag

Repeat last 2 rows 41 times more then 2nd row again. Fasten off.

Gusset

Using Raspberry commence with 28 ch.
1st Row: 1 tr into 4th ch from hook, 1 tr into each ch, 3 ch, turn.
2nd Row: Miss first tr, 1 tr into each st, 3 ch, turn.

Repeat last row 200 times more omitting turning ch at end of last row. Fasten off.

Damp and pin out to measurements.

Joining

With wrong sides together place gusset in position to front section and working through both sections attach Raspberry to last row and work a row of dc evenly along row ends having 3 dc into same place at each corner and working into foundation ch at lower edge of front section and over row ends of next side. Fasten off.
Join gusset to back section in same manner.

Top Edging

With right side facing attach Raspberry to first loop on last row of front section and work a row of dc evenly round top edge of bag ending with 1 ss into first dc. Fasten off.

Handle (make 2)

Using Raspberry commence with 7 ch.
1st Row: 1 dc into 2nd ch from hook, 1 dc into each ch, 1 ch, turn.
2nd Row: 1 dc into each dc, 1 ch, turn.

Repeat last row 8 times more turning with 2 ch at end of last row.

11th Row: Miss first dc, working into front loop only work 1 tr into each of next 5 dc, turn, working into back loop of same dc, 1 tr into each of next 6 dc, 1 ss over turning ch.
12th Row: 2 ch, 1 tr over bar of each of next 11 tr, 1 ss over turning ch.

Repeat last row until handle measures 38 cm (15 in) or length required from beginning working last ss into 2nd of 2 ch.

Next Row: Working through both thicknesses work 1 dc into same place as ss and into previous tr, (1 dc through next 2 tr) 5 times, 1 ch, turn.
Next Row: 1 dc into each dc, 1 ch, turn.

Repeat last row 8 times more omitting 1 ch at end of last row. Fasten off.

Chrysanthemum Trimming – First Section

Using White cut a piece of Mercer-Crochet 4.20 m (4½ yd) long and double to make cord.
Work over cord throughout.
1st Row: 20 dc over cord, 1 ch, turn.
2nd Row: 1 dc into first dc, 1 hlf tr into next dc, 1 tr into each of next 12 dc, 1 hlf tr into next dc, 1 dc into each of next 5 dc, 1 ch, turn.
3rd Row: 1 dc into each of first 8 sts, 12 dc over cord only, 1 ch, turn.
4th Row: 1 dc into first dc, 1 hlf tr into next dc, 2 tr into each of next 5 dc, 1 tr into each of next 7 dc, 1 dc into each of next 5 sts, 1 ch, turn.
5th Row: 1 dc into each of first 12 sts, 8 dc over cord only, 1 ch, turn.

Repeat 2nd to 5th row 10 times more then 2nd to 4th row again omitting turning ch at end of last row. Fasten off. (24 petals)

Second Section

Using White cut a piece of Mercer-Crochet 3.70 m (4 yd) long for cord.
Work over cord throughout.
1st Row: 20 dc over cord, 1 ch, turn.
2nd Row: 1 dc into each of first 5 dc, 2 dc into each of next 3 dc, 1 dc into each dc, 1 ch, turn.
3rd Row: 1 dc into each of first 5 dc, 15 dc over cord only, 1 ch, turn.
4th Row: 2 dc into each of first 8 dc, 1 dc into each dc, 1 ch, turn.
5th Row: 1 dc into each of first 7 dc, 13 dc over cord only, 1 ch, turn.
Repeat 2nd to 5th row 9 times more then 2nd to 4th row again omitting turning ch at end of last row. Fasten off. (22 petals)

Third Section

Using White cut a piece of Mercer-Crochet 2.80 m (3 yd) long for cord and work as second section having 16 petals instead of 22.

Fourth Section

Using White cut a piece of Mercer-Crochet 1.40 m (1½ yd) long for cord and work as second section having 8 petals instead of 22.

Centre

Using White commence with 2 ch.
1st Row: 6 dc into 2nd ch from hook.
2nd Row: 2 dc into each dc.
3rd to 7th Row: 1 dc into each dc. Cut thread leaving sufficient to lace through last row.

Small Flower

Using White cut a piece of Mercer-Crochet 1.80 m (2 yd) long for cord and work as second section of

Chrysanthemum having 10 petals instead of 22.

Centre

Work as centre of Chrysanthemum.

Leaf (make 3)

Using Mid Moss Green commence with 15 ch.
1st Row: 1 tr into 7th ch from hook, 3 ch, miss 1 ch, 1 tr into next ch, (3 ch, miss 1 ch, 1 dbl tr into next ch) twice, 3 ch, miss 1 ch, into next ch work 1 trip tr 3 ch 1 quad tr 3 ch and 1 trip tr, 3 ch, working along opposite side (1 dbl tr into same place as next dbl tr, 3 ch) twice, (1 tr into same place as next tr, 3 ch) twice, miss 2 ch, 1 ss into next ch.
2nd Row: 3 dc into same place as ss, 3 dc into next sp, 1 dc into next tr, into next sp work 1 dc 1 hlf tr and 1 tr, 1 tr into next tr, 3 tr into next sp, 1 tr into next dbl tr, 3 tr into next sp, 1 tr into next dbl tr, 3 dbl tr into next sp, 1 dbl tr into next trip tr, 3 dbl tr into next sp, into next quad tr work 2 dbl tr 3 ch 1 ss into last dbl tr and 1 dbl tr, 3 dbl tr into next sp, 1 dbl tr into next trip tr, 3 dbl tr into next sp, 1 dbl tr into next dbl tr, 3 tr into next sp, 1 tr into next dbl tr, 3 tr into next sp, 1 tr into next tr, into next sp work 1 tr 1 hlf tr and 1 dc, 1 dc into next tr, 3 dc into next sp, 1 ss into first dc. Fasten off.

Braid for Stems

Using Mid Moss Green commence with 2 ch, then holding this between the finger and thumb of the left hand work 1 dc into first ch made (diagram 1), turn, 1 dc into foundation loop of 2nd ch made inserting hook into back loop (diagram 2), * turn, insert hook into 2 loops at side (diagram 3), thread over and draw through 2 loops, thread over and draw through remaining 2 loops; repeat from * for length required. Fasten off. Make a length of braid 23 cm (9 in) for Chrysanthemum and 10 cm (4 in) for small flower.

Damp and pin out to measurements.

Making Up

Sew stems, leaves and flowers to front of bag as shown in illustration.

Cutting Out

Main Section – Cut 4 pieces from fabric 33 × 35 cm (13 × 14 in).
Cut 2 pieces from interlining 30 × 33 cm (12 × 13 in).
Gusset – Cut 2 pieces from fabric 8 × 102 cm (3 × 40 in), joining where necessary to obtain correct length.
Cut 1 piece from interlining 5 × 96 cm (2 × 38 in), joining where necessary to obtain correct length.

Sewing

1.5 cm ($\frac{1}{2}$ in) has been allowed for seams.
Baste one interlining main section centrally to wrong side of one fabric main section. Edgestitch interlining to fabric. Having right sides together baste a second fabric main section to interlined main section. Leaving one short edge open, stitch round three sides. Trim seams and turn to right side. Turn seam allowance on raw edge to inside and sew together inserting each end of one crochet handle 8 cm (3 in) from side edges. Make another main section in same way. Baste gusset interlining centrally to wrong side of one piece of gusset fabric. Edgestitch to fabric. Having right sides together baste a fabric gusset section to interlined gusset section, leaving one long edge open, stitch round three sides. Trim seams and turn to right side. Turn and sew together. Place gusset between main sections and oversew in place. Insert lining to crochet bag and sew round top edge.

Cheval Set

Materials Required

Coats Chain Mercer-Crochet Cotton No. 20 (20 g). 3 balls. This model is worked in shade 402 (Lt. Rose Pink), but any other shade of Mercer-Crochet may be used.
Milward steel crochet hook 1.25 (no. 3).

Tension

5 sps and 5 rows – 2.5 cm (1 in).

Measurements

Large Mat – 35 × 28 cm (14 × 11 in) approximately.
Small Mat – 18 × 20 cm (7 × 8 in) approximately.

Large Mat

Commence at A (see pattern on page 207) with 21 ch.
1st Row: 1 tr into 4th ch from hook, 1 tr into each of next 17 ch (6 blks made), 8 ch, turn.
2nd Row: 1 tr into 4th ch from hook, 1 tr into each of next 4 ch, 1 tr into next tr (2 increase blks made at beginning of row), 1 tr into each of next 15 tr (5 blks made over 5 blks), 1 tr into each of next 2 tr, thread over hook, insert hook into next ch and draw thread through, thread over and draw through one loop on hook (a foundation ch made), (thread over and draw through 2 loops on hook) twice, * thread over hook, insert hook into foundation ch and draw loop through, thread over and draw through one loop on hook (another foundation ch made), complete as tr; repeat from * 11 times more (4 increase blks made at end of row), 3 ch, turn.
3rd Row: Miss first tr, 1 tr into each of next 3 tr

Diagram 1

Diagram 2

Diagram 3

(blk made over blk at beginning of row), 11 blks, 2 increase blks, 3 ch, turn.
4th Row: 13 blks, 3 ch, turn.
5th Row: 13 blks, 1 increase blk, 2 ch, cut thread leaving an end.

Commence at B with 9 ch.
1st Row: 2 blks, 26 ch, turn.
2nd Row: 8 increase blks, 2 blks, 1 increase blk, 5 ch, turn.
3rd Row: 1 increase blk, 11 blks, 2 increase blks, 3 ch, turn.
4th Row: 14 blks, 1 increase blk, 3 ch, turn.
5th Row: 8 blks, 2 ch, miss 2 tr, 1 tr into next tr (sp made over blk), 6 blks, 2 increase blks, 5 ch, turn.
6th Row: 1 increase blk, 7 blks, 1 sp, 2 tr into next sp, 1 tr into next tr (blk made over sp) 8 blks, 3 ch, turn.
7th Row: 9 blks, 2 ch, 1 tr into next tr (sp made over sp), 1 sp, 7 blks, 3 ch, turn, do not cut thread, attach 2 ch of A to corresponding point on B.
8th Row: 7 blks, 1 sp, 10 blks, 2 ch, miss 2 ch, 1 tr into next tr, 13 blks, 3 ch, turn.
9th Row: 13 blks, 1 sp, 7 blks, 1 sp, 2 blks, 1 sp, 7 blks, 5 ch, cut thread leaving an end.

Commence at C with 12 ch.
1st Row: 3 blks, 5 ch, turn.
2nd Row: 1 increase blk, 3 blks, 2 increase blks, 26 ch, turn.
3rd Row: 8 increase blks, 6 blks, 1 increase blk, 3 ch, turn.
4th Row: 15 blks, 2 increase blks, 5 ch, turn.
5th Row: 1 increase blk, 17 blks, 1 increase blk, 3 ch, turn, do not cut thread, attach 5 ch of B to corresponding point on C.
10th Row: 19 blks, 1 tr into each of next 5 ch, 1 tr into next tr, 6 blks, 9 sps, 2 blks, 1 sp, 13 blks, turn.
11th Row: 1 ss into each of first 4 tr (1 blk decreased at beginning of row), 3 ch, 12 blks, 1 sp, 1 blk, 3 sps, 5 blks, 2 sps, 27 blks, 1 increase blk, 3 ch, turn.
12th to 47th Row: Follow pattern, 3 ch, turn.
48th Row: 12 blks, turn.
49th Row: Decrease 2 blks, 3 ch, 8 blks, turn.
50th Row: Decrease 2 blks, 3 ch, 3 blks. Fasten off.
48th Row: (continued): Miss 6 tr and 2 ch, attach thread to next tr, 3 ch, 4 blks, 1 sp, 3 blks, 1 sp, 2 blks, 2 sps, 4 blks, 1 sp, 16 blks, 3 ch, turn.
49th Row: 15 blks, 3 ch, turn.
50th Row: 15 blks, 3 ch, turn.
51st Row: 13 blks, turn.
52nd Row: Decrease 5 blks, 3 ch, 7 blks, 3 ch, turn.
53rd Row: 5 blks, turn.
54th Row: Decrease 3 blks, 3 ch, 2 blks. Fasten off.
49th Row: (continued): Miss 3 tr and 2 ch, attach thread to next tr, 3 ch, 5 blks, 1 sp, 11 blks, 3 ch, turn.
50th Row: 10 blks, 1 sp, 5 blks, 3 ch, turn.
51st Row: 15 blks, 3 ch, turn.
52nd Row: 14 blks, turn.

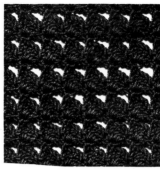

Close-up, worked section of Bag

Cheval Set

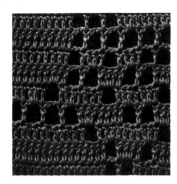

53rd Row: Decrease 1 blk, 3 ch, 13 blks, turn.
54th Row: Decrease 1 blk, 3 ch, 10 blks, turn.
55th Row: Decrease 1 blk, 3 ch, 8 blks, turn.
56th Row: Decrease 2 blks, 3 ch, 2 blks. Fasten off.

Small Mat (make 2)

Commence at A with 15 ch.
1st Row: 4 blks, 2 ch, cut thread leaving an end.

Commence at B with 15 ch.
1st Row: 4 blks, 5 ch, turn.
2nd Row: 1 increase blk, 4 blks, 3 ch, turn.
3rd Row: 5 blks, 2 increase blks, 2 ch, cut thread leaving an end, attach 2 ch of A to corresponding point on B.

Commence at C with 21 ch.
1st Row: 6 blks, 3 ch, turn.
2nd Row: 6 blks, 1 increase blk, 5 ch, turn.
3rd Row: 1 increase blk, 7 blks, 5 ch, turn.
4th Row: 1 increase blk, 8 blks, 5 ch, turn.
5th Row: 1 increase blk, 9 blks, 2 ch, cut thread leaving an end, attach 2 ch of B to corresponding point on C.

Commence at D with 21 ch.
1st Row: 6 blks, 5 ch, turn.
2nd Row: 1 increase blk, 6 blks, 2 increase blks, 5 ch, turn.
3rd Row: 1 increase blk, 9 blks, 3 ch, turn, do not cut thread, attach 2 ch of C to corresponding point on D.
6th Row: 10 blks, 1 tr into each of next 2 ch, 1 tr into next tr, 9 blks, 1 sp, 1 tr into each of next 2 ch, 1 tr into next tr, 7 blks, 1 tr into each of next 2 ch, 1 tr into next tr, 4 blks, 1 increase blk, 3 ch, turn.
7th to 29th Row: Follow pattern, 3 ch, turn.
30th Row: 5 blks, turn.
31st Row: Decrease 2 blks, 3 ch, 3 blks. Fasten off.
30th Row (continued): Miss 5 tr, attach thread to next tr, 3 ch, 1 blk, 1 sp, 3 blks, 2 sps, 6 blks, 1 sp, 5 blks, 1 sp, 5 blks, 1 increase blk, 3 ch, turn.
31st Row: (6 blks, 1 sp) twice, 4 blks, 1 sp, 3 blks, 2 sps, 2 blks, 5 ch, turn.
32nd Row: 1 increase blk, 4 blks, 8 sps, 6 blks, 1 sp, 7 blks, 3 ch, turn.
33rd Row: 8 blks, 1 sp, 4 blks, 1 sp, 5 blks, 2 sps, 6 blks, 3 ch, turn.
34th Row: 12 blks, turn.
35th Row: Decrease 1 blk, 3 ch, 10 blks, 3 ch, turn.
36th Row: 8 blks.
37th Row: Decrease 2 blks, 3 ch, 4 blks. Fasten off.
34th Row (continued): Miss 3 tr and 2 ch, attach thread to next tr, 3 ch, 3 blks, 3 ch, turn.
35th Row: 2 blks. Fasten off.
34th Row (continued): Miss 3 tr 2 ch and 6 tr, attach thread to next tr, 3 ch, 6 blks, turn.
35th Row: Decrease 1 blk, 3 ch, 3 blks. Fasten off.

Damp and pin out to measurements.

Pattern for Cheval Set

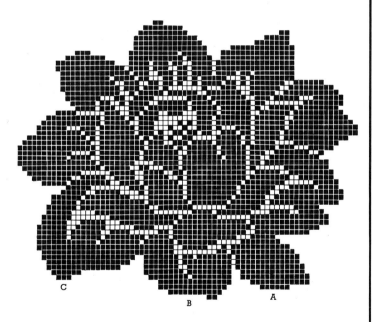

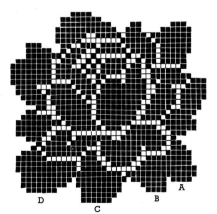

Chapter 13

CARE & REPAIR

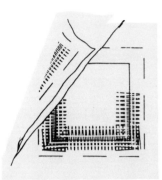

Diagram 1

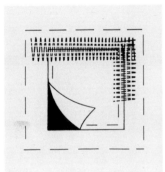

Diagram 2

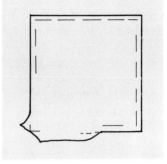

Diagram 3

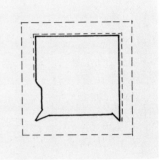

Diagram 4

Diagram 5

Diagram 6

Machine Darning and Mending

The high cost of living makes it imperative to save time and money by the machine darning and mending of household linens. Almost all mending can be done on the sewing machine, and the object of each operation must be invisible mending or as near to that as possible.

A darn is the best way to mend a small hole or a worn section in household linen. Use Anchor Machine Embroidery Thread No. 50 and a fine needle to ensure a soft flexible darn that is neat and serviceable. A heavier thread will produce a stiff darn which will look clumsy and unsightly.

Naturally the colour of the thread should always match, as closely as possible, the article to be mended. Where a two-toned fabric is involved, invisible mending can be done if the main fabric colour is used for the thread on the reel and the secondary fabric colour is used for the thread on the bobbin.

Machine Darning

Look at the instruction book for your sewing machine. Set the machine as instructed in the book, lowering the feed dog, or adding a plate and placing the worn part of the fabric in the embroidery hoops. Put the fabric over the embroidery hoops right side down, so that when the frame edge is turned up the darn can be made on the right side of the fabric. The article should always be stretched tightly over the hoops and in some cases, where the fabric is slippery, the inner edge of the hoops can be bound with tape for extra firmness. Lower the presser bar, bring up the lower thread, and the article is ready for darning. If the presser bar is not lowered, looped stitching is unavoidable.

The tension for darning is generally lighter than that for ordinary sewing, and the stitch should always be practised on a scrap of fabric before starting to darn. Always remember that a slow movement results in a short stitch while a quick movement results in a longer stitch. Thus the hoops should be moved at an even steady speed.

When working on fine fabrics, it is possible to strengthen the worn section before darning by backing the area to be darned with a fine fabric. Place it over the hole and stitch round 6 mm ($\frac{1}{4}$ in) from the edge of the hole, then commence darning. Move the hoops backwards and forwards across the section to be darned in closely spaced parallel rows, making the lines of stitching slightly longer than the worn section. This makes the darn less conspicuous and much stronger. The darn is finished by moving the hoops in the opposite direction and varying the length of the turns.

Fabrics have an uncanny way of wearing out at the edges. A worn-out edge can be filled in with darning stitches. To do this efficiently, place the article in the hoops so that the worn section lies in the middle, then attach the free edge to the taped edge of the hoops (diagram 1). Work the darn in the usual way, beginning at the outer edge and moving the hoops rapidly along this edge four or five times. Continue stitching in this way until the hole is covered. Turn work and fill in with short stitches, running at right angles to the edge. A worn corner may be darned in the same manner, using a fine fabric as a foundation for the darn and strengthening the finished darn at the outside edges with plain or buttonhole stitching.

Patching

Much larger holes are not infrequent occurrences in household linens. It is only too easy to catch a big toe in a small hole and make an ugly casualty of a sheet otherwise still capable of years of use. Such holes call for a darned patch rather than a darn. It would be a hopeless and time-consuming task to attempt to darn such a hole.

Obviously, the patch should be of the same fabric and colour as the damaged article. Often it happens that a piece of the original fabric can be cut from a hem, or from some section of the article where it will not show. If you cannot use the original material, do try hard to get as close as possible to the original to avoid an unsightly patch. It is not advisable to patch an old article with a new fabric as this will make the patch more noticeable. However, if new fabric has to be used, wash it first so that it will lose its new appearance.

Machine Darned Patch

For a machine darned patch on light and medium fabrics, cut the patch 2.5 cm (1 in) larger all over than the hole. Place the patch under the hole matching the grain or pattern of the fabric. Baste the patch to the article. Trim the hole to an even shape then darn across the cut edge from the right side, running the darning about five stitches beyond each side and crossing the stitches at the corners (diagram 2). Next trim the edges of the patch to the stitching on the wrong side. You should now have a neat patch impossible to detect.

Inserted Patch

The patch for a hole in a thick, heavy fabric should be cut exactly to the size of the hole. The hole should be trimmed to an even shape before cutting the patch.

Place the patch edge to edge in the hole (diagram 3). Now cut a piece of net curtain mesh or similar old fabric about 2.5 cm (1 in) larger than the patch. Place it under the patch on the wrong side of the fabric and baste it to the fabric. Darn as for previous method and trim the edges of mesh when finished.

Straight Stitching Patch

For an extra large hole or worn section, particularly in bed linen, use a flat fell patch. Trim the edges of the hole to a square or rectangle and cut the patch about 6.5 cm ($2\frac{1}{2}$ in) larger. Place the right side of patch to the wrong side of the article, matching grain. Turn in raw edges of patch; baste and stitch. Turn the article to the right side, clip corners of article diagonally to within $1 - 1.5$ cm ($\frac{3}{8}-\frac{1}{2}$ in) from the stitching; turn under raw edges and stitch as before (diagrams 4 and 5).

Patching with Swing Needle Machine or Zig-Zag Attachment

For fabrics which stretch, such as jersey, the best method of patching is to apply the patch with the grain matching, and zig-zag stitch round the edge of the patch. Use a wide zig-zag stitch of medium length and this will allow for the elasticity of the fabric. Trim the worn section to the stitching (diagram 6).

Mending by Hand

All rips, tears or holes should be repaired at once, before the article is cleaned or put away.

Buttons

Cut away and unpick the surplus worn thread. Sew the buttons on securely.

Hand Darning a Hole

To repair a hole invisibly from a fabric with easily withdrawn threads, cut a piece of fabric from the hem or seam. The size of the patch must be at least 4 cm ($1\frac{1}{2}$ in) larger on all sides than the hole or tear.

Draw out the threads from all four sides of this patch until you have a piece of the fabric which covers the hole with a 6 mm ($\frac{1}{4}$ in) overlap all round, and a fringe of at least 3 cm ($1\frac{1}{4}$ in) on all sides (diagram 7).

Place this patch over the hole on the right side of the article, then pin and baste it firmly in position, carefully matching it with the pattern and keeping all threads running with the weave of the fabric. Thread a darning needle with one strand of the fringe and pass the needle and strand together through to the wrong side of the fabric. Pull all the fringe, strand by strand, through to the wrong side, taking care to blend it with the weave of the fabric (diagram 8).

Turn the work to the wrong side and darn each separate strand of the fringe into the surrounding fabric, making sure that the darning stitches do not penetrate to the right side of the article (diagram 9). Trim away the ends of the fringe when a sufficient length (about 1.5 cm ($\frac{1}{2}$ in)) has been darned in.

It is important that the darning is worked in the same direction in which the strands are lying. If they are folded back and darned over the original hole they cause a ridge all round the edge of the patch.

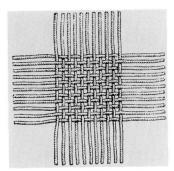

Diagram 7

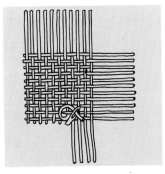

Diagram 8

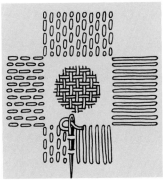

Diagram 9

Diagram 10

Ripped Hem

Unpick the broken threads for a few centimetres (inches), and then secure them with a few small stitches. Sew the hem in position with slipstitching or Herringbone Stitch.

Ripped Seam

Turn the article to the wrong side and mend with a line of Back Stitch. If the rip is long, it is well worth the extra trouble of restitching by machine, running over the original stitching at each end.

Tears

A tear in tweed or woollen fabric may be invisibly mended quite successfully by first removing a few threads from the hem or seam. Using this thread, darn carefully on the right side (diagram 10). If the fabric is lightweight, use extra small, neat stitches. When the darning is complete, press well on the wrong side, using a damp cloth. For greater strength a piece of fine net may be placed under the tear on the wrong side and secured with the darning stitches.

Worn Fabric

Fabric which is wearing thin may be repaired with small regular darning stitches. These may be worked diagonally across the weave to make them less visible,

Stain Removal

Stains should be removed wherever possible while still fresh. Stain removal is comparatively easy if the article is washable, but never use very hot water, as this may set the stain and so make it impossible to remove. Certain stains will require the use of chemicals for their removal; in these cases always test a scrap of the fabric or the inside of a seam first, as the dye may be unstable. Make sure that it does not leave spots on the fabric. To avoid rings caused by the action of the stain remover, make a jagged shape round the stain and work from the outside to the centre with a light feathery motion. If the stain is very bad and its origin is unknown, do not run the danger of fixing the stain by incorrect treatment, but instead take it to a reliable dry cleaner.

Remember that care must be exercised in the use of the highly inflammable grease solvents. Keep them well away from an open flame and do not breathe in their fumes.

Here is a list of the more common stains and processes which may help to remove them:

Blood

Soak the article in cold salted water (1 teaspoonful to 500 ml or 1 pint) for about an hour. Wash in cool, soapy water. Treat blood stains as soon as possible.

Cocoa

Sponge the stain with a warm solution of borax and

water, 15 g to 250 ml ($\frac{1}{2}$ oz to $\frac{1}{2}$ pint). Rinse well.

Coffee

Treat as for cocoa. It may be necessary to repeat the process a few times.

Egg

The white of egg may be removed by sponging with a lukewarm solution of salt and water (1 teaspoonful to 500 ml or 1 pint). To remove the yolk, wash and then remove the greasy mark with a grease solvent (benzene or carbon tetrachloride).

Fruit Juice

Treat as for coffee.

Grass

Treat with methylated spirits, but test all synthetics before applying.

Grease

Place an absorbent pad below the stain, dampen a piece of muslin with a grease solvent (benzene or carbon tetrachloride) and work from the outside edges of the stain towards the centre. If it is a surface grease stain, place a piece of clean blotting paper over the stain and press with a hot iron until the grease is entirely absorbed.

Ink, Ball-point

Sponge with methylated spirits. Test synthetics first.

Ink, Writing

Wash a washable fabric at once. If any stain remains, soak it in milk. If the ink stain has been in the article for some time and is dry, sponge with oxalic acid solution, 1 teaspoonful to 500 ml (1 pint) of hot water.

Lipstick

On washable fabrics, wash in warm soapy water; otherwise use a grease solvent, ie benzene or carbon tetrachloride.

Mildew

This is one of the most obstinate stains to remove. If it is on white fabric, try bleaching lightly with hydrogen peroxide.

Milk

Wash with warm soapy water, rinse and then treat with a grease solvent.

Nail Polish

Rub lightly with acetone or nail varnish remover. (Test all synthetics first and on no account use on acetate rayons.)

Paint

Treat at once by rubbing with turpentine.

Rust

Sponge with oxalic acid solution (1 teaspoonful to 500 ml or 1 pint) of hot water.

Scorch Marks

There is no treatment for really bad scorching. For slight scorching, sponge with a warm solution of borax and water, 15 g to 250 ml ($\frac{1}{2}$ oz to $\frac{1}{2}$ pint), or on a heavy fabric rub lightly with a cake of damp soap.

Tar

Scrape off all surplus tar at once, and then rub the stain immediately with benzene or carbon tetrachloride.

Tea

Stretch the fabric over a basin, dampen and sprinkle with borax. Pour hot water through. Rinse and wash. Sponge coloured fabrics with a warm solution of borax and water, 15 g to 250 ml ($\frac{1}{2}$ oz to $\frac{1}{2}$ pint). Rinse well.

Dyes and Dyeing

Today it is both easy and economical to give a new look to your existing clothes and household linens by dyeing them to the colours of your choice – bright greens, blues, reds, purples and yellows, or pretty pastels.

Curtains, blankets, towels, sheets, pillowcases and clothing can be machine or hand dyed to any colour you want. Most fabrics, except acrylics, can be dyed successfully, with the minimum of trouble. Observe the following simple rules to ensure perfect results.

1. Choose a fabric suitable for dyeing, and use the correct dye for the fabric.
2. Use the right method. If you don't have a washing machine, you can use a large saucepan or bucket on top of the cooker for hot dyeing, or a plastic bowl or the sink for cold dyeing.
3. When choosing your colour, remember to take into account the colour you start from – this will have some effect on the shade achieved after dyeing. It is also important to use the correct amount of dye for the dry weight of fabric.

The instructions below are for Dylon dyes.

Choosing a Dye

Cold Dye dyes natural fibres to true bright colours. It is very easy to use in cold water. Results have excellent fastness to light and washing. For each colour use 1 tin of Dylon per 200–225 g (6–8 oz) dry fabric (2–3 sq m/yd of medium weight fabric); ie a 450 g (1 lb) dress to be dyed in blue and red needs 2 tins of blue and 2 tins of red dye.

Multi-Purpose Dye dyes natural and most synthetic fabrics. There is a range of 47 colours. They can be used with hot water, but simmering gives greater density of colour. For each colour use 1 tin of Dylon per 225 g (8 oz) dry fabric (2–3 sq m/yd of medium weight fabric).

Liquid Dye is a ready-mixed, very convenient alternative to Multi-Purpose dye, available in 15 colours. It comes in a plastic bottle, and dyes up to 900 g (2 lb) dry fabric (8–10 sq m/yd of medium weight fabric). Part can be stored for future use.

Fabric Guide

Woollens, polyester/wool mixtures, acrylics (Orlon, Acrilan, Courtelle, Neospun), Tricel and acetate should not be dyed.

For cotton and linen, use Cold, Multi-Purpose or Liquid dye, but choose Cold dye for tablecloths, sheets, pillowcases, towels and other items washed frequently.

For cottons with special finishes, such as drip-dry, etc., Cold dye often gives paler results than the shade specified on the pack.

For silk, use Cold, Multi-Purpose or Liquid dye; the two latter give richer shades on silk.

Viscose rayon can be dyed in Cold, Multi-Purpose or Liquid dye.

For polyesters like Terylene, Crimplene and Dacron, treble-strength Multi-Purpose or Liquid dye in dark shades will give pretty pastel shades.

For polyester/cotton mixtures, use Cold, Multi-Purpose or Liquid dye; it is best to use Cold dye for shirts or other items washed frequently.

How to Tie-and-Dye

The principle behind this fascinating craft is quite simple; when fabric is folded, bound and then dyed in one or more colours, the dye penetrates some areas and not others, giving highly individual patterns and effects.

When you have an article to tie-and-dye, first choose your dye and colours, then your design (see below), then proceed, following the instructions given with the dye.

If you choose two or more colours they will, of course, blend with each other, eg blue on yellow gives green. Other factors also affect the final colour achieved – the length of time you leave the fabric in the dye, for instance.

When you start to tie-and-dye the element of surprise is a great part of the fun. As you gain experience, however, you will enjoy controlling the results more closely.

To remove existing colour from an article, use Dygon Colour and Stain Remover. Test a small sample first to see if the dye is fast.

Tie-and-Dye Designs

Here are some easy basic techniques to try. You can combine them or adapt them as you wish. For example, a T-shirt could have the sleeves knotted and the front clump-tied.

For binding, use cotton or linen thread, string, cord, raffia or elastic bands. As the idea is to restrict the penetration of the dye, be sure to fasten off securely.

Tip 1 — Leave 5 cm (2 in) of thread when you start binding, and when finished return to starting point and tie the two ends together.

Tip 2 — If you are doing several bindings on one garment simply use a slip knot and carry the thread on to the next binding.

Simple circles can be any size. Pick up the centre of the circle to form a peak. Furl like an umbrella. Bind tightly with rubber bands or string at intervals according to required size of circles.

For further information on all aspects of home dyeing, free fabric analysis and advice on colour-matching, write to Annette Stevens, Dylon International Limited, Lower Sydenham, London SE26 5HD.

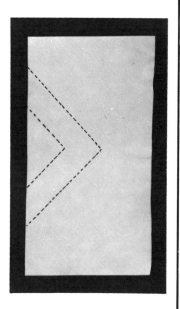

Sewing can be used to produce many different effects, here diamonds. Fold fabric in half. Draw half diamonds with pencil or chalk. Stitch round it, pull thread up tight. Bind around stitching.

Clump-tying: tie in a stone and criss-cross it with thread. Bind at intervals to make a circle design.

214

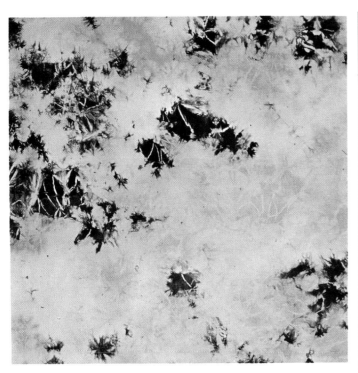

Marbling: crumple up fabric in your hand. Bind into a hard ball. Crumple up in different places for each colour you use. For a large garment, bunch along the length, section by section, making a long firm roll.

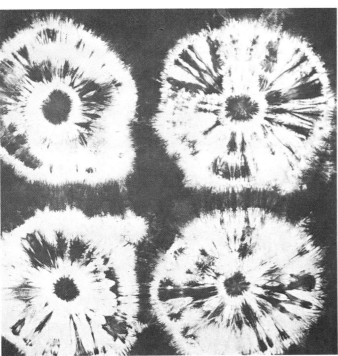

Knotting: pick up points of fabric and knot them. Mark out their position with a pencil or chalk first.

215

Clump-tying: tie in a stone and butter beans for a pattern of circles (or try corks, coins, dried peas, rice or shells).

Knotting: pick up points of fabric and knot them. Mark out their position with a pencil or chalk first.

216

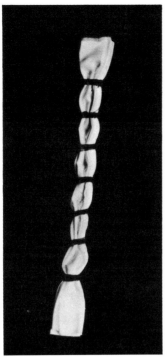

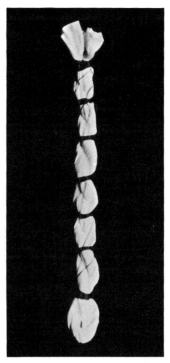

Pleating: gather in regular folds like an accordian, and bind to form a firm strip of fabric.

Twisting: twist fabric until it coils back on itself like a skein of wool. Bind at ends and at intervals.

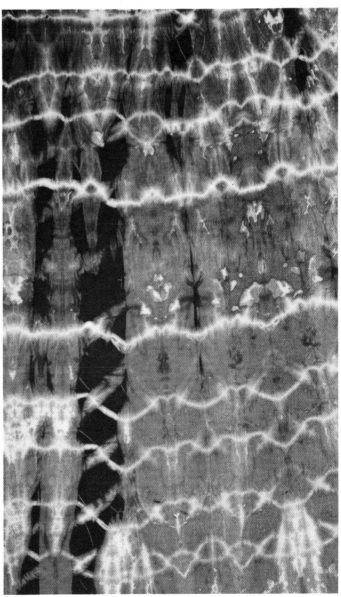

217

Spring clean or spring colour?

Greying nylon sheets and pillowslip dyed deep pink, Carnival, with Dylon Liquid Dye.

Off-white wool blankets dyed deep pink in the washing machine with Dylon Wash'n Dye.

Faded yellow cotton lace bedspread colour-stripped with Dygon and then dyed deep pink with Dylon Liquid Dye.

Blind made from cotton dyed deep pink, Tahiti Rose, with Dylon Cold Dye. Red border painted on using Dylon Cold Dye, Mexican Red, mixed with Paintex.

Cushions and lampshade made from cotton and silk remnants dyed and tie-dyed with Dylon Cold Dyes. The acetate fringe was colour-matched with Dylon Multi-Purpose Dye.

Batik pictures on cotton mounted on cardboard. Hot wax was painted on to the fabric which was then dyed in Dylon Cold Dye. The waxed areas resist the dye. Repeating the process several times builds up an interesting and unusual picture.

Dried grasses dyed a variety of toning colours with Dylon Multi-Purpose Dyes.

Terylene curtains kept white and fresh with Dylon-CC Curtain White.

White tumbletwist rugs make a deep-pile luxury carpet and can be easily lifted and washed in the washing machine with Dylon Super White, or dyed to blend with the new décor.

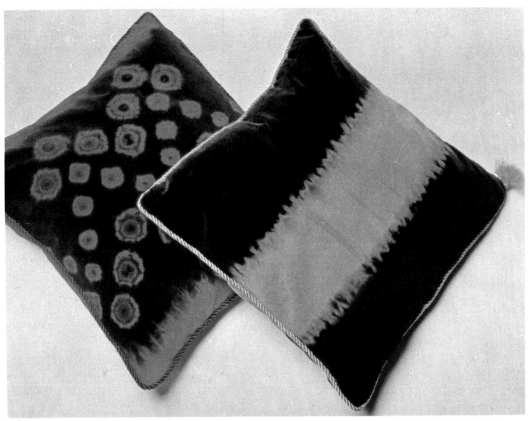

*Tie-dyed velvet cushion covers
Small stones were tied into the
orange cover to give an
interesting design of small
circles. The broad stripes on the
yellow cover were achieved by
sewing two lines of small
stitches, ruching tightly and
binding the centre panel with
polythene.
Both covers were then dyed in
Dylon Multi-Purpose Dye,
Coffee.*

*A co-ordinated theme for the
nursery. Cotton twill sheeting,
tie-dyed using the sewing
method to create an attractive
paisley design, makes ideal
curtains and a matching cot
cover. Use Dylon's non-toxic
colourfast Cold Dyes in
Nasturtium, Radiant Pink and
Mexican Red. Colour-match
cotton sheets and pillowslips
with Coral.*
    *Whitewood cot dyed with Mr
Dylon Wood Dye, Swedish
Dawn, (also non-toxic) and
sealed with Mr Dylon
Polyurethane Wood Seal.*

219

Index